THE RHINE
ENDEAVOUR

Above: Detail from picture on p. 132. (*Imperial War Museum BU-480*)
Previous page: Detail from picture on p. 64. (*Imperial War Museum BU-10279*)

THE RHINE ENDEAVOUR

WAR AND PEACE
SEPTEMBER 1944 NW EUROPE

PATRICK DELAFORCE

AMBERLEY

For my sweet wife with very many thanks for her help with this book.

First published 2010

Amberley Publishing Plc
Cirencester Road, Chalford,
Stroud, Gloucestershire, GL6 8PE

www.amberley-books.com

Copyright © Patrick Delaforce, 2010

The right of Patrick Delaforce to be identified as
the Author of this work has been asserted in
accordance with the Copyrights, Designs and
Patents Act 1988.

ISBN 978 1 84868 825 4

British Library Cataloguing in Publication Data.

A catalogue record for this book is available
from the British Library.

Typeset in 10pt on 12pt Sabon.
Typesetting by FonthillMedia.
Printed in the UK.

Contents

	Foreword and Acknowledgements	7
1.	War and Peace	9
2.	Hitler's Miracles: Hitler's 'Fireman'	17
3.	Von Zangen's Dunkirk Evacuation	22
4.	The Capture of Antwerp: the key fulcrum	28
5.	Operation Astonia: Capture of Le Havre	40
6.	The Cinderella Army: Canadians in the Scheldt Campaign	50
7.	The *Verdronken* Land of Polders and Peel Country	61
8.	Dilemma of the Allied Airborne Army	71
9.	War of the Generals	75
10.	Monty's Greatest Gamble	78
11.	The Bitter Triangle	85
12.	Monty's Forlorn Hope: 1st Airborne Division	89
13.	Frost's War	109
14.	Taylor's 101st US Airborne Division: The Screaming Eagles	116
15.	Gavin's 82nd US Airborne Division: The All American	121
16.	Guards Armoured: 'Ever open eye'	130
17.	'Von Thoma's' 43rd Wessex Wyverns Division	147
18.	Last Battle of 50th Tyne-Tees Division	164
19.	Polish Brigade Tragedy	176
20.	Black Bull: 11th Armoured right flank protection	181
21.	Monty's Ironsides: 3rd British Division	193
22.	The Netherlands' unique Tank Battle	203
23.	Desert Rats: 7th Armoured Division left flank	209
24.	Red Crown & Dragon: 53rd Welsh Division	221
25.	The Red Lion Rampant: 15th Scottish Division	232
26.	Monty's Marauders	247
27.	Student's Ferocious Counter-Attacks	257
28.	Who Won?	263
29.	The Island, 'No Man's Land' and the Polar Bears	269
	Bibliography	276
	Glossary	277
	Index	281

Detail from picture on p. 196. (*Imperial War Museum B-6683*)

Foreword

This book is written as a tribute to the modern British Army, which has exactly the same problems as the 1944/45 British Liberation Army - a very difficult enemy, unpleasant battle terrain and imperfect weaponry - but, thank goodness, it has the same *esprit* and good leadership. In the original British Liberation Army, in the first four months of the campaign, we freed about 20 million people in France, Belgium and Holland from Nazi tyranny. In the second phase, to be described in my next book *Operation Eclipse: The Invasion of the Third Reich 1945*, we fought in five dangerous river crossings in Germany before beating the Russians to the Baltic and completing the liberation of Denmark, Norway and the rest of Holland, thus again liberating over 20 million fairly grateful Europeans. In 11 months of attritional fighting my division, the 11th Armoured (Black Bull), lost 2,000 young soldiers killed in action and a further 8,000 wounded. We had good 'management' under Major General 'Pip' Roberts and had immense confidence in him. We were very fortunate to fight and to survive.

Detail from picture on p. 222. (*Imperial War Museum B-0137*)

CHAPTER ONE

War and Peace

The British Liberation Army (BLA) brought devastating war to Adolf Hitler's disorganised armies in the Low Countries in September 1944. It also brought peace and freedom from four years of Nazi rule to some 20 million French, Belgian and Dutch citizens. The BLA, with its handsome insignia of a crusader's white shield and a gold and blue sword, surged ashore on the Normandy beaches. There were very few 'liberated' French emerging from the ruins of Caen, and a score of small towns and villages were all rubble and confusion.

September 1944 was the *mensis mirabilis* when the BLA swept through most of western and northern France, then through Belgium and into Holland, and received an ecstatic welcome everywhere. It was a milestone in the history books, a military adventure unique for any army, anywhere, any time. In the annals of the exploits of the British Army over many centuries, September 1944 is in a class of its own.

Normandy in that long, hot summer had been a blood bath, often of First World War intensity. The Germans and a few co-opted Slav and other nationalities had fought brilliantly to defend their ownership of a land of milk and honey in which they had absolutely no right to be. The Allies, American, British, Canadian, Polish, with a little bit of help from de Gaulle's French, had planned and planned for Operation Overlord. The unusual combination of the Royal Navy, Airborne paratroops, Marine commandos, and British, American and Canadian Armies had thrust ashore on 6 June. The RAF had ruled the skies and Bletchley Park's Ultra decrypted the 100,000 German Enigma machines, which helped produce – eventually – a stunning victory.

But there were some disquieting aspects of the Allied 'citizen' armies as Lt General Brian Horrocks discovered on his return to Normandy to command a corps, after recovering from the severe wounds he had sustained in Africa:

Seven weeks hard slogging in the thick *bocage* country had taken their toll and the gloss had gone from the magnificently trained army that had landed in Normandy. I have always said that in a section of ten men, as a rough guide, two lead, seven follow and one would do almost anything not to be there at all. The two leaders take most of the risks and are usually the first to become casualties. When this happens on a large scale as it had occurred

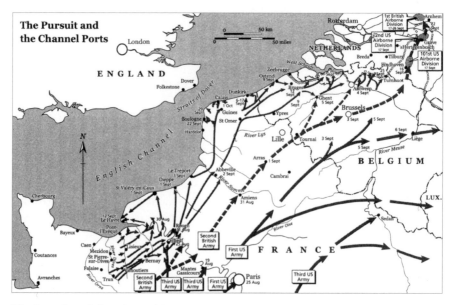

The Pursuit and the Channel Ports.

in the Normandy beachhead battle, so much better suited to defence than to attack, the cutting edge of a division becomes blunted.

And Colonel Trevor Dupuy, an experienced New Zealand soldier-observer, wrote in his book *A genius for war*: 'On a man to man basis the German ground soldier consistently inflicted casualties at about a 50 per cent higher rate than they incurred from the opposing British, Canadian and American troops *under all circumstances*. This was true when they were attacking and when they were defending, when they had a local numerical superiority and when, as was usually the case, they were outnumbered, when they had air superiority and when they did not, when they won and when they lost.' This was truly evident: the SS panzer grenadiers and the Hitler Jugend fought like fiends.

The Allies in Normandy faced the finest fighting army of the war, one of the greatest that the world has ever seen. This is a simple truth that some soldiers and writers have been reluctant to acknowledge, partly for reasons of nationalistic pride, and partly because it is a painful concession when the Wehrmacht and SS were fighting for one of the most obnoxious regimes of all time. The quality of the German weapons – above all, tanks – was of immense importance. Their tactics were masterly: stubborn defence, concentrated local fire-power from mortars and machine-guns, and quick counter-attacks to recover lost ground. Units often fought on, even when cut off.

By the end of August 1944, 11 weeks of bitter attritional fighting had caused total battlefield casualties of 460,000 men killed in action, wounded, missing and taken prisoner, plus untold thousands of French civilians. On average there were about 7,000 casualties *every day*.

The closing of the Argentan-Falaise Gap had left Hitler's storm troopers in disarray. It was impossible for any army, however strong and determined they might be, to withstand the incessant pounding night and day by the RAF, night and day by the massed Allied artillery, and the bravery of the PBI (Poor Bloody Infantry). Twenty-six British formations including one division were disbanded or forced to merge. Britain's armed manpower was slowly running down.

But on 1 September 1944 everything changed!

General Bernard Montgomery (Monty) had been rewarded for the eventual success of Operation Overlord (and the many unsuccessful operations: Epsom, Charnwood, Jupiter, Goodwood, Totalise and a score of others) – by being promoted to Field Marshal, the highest rank in the British Army. At the same time he was demoted to the sole command of 21st British Army Group as General Dwight D. Eisenhower arrived from England and became Supreme Commander of Allied Forces in north-west Europe.

This book is about the astonishing events that then followed. Briefly, the four armoured divisions under Montgomery's command were unleashed like 'the dogs of war' and raced northwards over the Seine, through the sad First World War battlefields of Northern France and into Belgium: 300 miles in three or four days. It was a feat unique in history and Lt General Brian Horrocks was the hunt master who urged on 11th Armoured (Black Bull), Guards Armoured, 7th Armoured (Desert Rats) and 1st Polish Armoured Division into the green pastures and infinite pleasures of the capture of Brussels. The 'Great Swan' and the capture of a country's capital city were astonishing successes. Then came the three-day battle to capture Antwerp, the largest port for hundreds of miles and vital for the future supply of all of Eisenhower's armies.

Major Edward Elliot, a company commander in the 2nd Glasgow Highlanders, 15th Scottish Division, fought hard in Normandy, kept a diary and, advancing up the Belgian border, wrote:

Wherever we stopped crowds ran forward to shake our hands and clamour for autographs. Fruit and flowers were thrown into jeeps and [Bren gun] carriers as we drove past dense and enthusiastic people. In return we threw our cigarettes and sweets onto the pavements, immediately seized upon … The windows and shops were bedecked with colours and flags and patriotic slogans hung across the main street of every town and hamlet … This was victory indeed! Now for the first time we understood why the British Expeditionary Force had been renamed the **British Army of Liberation** … as if a veil draping the inner soul of France and hiding her true visage had suddenly been lifted to reveal a shining and cheerful countenance, a menace which had hung over her life for four long weary years was gone – gone they hoped for ever.

5th Royal Tank Regiment of the 'Desert Rats' Division took part in the capture of Ghent. They were given an incredible welcome. Thousands of people were in the streets, including German patrols, milling around the tanks, all laughing, cheering and crying. On 6 September the editor of *La Flandre Liberale* wrote (translated): 'The unforgettable hour came. Each man keeps in his heart the memory of the first Tommy to be spotted. We have awaited this day for four years. Four long black years with only our patriotic faith giving us the strength to hope ...'

Two intensely sentimental journeys took place early in September. On 19 August 1942 in Operation Jubilee the Canadian Army launched a massive one-day raid on Dieppe to see if a head-on combined operations assault on a well-defended French port would be successful. It was an appalling failure, and thousands of young Canadians were killed, wounded and taken prisoner.

Guards Armoured Cromwell tanks swamped by joyful *citoyens* of Brussels. (*Imperial War Museum BU-509*)

When the Canadians did capture Dieppe on 1 September 1944 they spent three days of sorrow, with memorial services and visits to the local cemeteries.

The 51st Highland Division, as part of the British Expeditionary Force in June 1940, was temporarily under command of the French Army. At St Valéry-en-Caux, 30 kilometres west of Dieppe, General Rommel's panzers cut off the Division from a withdrawal to Dunkirk and it was forced to surrender. 3 September 1944 was declared 'St Valéry Day' as the Highlanders returned as avengers. In the cemeteries there were many graves dedicated to 'L'Ecossais Inconnu', and the divisional pipers and buglers played the Lament, Last Post and Reveillé in several moving ceremonies.

In mid-September the classic all-arms Operation Astonia by the Royal Navy and RAF, and then by two British divisions, ended in the capture of another great port, Le Havre.

An eight-day drama, from 17 to 25 September, took place during Monty's dramatic, and rash, Operation Market Garden; although a large salient and two river crossings were achieved, the 'Forlorn Hope' of 1st Airborne Division was sacrificed. The whole of Montgomery's 21st Army Group (30th, 8th and 12th Corps) was involved. At the end of the affair the gallant 50th (Northumbrian) Tyne-Tees Division, which had fought so bravely in North Africa, where it was awarded three Victoria Crosses, and in Sicily and Normandy, where a D-Day Victoria Cross was earned, was eventually disbanded, much to the distress and anger of Prime Minister Winston Churchill.

There were two more surprises.

No army has successfully invaded the *verdronken* (drowned) land of Holland. It is unique in the world with its polders of land reclaimed from the sea, and its infamous Peel country of swamps and marshes covering a third of the land. All the Allied generals and the Field Marshal were totally ignorant of the battlegrounds that would cause infinite pain, bewilderment and losses in the next four months. The *bocage* country in Normandy had proved to be ideal for defensive warfare and in many ways the polders and the Peel countryside were similar. This author writes with feeling. He fought in Market Garden amongst the polders and in the Peel country for those wicked months of winter 1944.

And the second surprise was that the only tank versus tank battle ever fought in Holland was between the 11th Armoured (Black Bull) Division, in which the author served, and a bold Kampfgruppe well equipped with Panther tanks. The author's 21st birthday was spent as a Royal Horse Artillery forward observation officer (FOO) near the river Maas on the eastern edge of the Peel country, in his Sherman tank under mortar bombardment for most of the day.

Early in 1944 Winston Churchill wrote to the War Office: 'It is a painful reflection that probably not one in four or five men who wear the King's uniform even hear a bullet whistle, or are likely to hear one. The vast majority run no more risk than the civil population in southern England. It is my

2nd Battalion Grenadier Guards approaching the Belgian frontier.

unpleasant duty to dwell upon these facts. One set of men are sent back again and again to the front while the great majority are kept out of all fighting, *to their regret.*' After being wounded in Holland and again in Germany, the author returned to fight with the Black Bull Division. He had no regrets!

September was the extraordinary month of LIBERATION! Every city, town and village between the Seine and across the Dutch frontier went mad with joy. The first inkling would be an armoured car, perhaps from the Cherry Pickers, the Household Cavalry or the Inns of Court, cautiously feeling the temperature. What was going to be the reception? A bazooka, a defended roadblock, an ambush … down the road and into the main square went the tough little Daimler with its long radio antenna as the message went back to the squadron leader. And if the dreaded *moffen* (the Dutch equivalent of 'Jerry') had gone, delirious crowds appeared from every corner. 5 September was later to be known in Dutch history as *Dolle Dinsdag* or 'Mad Tuesday'.

Alan Moorehead, the intrepid journalist who had covered the British Army's defeats and victories in North Africa, was now at the forefront in north-west Europe. He described the liberation of Brussels. He could equally have been describing the liberation of Paris, Antwerp, Ghent or hundreds of other places:

Brussels Liberation Extravaganza. (*Imperial War Museum BU-482*)

The taking of Brussels was a crazy headlong skirmish. Nearly all the Germans had decamped and those that remained at the southern approaches found themselves overwhelmed with a tank charge [Guards Armoured] that burst through the streets and the centre of the capital. Mad with excitement the million people of Brussels rushed out into the open, screaming and shouting and waving flags. The joy of Paris was a pallid thing compared to this extravaganza. At one moment women would be spitting and kicking at the German prisoners: the next they would rush at the British soldiers with bottles of wine and cakes and flowers. Someone discovered the German wine dump – some eighty thousand bottles of a remarkable claret. A kind of frenzy, utterly uncontrollable, seized the people. They danced wildly all night through the streets, the hotels and the cafés. They scrawled their names over the tanks and trucks. They carried off the autographs of the soldiers as though they were precious manuscripts … Every house was flung open and every passing soldier – even though he might be engaged on a mopping-up operation [liberation seriously impeded Allied troop battle progress in Antwerp, Ghent, Eindhoven and Nijmegen!] – was dragged inside and given a meal, a bed, anything he wanted. Effigies of Hitler were paraded through the streets. Tunes like 'Tipperary' and 'We'll hang out the washing on the Siegfried Line' became the steady monotonous background of the wild shouts and screams in every street … And Brussels continued with this madhouse atmosphere for ten long days and nights on end.

Moorehead observed the fantastic happiness of the liberation of Brussels on 3 September. The next day this author encountered exactly the same welcome in Antwerp.

September 1944 started full of hope with success after success, then there was a magnificent failure, followed by four months of dreary fighting, particularly on the 'Island' of polder land between Arnhem, Nijmegen and points west and east. And there were still five more huge German rivers plus the Siegfried Line to cross …

The first was the Rhine endeavour.

Detail from picture on p. 15. (*Imperial War Museum BU-482*)

CHAPTER 2

Hitler's Miracles:
Hitler's 'Fireman'

On 25 August, the day after the fall of Paris, the SHAEF intelligence summary declared: 'Two and a half months of bitter fighting, culminating for the Germans in a bloodbath big enough even for their extravagant tastes, have brought the end of the war in Europe within sight, almost within reach. The strength of the German armies in the West has been shattered, Paris belongs to France again and the Allied armies are streaming towards the frontiers of the Reich.' And Eisenhower said: 'The enemy was momentarily helpless to present any continuous front against our advance.' With the capture of Brussels on 3 September and Antwerp the next day euphoria was everywhere, from the top (SHAEF) downwards. 'On to Berlin' was the cry. Eisenhower now had five armies under his command, more or less poised to smash eastwards to the Ruhr. The combined Allied Intelligence Committee in London estimated that 'organised resistance under the control of the German high command is unlikely to continue beyond 1 December ... and may end even sooner'. Major General John Kennedy at the War Office in London noted, on 6 September: 'If we go at the same pace as of late, we should be in Berlin by the 28th ...'

When Adolf Hitler in his *Wolfchancellery* in Rastenburg, East Prussia, heard of the capture of Antwerp there was consternation and great shock. On the same day, 4 September, he reappointed the 69-year-old Field Marshal 'Gerd' von Rundstedt, the senior and most dependable of all of Hitler's generals, as commander in chief in the west, and Field Marshal Walther Model, the Führer's 'fireman', to continue as Commander of Army Group B to direct the critical battle for Holland and Belgium. Hitler ordered that the Scheldt fortresses be defended at all costs and that both sides and banks of the estuary be held. He ordered General Kurt Student, C-in-C Paratroops, to form the new First Parachute Army and hold the line of the Albert canal from Antwerp to Maastricht, a front of 60 miles. Student was given command of the forces already on the Dutch mainland, and portly Reichsmarschall Hermann Göring revealed on 4 September, to everyone's surprise, that he had six parachute regiments in various stages of training or re-equipment. Also that he could raise two more regiments from paratroops in convalescent depots, making a total force of 20,000 mainly fit, tough young men. He then added another 10,000 from the Luftwaffe ground and air crews whose operations and training had been stopped by a shortage of petrol. They were classed as

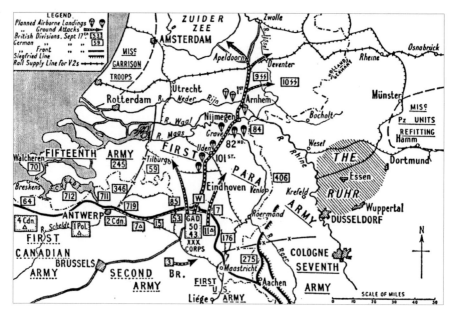

British and German Army units in the region comprising the Scheldt and Upper Rhine, 17 September 1944.

Field Marshal Walter Model, the C-in-C of German Armies in the west.

Fliegerhorst battalions, and as members of the German Air Force they were all dedicated Nazis.

Dr Josef Göbbels, C-in-C Home Army, had already lowered the call-up age from seventeen and a half to 16 years and this provided 300,000 men in August, 200,000 in September and another 200,000 in October. Many of these Hitler Jugend were drafted into 25 new Volksgrenadier divisions. The German Navy disgorged tens of thousands of under-employed officers and ratings; submarine crews and water police were also mobilised. In August, despite Albert Speers' protests, Hitler transferred 250,000 young men from industry into the army. A brigade of seriously deaf men was formed and the White Bread Division appeared – all 'patients' with gastric problems. Other earless, even limbless men were absorbed into Kranken units.

Practically every one of Hitler's fortresses had regiments of OST (eastern territories) troops, or Hiwis or Hilfswillige pressed men, mainly Poles, Czechs or Alsace Germans. They were unreliable and deserted whenever they could.

The final group – fortunately quite small – was the dedicated young Dutch or Belgian youths who preferred to become members of SS battalions. In the Arnhem battle the III Dutch SS Landsturm Niederland was an active member of Sperrverband Harzer, and there were presumably at least two other Dutch SS formations. In Belgium there were several Belgian SS units, one of which guarded Breendonck concentration camp on the outskirts of Antwerp.

The Kettenhunde (chain dogs), the efficient German police, had a field day. In all the towns and cities they 'captured' men on leave and took them to the nearest barracks, or perhaps made sure that they returned immediately to their unit at the front. They were deployed in Holland to waylay stragglers from Normandy and men from the 15th Army who had lost their unit. These stragglers were shoved together into kampfgruppen or emergency battle groups. In the battle for Arnhem and Oosterbeek Field Marshal Model and Generals Bittrich and Student had no fewer than 24 kampfgruppen, including ten SS. In Alan Moorehead's book *Eclipse* he noted: 'We began to collect extraordinary prisoners – near-sighted clerks who had left their city offices three weeks before, men with half-healed wounds, even cripples and children of 15 or 16. It was a makeshift, hotch-potch army, an emergency army put in simply to hold the gap, simply to fight for time while the German generals reorganised on a sounder basis.'

Field Marshal Model told the Führer he needed six weeks to buy time to get the half-abandoned Siegfried Line revitalised and strengthened. Model's career was spectacular. He had no social graces, no military background and a rough manner. In 1941 he commanded a panzer division in Russia and led the drive to the Dnieper. Hitler then promoted him to command an army and during the harsh winter of 1941–42 Model was as resolute in defeat as he had been aggressive in attack. Hitler often sought his advice and generally accepted it. He had many more successes on the Russian front and Hitler called him 'the

Lt General Willi Bittrich, the debonair and gifted GOC of the 2nd SS Panzer Corps which happened to be refitting in the Arnhem area.

saviour of the Eastern Front'. Regarded as a master of defensive strategy and improvisation, his stocky, bustling figure was often seen up at the Front and his troops trusted him. His ruthless energy was just what Hitler wanted and he gave himself the nickname of the 'Führer's fireman', capable of dealing with any emergency.

Two full days before Market Garden was launched (0752hrs on the 15th), the Ultra intelligence from Bletchley Park revealed: 'New location Flivo Army Group B 07hrs 14th Oosterbeek 4 kilometres W of Arnhem.' This proved conclusively that Hitler's most reliable and experienced field marshal and his HQ were between the Arnhem bridge and the drop zones for the British Airborne Division. This should have rung every possible alarm bell. Seventeen Allied airborne army drops had been cancelled or deferred at the last moment. It should have happened for the 18th time.

When the news of the airborne drop reached Hitler in his HQ in East Prussia, an eyewitness described the scene:

On the previous day, 16 September, a very important conference had taken place at Wolfschanze, Hitler's headquarters in East Prussia, when the Führer had outlined his plan for the Ardennes offensive. All was calm. But the next day things were very different. As reports of the airborne landing came

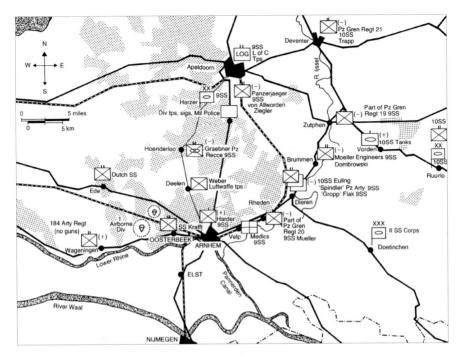

German Troops around Arnhem, 15 September 1944.

in, excitement mounted. The major part of the daily situation conference was taken up with discussions of the air landing, constantly interrupted by telephone calls as fresh reports came in. Hitler himself was chiefly impressed with Model's narrow escape and he became increasingly worried about the safety of his own headquarters. In his own words – 'At any rate if such a mess happened here – here I sit with my whole Supreme Command: here sit the Reichsmarschall (Göring), the OKH, the Reichsführer SS (Himmler), the Reich Foreign Minister (von Ribbentrop); well then, this is the most worthwhile catch, that's obvious. I would not hesitate to risk two parachute divisions here if with one blow I could get my hands on the whole German command.' He then screamed, 'Holland overshadows everything else'.

As reports of more air landings arrived the Führer became violent and raged about the failure of the Luftwaffe. As a result of all the excitement Holland was given top priority and every available reserve formation in Germany, and even those as far afield as Denmark, was alerted and ordered to move down to defeat the British/US penetration.

CHAPTER 3

Von Zangen's Dunkirk Evacuation

Operation Fortitude had been a brilliant success. The plan was to convince Hitler and the German General Staff at OKW that the main Allied onslaught into France would come in the obvious place – the Pas de Calais. It was the closest land point to south-east England; through it lay the easiest route to the Rhine and the Ruhr; and it contained the main sites for Hitler's 'vengeance' weapons, the V-1s and V-2s. A successful landing there would probably mean the loss of all France for the Nazis.

A combined but bogus operations HQ had been built at Dover. The pumping head for one of the PLUTOs (Pipeline under the Ocean) had been set in the cliffs facing Boulogne, and General Patton commanded a 'paper' army in the south-east of England whose extremely busy radio networks were preparing for the invasion.

So, the German 15th Army stayed in the Pas de Calais area under General von Salmuth. It was composed of 346th, 84th, 17th GAF, 348th, 245th, 85th, 344th, 49th, 326th, 2nd Panzer, 331st, 47th, 18th GAF, 148th and 712th Divisions. On top of this there were three more divisions based in Holland. They all remained idle! Even into mid-July the German High Command expected General Patton's Army Group to come sailing across the Channel in the *main* attack on France.

General von Zangen (Salmuth's successor), GOC German 15th Army, wrote later: 'When we retired from the Somme about 1 September I planned slowly to fight my way [back] to Brussels and Antwerp and then take up a line in Holland. I had no fear that Antwerp would be taken since it was far behind the front line and there was a special staff organised to defend it. When I heard on 4 September that it had been captured it came as a stunning surprise. The reason for the fall of Antwerp was the failure of the High Command to appreciate how badly beaten 5th Panzer Army really was. Instead of an army on my left flank there was an empty gap. My own forces were neither strong enough nor fast enough to get back to Antwerp in time to defend it. We were constantly being attacked by armoured columns.' 11th Armoured Division had advanced 230 miles in six days and nights; the sheer speed and brutality of this action had foxed the Germans.

On the face of it the British armour had pulled off a magnificent coup, but it could have been so much better if there had been a back-up infantry division available to strengthen the bridgehead over the Albert canal and force the defenders out of the Merxem suburb. An advance 15 miles north-west of Antwerp would have proved extremely embarrassing to General von Zangen. On hearing the amazing news of the capture of Antwerp, Hitler's immediate command to German Naval Group West was to 'mine and obstruct the Scheldt energetically'. And they did just that!

The original six divisions that came under command of General von Zangen were joined in early September by the remnants of five divisions escaping from the Falaise Gap slaughter in Normandy. Von Zangen wrote:

> It was only by the greatest of efforts that we succeeded in withdrawing at all. One of my divisions marched 90 kilometres in one day during this retreat. With Antwerp in enemy hands there remained only two courses of action open to me – evacuation by sea or breakthrough to the northeast. I decided on the latter course and on 5 September I ordered my troops to assemble in the neighbourhood of Audenarde with the object of attacking in the direction of Brussels. However, before this operation could get properly under way I received word from the Commander-in-Chief West on 6 September to abandon this breakthrough attempt since the enemy line was already much too strong in the area between Brussels and Antwerp. Instead I was told to make preparations for the evacuation of my army across the Scheldt to the islands of Walcheren and South Beveland.

Field Marshal von Rundstedt, Commander-in-Chief West, ordered the 15th Army to hold out tenaciously in all the fortress-ports of Le Havre, Boulogne, Calais and Dunkirk and, importantly, the new 'fortresses' of Walcheren, Breskens and Flushing to deny maritime access to the port of Antwerp. The main bulk of the 15th Army would be evacuated through Breskens on the south bank of the river Scheldt, to the port of Flushing on the north bank, and then march across Walcheren Island eastwards to the mainland north of Antwerp. If the British and Canadians sealed the South Beveland route to the mainland, then the German defences in Holland west of the river Maas were at risk.

General von Zangen now made sure that the fortress commandants of Le Havre, Boulogne, Calais and Dunkirk were reinforced. He brought the 719th Infantry Division from northern Holland to help defend the canal line between Bruges and Ghent, and the vital area north of Antwerp. The crucial retreat of the 15th Army across the river Scheldt he entrusted to the unfortunate General Eugen-Felix Schwalbe. Unfortunate not because he was deaf, but because he had lost his division trying to stop the Allied forces at the river Seine. Schwalbe said:

When I was told what my new job was to be I immediately set up my headquarters in Breskens, from where I could control the situation. Gathering about me as many officers as I could find, I sent them along the roads leading to Breskens, where they set up collecting posts for the assembling of the retreating units. They would telephone to me telling me what formation had arrived and was ready to cross, and I would allot it a specific hour when it was to be evacuated. Until that hour it was to remain well camouflaged and hidden along the roads.

For the task of crossing the Scheldt I had assembled two large Dutch civilian ships, three large rafts capable of holding 18 vehicles each, and 16 small Rhine boats with a capacity of about 250 men each. The trips were made chiefly at night, although since time was pressing, some crossings had to be made during the day. Allied planes constantly harried the ships and a number of them laden with troops received direct hits. However, in 16 days we managed to evacuate the remnants of nine shattered infantry divisions – 59th, 70th, 245th, 331st, 344th, the 17th Luftwaffe Field, the 346th, 711th and 712th. We left one division *in Dunkirk* to defend the approaches to Antwerp. In terms of men and equipment we brought to safety by this operation some 65,000 men, 225 guns, 750 trucks and wagons and 1,000 horses. By 21 September my task was completed and the bulk of the 15th Army had been rescued from encirclement.

I was in constant fear that the Allies would cut off the Beveland Isthmus by an advance north of Antwerp and thereby trap such troops as were in the process of moving out. If this had happened our alternative plan was to evacuate the troops by sea through the Dutch islands to Dordrecht and Rotterdam. But such a journey would have been slow and dangerous. It would have meant a 12-hour voyage by sea rather than the three-quarters of an hour needed to cross from Breskens to Flushing. We could not have hoped to rescue anything but the troops themselves had it been necessary to adopt this course.

On 4 September Adolf Hitler issued a new directive: 'Because of the breakthrough of enemy tank forces toward Antwerp, it has become very important for the further progress of the war to hold the fortresses of Boulogne and Dunkirk, the Calais defence area [inc Cap Gris Nez], Walcheren island with Flushing harbour, the bridgehead at Antwerp and the Albert Canal position as far as Maastricht. For this purpose the 15th Army is to bring the garrisons of Boulogne and Dunkirk and the Calais defence area up to strength by means of full units. The defensive strength of the fortresses is to be increased by means of additional ammunition supplies, from the supplies of 15th Army, especially anti-tank ammunition by bringing up provisions of all kinds from the country and by evacuating the entire population. The Commanders of the Calais defence area and of Walcheren island receive the same authority as a fortress commander.'

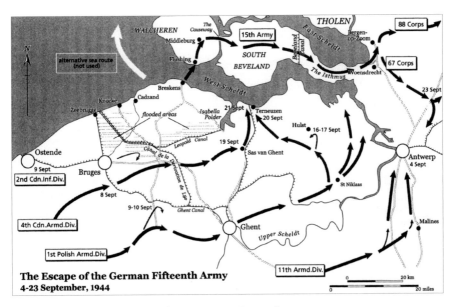

The Escape of the German Fifteenth Army
4-23 September, 1944

The escape of the German 15th Army, 4–23 September 1944.

General Gustav von Zangen had six divisions still under command and by a vital Allied strategic error, managed to follow his Führer's instructions perfectly. The three coastal fortresses were manned and provisioned, and in addition 80,000 men, 616 guns and 1,200 vehicles eventually managed to escape to continue the war in Holland and Germany. On Winston Churchill's journey to the Quebec Conference of 10 September he wrote, 'It is difficult to see how 21st Army Group can advance in force to the German frontier until it has cleared up the stubborn resistance at the Channel ports and dealt with the Germans at Walcheren and north of Antwerp'.

On the day after the 1st Canadian Army started the Herculean task of clearing the defences to the Scheldt estuary, General Von Zangen sent out this message to all his troops:

Commander-in-Chief Fifteenth Army. Army Headquarters
7 October 1944

ORDERS

The defence of the approaches to Antwerp represents a task which is decisive for the further conduct of the war. Therefore, every last man in the fortification is to know why he must devote himself to this task with the utmost strength. I have confirmed that so-called 'experts' among the local population are attempting to confuse the German soldiers in this battle task ordered by the Führer.

Whether know-it-alls in some headquarters are participating in such nonsense, which then quickly reaches the troops, I do not know. This I have reason, however, to fear. Therefore, I order commanders, as well as the National Socialist indoctrination officers, to instruct the troops in the clearest and most factual manner on the following points: Next to Hamburg, Antwerp is the largest port in Europe...

After overrunning the Scheldt fortifications, the English would finally be in a position to land great masses of material in a large and completely protected harbour. With this material they might deliver a death blow to the north German plateau and to Berlin before the onset of winter.

In order to pretend that the battle of Antwerp is unimportant and to shake the morale of its defenders, enemy propaganda maintains that the Anglo-American forces already possess sufficient ports which are intact, with the result that they are not at all dependent on Antwerp. That is a known lie. In particular, the port of Ostend, of which the enemy radio speaks frequently, is completely destroyed. Current delays in the enemy's conduct of the war are attributable in great measure to the fact that he still must bring all his supplies through the improvised facilities of Cherbourg. As a result, he has even had to lay a temporary oil pipe-line from these to the interior of France....

In his last speech, Churchill said again, 'before the storms of winter we must bring in the harvest in Europe'. The enemy knows that he must assault the European fortress as speedily as possible before its inner lines of resistance are built up and occupied by new divisions. For this reason he needs the Antwerp harbour. And for this reason, we must hold the Scheldt fortifications to the end. The German people are watching us. In this hour, the fortifications along the Scheldt occupy a role which is decisive for the future of our people. Each additional day that you deny the port of Antwerp to the enemy and to the resources that he has at his disposal, will be vital.

(signed) Von Zangen
General of the Infantry

Von Zangen had left behind two unusual divisions to obey Hitler's orders to delay the Allied clearance of the Scheldt estuary. On Walcheren Island the curious 70th Infantry Division (with 1018th, 1019th and 1020th Regiments), together with the usual Luftwaffe flak anti-aircraft weaponry, 89th Fortress Regiment and Kriegsmarines formed the garrison. The 10,000 men of the 'White Bread' Division of special stomach (Magen) battalions all suffered from stomach ailments of one form or another. After five years of war, bad food, hard living conditions and above all nervous tension, the Wehrmacht was swamped with soldiers complaining of internal gastric trouble. Most of them were genuine sufferers, but others were malingerers. Occupying the polderland bunkers of the island defences were soldiers with acute ulcers, dyspeptic and inflamed stomachs, and veterans suffering from wounded abdomens. The food in Holland was ideal; fresh vegetables, eggs, milk, fish and, in particular, white bread was readily available, hence the divisional nickname. Behind Spandaus, Schmeissers, bazookas, nebelwerfers, 88mm dual purpose and coastal guns, the 'White Bread' Division was just as potentially dangerous as any of the Wehrmacht troops.

On the south side of the Scheldt Major General Knut Eberding's 65th Infantry Division, known as the 'Leave' Division, had been hastily formed. Almost all soldiers *on leave* in every German city or town, and from Italy and Norway, were required by the military police to join the 65th, which was rushed up to the Walcheren front. They were mainly experienced (but indignant) soldiers, torn away from their families.

Detail from picture on p. 98. (*Imperial War Museum MH-3956*)

CHAPTER 4

The Capture of Antwerp: the key fulcrum

Hitler had not designated Antwerp a 'fortress' and no proper fortress division was available, but Major General Graf Stolberg-zu-Stolberg arrived from Brittany on 5 June to take command of the Antwerp garrison. A week later the headquarter staff of 136th Infantry Division arrived. The 15,000-17,000 defenders consisted of the usual mixture: a security battalion, a 'stomach invalid' battalion, a Belgian renegade battalion, an OST Russian prisoner of war battalion, Luftwaffe ground crews, anti-aircraft batteries, transport guards, and various Kriegsmarine troops for naval servicing. There were no specialist anti-tank weapons, but all the many 88mm anti-aircraft guns were now dual purpose. There were two lines of defences. One of roadblocks and pillboxes at main road junctions, with a line of forts stretching from a bend in the river Scheldt to Fort Ste Marie and Kruisschans village at the far end of the docks. The second line of defence was based on the ancient inner forts that reached as far as Merxem, the northern suburb over the Albert canal. In the main Central Park, Stolberg had his headquarters in three large bunkers.

From June, in accordance with Hitler's instructions, plans had been made for the destruction of the huge docks. The massive 1,000-acre deep-sea complex, with warehouses, cranes, bridges, six miles of wharves, quays, locks, electrically controlled gates and railway rolling stock, extended along the river Scheldt below the city. The whole area was criss-crossed by long water barriers. Antwerp, a major city at that time, had a population of 2.5 million.

Fortunately for the Allies the Belgian Resistance movement was substantial – with 3,500 men – and well organised. M. Eugene Colson, codenamed 'Harry', was the chief co-ordinator of the Resistance in the Antwerp port area. Although the Gestapo arrested several key Resistance members on 25 August, Colson's groups captured the port commandant, Captain Mohr and his staff, and then took control of the south-east of the port area. The White Brigade Resistance locked many of the lifting bridges in the down position to make the road access easier for the British.

Hitler's other sea fortresses of Brest, Boulogne, St Malo, Calais and Le Havre were commanded by dedicated soldiers who systematically carried out their Führer's orders to destroy all the port facilities. 'Harry' and his friends had achieved a miracle by preventing this happening in Antwerp.

Antwerp was the jewel in the crown and although Eisenhower, Montgomery and even Horrocks, appeared to be totally unaware of its importance, other VIPs were. Adolf Hitler and Winston Churchill were, unwittingly, both appreciative of the logistical supply problem facing the Allies. Lt General Brian Horrocks, GOC 30th Corps, had allocated various objectives to his three brilliant armoured divisions. The Guards Armoured had taken Brussels, the 7th Armoured (and 1st Polish) Divisions had taken Ghent, and the 11th Armoured, by a *coup de main*, had taken Antwerp. As Churchill noted at the time: 'Without the vast harbours of this city no advance across the lower Rhine and into the plains of Northern Germany was possible.' The potential of Antwerp was enormous. In pre-war days 11,000 seagoing vessels entered it each year with cargoes of 24 million tons. Additionally, 44,000 smaller river craft shipped in a further 12 million tons annually. Admiral Bertram Ramsay sent a signal on 4 September to SHAEF headquarters and 21st Army Group headquarters, so Field Marshal Montgomery *must* have seen it:

> It is essential if Antwerp (and Rotterdam) are to be opened quickly enemy must be prevented from:
> 1. a) Carrying out demolitions and blocking ports.
>   b) Mining and blocking Scheldt (and new waterway between Rotterdam and the Hook).
> 2. Both Antwerp (and Rotterdam) are highly vulnerable to mining and blocking. If the enemy succeeds in these operations the time it will take to open the ports cannot be estimated.
> 3. It will be necessary for coastal batteries to be captured before approach channels to the river routes can be established.

In his diary the Admiral wrote: 'Antwerp is useless unless the Scheldt Estuary is cleared of the enemy.'

Major General 'Pip' Roberts had spurred on and led his great 11th Armoured Division, the 'Black Bull', over 230 miles in six days since crossing the Seine at Vernon. He had thrust vigorously from the Seine to Beauvais, captured the German General Eberhardt and the headquarters of the 7th Army at Amiens, and then passed Arras, Lens, Vimy Ridge, Tournai, Alost, Malines towards Boom. In his memoirs he wrote: 'I did not want to try getting into Antwerp in the dark – the possibility of absolute chaos was much too great – but we had to start at first light.' He had an excellent plan that encouraged an element of competition between 23rd Hussars on the left flank route and 3rd Royal Tank Regiment on the right. The third armoured regiment – 2nd Fife and Forfar Yeomanry and 159th Infantry Brigade with 3rd Monmouthshires, 1st Herefords and 4th Battalion King's Shropshire Light Infantry in their trucks, guarded by 15/19th Hussars – followed closely behind. The Inns of Court, a brilliant and brave reconnaissance regiment, guarded both flanks and checked that the outskirts of Boom were mined and guarded by anti-tank guns.

Just south of Boom to the right of the road was Fort von Breendonk, a large sinister grey fortress near the main crossroads. Patrick Delaforce, with 13th

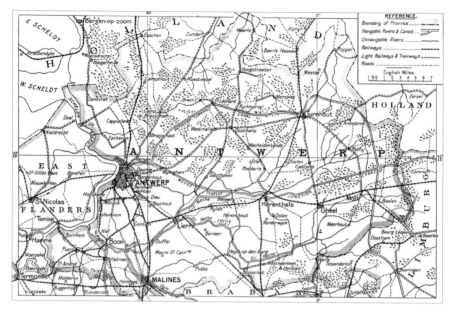

The region of Antwerp.

Royal Horse Artillery, stopped his half-track briefly and was immediately asked by a group of Belgian White Brigade to look inside the building. In *Eclipse* Alan Moorehead describes what he saw there later: 'Fifty of the Belgian White Army were handed over to the Gestapo. Ten days was the usual length of the torture. That is to say the special torture used to get members of the Resistance to give away the names of their comrades. It was very severe. When the Gestapo constructed this concentration camp [at Breendonk] they made special runnels in the cement floors for the blood.' The bodies, the blood and the smell of horrible death were there early on the morning of 4 September.

Near Breendonk Lieutenant Robert Vekemans, a Belgian engineer dressed in a grey shabby raincoat, stopped or tried to stop the Sherman tanks of 3rd RTR. By skill, guile, luck and bravery this patriotic repatriated prisoner of war, having discreetly surveyed the two main well-guarded road bridges over the river Rudel, decided he would stop the British armoured column short of a large railway viaduct and lead them over the Breendonk crossroads to cross the canal at Willebroek, half way to Boom. The tanks would be concealed by buildings and, it was hoped, would be able to reach the Pont van Enschodt before being identified as hostile. Vekemans confirmed that the minor road bridge would take the 35-ton weight of a loaded Sherman across 160 yards of river. Vekemans suggested that the leading tanks should turn their guns to face backwards and that they should be covered with camouflage netting Lieutenant Stubbs's troop led the armoured column and crossed the bridge. The resourceful Vekemans, halfway over, cut the firing leads to the mines below the bridge, which was later guarded by 8th Battalion Rifle Brigade.

The RTR Shermans turned left through the narrow waterside streets of Boom into the town square. The Belgian White Brigade freedom fighters appeared at 1300hrs and all together charged up the main road to seize the great bridge from the rear, taking the Germans by surprise. The bridge guard of about 50 tried to hold off the tanks as the German engineers rushed to the bridge with primers, detonators and leads. Faced by the guns and machine-guns of a squadron of tanks, the bridge guard surrendered and the indomitable Vekemans, at revolver point, found the leads to the explosives and cut them. The other canal bridge was destroyed, but divisional sappers put a Bailey bridge across the canal that night. Now Vekemans was joined by Edouard Pilaet, codenamed 'Francois', one of the Resistance leaders, who clambered onto Lt Colonel Silvertop's tank, and the RTR, Rifle Brigade and the White Brigade drove briskly down the main road 12 miles north to Antwerp. Major Bill Close, 3rd RTR, meanwhile took his squadron on the left by the river bank route through Niel, Hemiksem and Hoboken to enter Antwerp along the bank of the river Scheldt led by M. Gaston de Lausney, another brave Resistance leader, also in a dirty mac, but armed with a Sten gun. The route to Antwerp of another armoured regiment of the Division, the 23rd Hussars, was via Malines, Mechelen and Kontich. They encountered a flak site with several 88mm anti-tank guns, which was dug in and sandbagged but was promptly shelled heavily by the Sexton Ram 25-pdrs of 13th RHA.

3rd Monmouthshires had driven through the night of 3–4 September in their TCVs. After a small action at Londerzeel, a few miles south of Breendonk, 3rd Mons crossed the river Rupel at Boom and entered Antwerp by the main road.

Antwerp: View of the quays and the Steen.

After passing the inner line of forts they turned off left to the west, heading for the Scheldt and the docks. They were ordered to secure the sluice gates vital to the port, and these they captured intact. Near the river, 'A' Company came under fire at a narrow bridge. After several attempts and casualties they established a firm bridgehead in the darkness. On the east side of town the 23rd Hussars had a more difficult time. On their advance line the roads were mined and covered by a flak unit, and anti-tank guns had been placed in some of the forts and on the roofs of houses. 'C' squadron brewed up a number of staff cars leaving the town. Despite Captain Budgen, 13th RHA, firing stonks, the impasse continued. 'H' Company 8th RB did not have enough manpower to clear the area dominated by anti-tank guns and mined roads. Eventually 23rd Hussars withdrew and spent a very comfortable night at Kontich.

Colonel Ivor Rees, CO 4th KSLI, described part of his 'O' group given out at 1500hrs on the outskirts of Antwerp on the Boom road:

> The difficulties of collecting one's 'Order-Group', thinking and giving out orders, making oneself heard, linking various sub-units together among this mass of the populace crowding round, still kissing you, asking you to post a letter to America, to give them some petrol, some more arms for the White Brigade, holding a baby under your nose to be kissed, trying to give you a drink, inviting you to their house, trying to carry you away, offering information about the enemy, had to be seen to be understood, and were the same, but about three times as great, as in Amiens. In addition Brigadier [Churcher] would say at intervals, 'I want you to be as quick as possible'.

General Graf Stolberg-zu-Stolberg reported to Field Marshal Model by radio that British tanks were across the river Rupel in Boom, and the Belgian Resistance in Antwerp was now very active indeed. He was told to withdraw across the Albert canal or if that was impossible, to fight or take flight to the south-east of the city.

The Resistance leaders estimated that 5,000 enemy infantry were in the city, with General Stolberg's HQ in a network of bunkers in the Central Park. General Roberts ordered 4th KSLI plus 'C' squadron 2nd Fife and Forfarshires to take on the Central Park garrison at 1600hrs, and 3rd Mons to move to and occupy the dock area. Maps were very poor and neither the general nor his two brigadiers realised that the vital Albert canal did not go through the *centre* of the city, but was in fact in the northern suburbs, separated from the suburb of Merxem. Horrocks admitted that the Division simply did not have sufficient troops to clear the town, seize the docks, and force and occupy a strong bridgehead over the canal. Nevertheless that is what the Division now proceeded to try to do.

Under cover of the artillery smokescreen 3rd RTR plus 'G' Company 8th RB attacked and cleared the defences and by 1400hrs had reached the dock area. Captain Noel Bell, 8th RB reported:

As we arrived at the city itself shots rang out, Germans began throwing grenades on to us from a window of a high building near us, 20mm guns opened up and we knew we should have to fight for it. The main streets were densely packed with crowds awaiting us. Our vehicles were unable to move and were smothered with people; we were overwhelmed by flowers, bottles and kisses. Everyone had gone mad. We had to get to the docks at all costs to save them from being destroyed by the Germans who might now be getting organised.

But the riflemen in their carriers were separated from the tanks by the immense crowds: 'We then came under fire from the far bank of the Scheldt at the same time as we were engaged in two different street battles on the near side. I began to wonder whether we should ever see the tanks again. It was difficult to describe over the wireless exactly where we were.' Eventually 3rd RTR arrived, running a gauntlet of German bazooka fire. There were snipers everywhere, as Major Bill Close, 3rd RTR, wrote: 'I found myself crouching in the turret looking for the source of the bullets pinging about, while pretty girls waved madly from blocks of flats pointing out the enemy positions.' John Dunlop's 'C' squadron went for the docks with 8th RB and Bill Close took his squadron to Antwerp-South railway station. The White Brigade Resistance fighters conducted their own private wars, often vendettas, settling old scores with the Germans or collaborators. The Shermans were pelted with fruit and flowers and every head exposed was offered a glass of cognac or champagne, plus cigars. John Dunlop led 3rd RTR to the docks. He had stayed in Antwerp before and spoke French and enough Flemish to get by:

We never closed the lids of our turrets, because we then became so blind and so deaf that we felt too vulnerable. We felt a lot safer with them open. But that afternoon I remember seriously considering closing down. Sporadic firing from above (from Germans at the upper windows of houses) was confined to the outskirts of the town and later rather more intensively to some parts of the centre. Civilians climbed on our tanks. We kept on meeting bursts of small arms fire and an occasional grenade and there were civilian casualties.

Lieutenant Gibson Stubbs's troop sank a small steamer full of Germans in the Scheldt river. He fired AP at 1,000 yards and the boat went aground enveloped in steam.

4th KSLI marched two miles in a straight line from the Boomse-Steenweg roundabout towards the Central Park, cheered on by the hordes of well-wishers thronging the tightly packed pavements. The large triangular park, each side a quarter of a mile long, was covered with bushes and tall trees and overlooked by high buildings. Three substantial bunkers, screened by thick shrubs, sheltered the main German HQ and there was a subway under the road to the Kommandantur building. A large lake was another obstacle while snipers on the rooftops were a distinct menace. 'A' Company attacked from the west and 'C' Company from the east; by 2200hrs the park HQ was taken. 'C' squadron 2nd Fife and Forfarshires did a good deal of intimidation by milling about in the park, and certainly helped compel the complete surrender. Captain Fruin took his tank and another off to deal with the SS HQ and shelled the building briskly. Each time an empty shell case was pushed out of the tank's open port, a Belgian civilian put a hand in with a large glass of wine!

The Ayrshire Yeomanry FOO, Captain Robin Burton, used his Sherman machine-guns to good effect, since he was not allowed to call down pinpoint fire on the bunkers.

Captain Ted Jones with 'A' Company 4th KSLI noted that his platoon sergeant, Paddy Cahill, was offered a precious bottle of White Horse whisky, which had been kept safe for the day of liberation. 'When we finally reached the park we found a high bank covered in shrubs and trees. The only access was over a narrow footbridge covered from the far side by two enemy machine-gun posts.' Sergeant Cahill, Major Tom Maddocks and the determined 'A' Company fought their way through the park and captured 280 prisoners in the bunkers, including General Stolberg and a resplendent chap who turned out to be the bandmaster.

Ned Thornburn, with 'D' Company 4th KSLI, was given the task of capturing the Kommandantur in the Banque Hypothecaire, half a mile north-west of Central Park. Supported by a troop of 3rd RTR, the three platoons attacked the building from various angles with Sten guns and grenades. Bill Close ordered a Firefly to fire its 'beeg cannon' at the main doors. The KSLI platoon commander, Jimmy Bratland, was a Norwegian and with his fluent German helped Ned Thornburn negotiate the surrender. Eventually seven officers, including the smartly dressed commandant and 84 other ranks, came out and were marched

Heil de 11de Britse pantserdivisie. (*Antwerp newspaper photo*)

off to Antwerp Zoo which had been organised by the Resistance as a collecting centre for prisoners and collaborators. After that very successful little battle Ned drank Pils with the Resistance leaders in a nearby café until 0200hrs and slept on a doormat at Taymans toy shop in the Huidvetter-Straat.

The third KSLI battle on 4 September involved 'B' Company under Dick Mullock. They were ordered to seize a bridge on the south-east perimeter and block one of the main east-west roads in the southern suburbs. Admiring crowds impeded their march and the KSLI burst into song with 'Tipperary' and 'Pack up your troubles', many arm in arm with the (prettier) Belgians. It was just as well that Colonel Reeves did not see them. CQMS Bob Howells arrived with a proper hot meal: 'The locals were amazed to see such delicious food being ladled out to us.'

Their FOO, Captain Burton, mowed down a column of German troops and horse-drawn vehicles; the dead horses were then hung, skinned and quartered by a local *boucher*. Later, Sergeant Hughes almost single-handedly destroyed a retreating column of 15 vehicles, causing 45 casualties. Altogether 4th KSLI had a marvellous day. The city of Antwerp was in their hands and 2,000 prisoners had been captured, including the German GOC and town commandant.

'It was unrestrained joy – mad and crazy,' according to Captain C.K.O. Spence, Ayrshire Yeomanry, 'and all the time sporadic firing [continued] against stubborn remnants of resisting Germans. No war can have been more crazy.' Spence tried to capture a beautiful Mercedes staff car but the Belgians got there first, so he had to settle for a moth-eaten Volkswagen, which did at least 60 miles to the gallon.

That night was chaotic. Café parties went on until dawn. Snipers fired and were hunted down by the Resistance. There was dancing in the streets. A

Celebrations in Antwerp, 4 September 1944. (*R.T. Lancaster*)

company commander of the Herefords told Bill Close that he hadn't a clue where half his men were!

Captain Moody, 2 i/c 'C' Company 3rd Mons, had a strange visitation during the night of 4–5 September: 'The sound of approaching tracks brought the company to "stand to". It was a Bren carrier painted white with gun etc, in perfect order, manned by the Resistance, furious that 3rd Mons had arrived in their patch "so early". The Belgian crew had hidden and serviced the vehicle and weapons since it had been abandoned by the BEF in *1940*!'

At first light on 5 September the Herefords started to clear the eastern and south-eastern part of the city. Slowly but surely they succeeded, taking many prisoners. Major John How, 3rd Mons, noted:

> Even at this early hour (0600hrs) the people of Antwerp thronged into the roadway to greet the advancing troops as they made their way in long files on either side of the road. Fair ladies of Antwerp, showing signs of having been hurriedly disturbed from their slumbers, pressed bunches of flowers on the soldiers who, not wishing to appear ungrateful by throwing them into the gutter, continued on their way with bouquets in one hand and their firearms in the other.

At 0900hrs General 'Pip' Roberts received an unpleasant shock. The main bridge over the Albert canal had been blown up: 'This was a blow to me and I realised that I had made a great error in not going into the city the evening before. I had thought that the canal went through the centre of the city … had I braved the crowds and gone into the city myself I would have realised the situation.' In the absence of adequate maps, patrols of 4th KSLI were sent out to locate the Albert

Noel Bell's half track enters Antwerp.

canal and to discover whether it could be crossed. The Schijnpoort-Weg carried the main road to Breda and to the west in the dock areas was the Yserbrug bridge. Major Andy Hardy, commanding 'C' Company 4th KSLI, said:

> My task on the 5th was to seize a main road bridge over the [60-yard wide] Albert canal somewhere west of Merxem. The scene was as usual [with] dense accompanying crowds making control difficult, all mysteriously vanishing as we approached the bridge and shortly before we came under fire from MGs across the canal. I must say that I regarded the task of rushing the bridge as doomed to bloody failure.

As one platoon got across there was a loud explosion and the middle span dropped into the canal. Major Hardy's men remained in their positions until dusk.

At 2000hrs Colonel Reeves, CO 4th KSLI, was ordered to put the whole battalion across the Schijnpoort-Weg bridge. The maps were unreliable, there was no time for a detailed reconnaissance and the Belgian guides disappeared. The assault boats carried from Normandy on the sides of TCVs all had holes in the canvas and leaked badly. Colonel Reeves' Ayrshire Yeomanry FOO's key wireless set failed to work. Nevertheless the indomitable Sergeant Ted Jones, 'A' Company, found some local boats and, despite a strong current, rowed across a 150-yard stretch of canal. During the night three companies got across and, backed by their own mortar sections, formed a bridgehead near the Sports Palace south of the canal. The Sextons of 1 Battery 13th RHA were ready for action in the Central Park; they could not fire on targets within the city but they were soon to be in action. Patrick Delaforce noticed that his troop commander's Sherman OP tank had 18 civilians clustered on it. Norman Young was a good looking chap and he had lost his beret, his steel helmet, his RHA insignia and much of his dignity, but not his nerve! Delaforce visited the lion house in the zoo, a broad high building with barred cages on both side. Two pretty Belgian girls checked in the new arrivals. Each cage had a different category of prisoner: male collaborators, female collaborators, important Belgian traitors, German NCOs, German other ranks and finally, German officers. When Alan Moorehead visited the zoo he compared it to the Colosseum in Rome in the time of Emperor Caligula. A large crowd was permanently baying at the entrance to the zoo; they wanted to get inside and carry out a lynching party. 'These,' explained the Belgian officer in charge, indicating the Germans, 'we will turn over to the British authorities. These,' indicating the collaborators, 'will be shot this evening *after a fair trial*.' A couple of photographers had gone into the cages and were arranging the condemned men in convenient and artistic groups to have their photographs taken. The models stayed rigid like wax figures. Another man was going among them taking their watches. By midday on the 5th Brigadier Churcher gave orders that the 6,000 German prisoners in the zoo should be marched out of the city and escorted by the carrier platoons of the three infantry

De Engelsen rukken op! (*Antwerp newspaper photo*)

battalions to protect them from acts of retribution. Three months later Brigadier Churcher, then on the Maas, received a letter from Switzerland accusing him of contravening the Geneva Convention by placing German prisoners in a zoo and thus humiliating them! Appropriately most of the German PoWs were marched to the infamous Breendonk concentration camp.

Colonel Ivor Reeves, CO of 4th KSLI, described his bridgehead at dawn on 6 September:

> We found ourselves in the most ghastly factory area, one mass of small streets, lanes, passages, walls, walls within walls, piles of iron and waste of every description. We soon discovered some machine-gun posts and started to clear them. That started two days and a night's street fighting, the most tiring and trying type of fighting even under the best conditions. The Boche found us and soon [1100hrs] had five tanks among us. We knocked out two and then ran out of all PIAT anti-tank arms. They shot us up with machine-guns, AP shot and HE, knowing we couldn't touch them, stalking round and round day and night, blasting us out of houses as they discovered us.

General Roberts wrote:

> With the object of entering Merxem from the flank and taking pressure off the 4th KSLI, the 3rd Mons (less one company who were down at the main lock gates) and two squadrons of 23rd Hussars organised an attack on Merxem from the flank. At the second of two bridges on their route, this force was held up by a road block protected by mines and covered by heavy fire.

Colonel Reeves, 4th KSLI, asked Brigadier Churcher for permission to withdraw his battered, defenceless three companies on the night of 6

September. Churcher sought permission from the general. His intention was still for the Division to move north with 29th Brigade leading and 159th Brigade clearing up Merxem. The sappers were ordered to construct one or more bridges in the night. So that evening 4th KSLI clung on to their small factory area bridgehead, 3rd Mons beat off a counter-attack on the vital sluice gates, while 23rd Hussars/3rd Mons were also in trouble.

The divisional historian, Edgar Palamountain, wrote: 'Nor were we ourselves to find Antwerp a rose without a thorn, for besides the intermittent shelling which continued for some weeks, we were to fight a battle there and an unsuccessful battle at that!' General Roberts wrote: 'The 4 KSLI situation was becoming worrying: they were suffering steady casualties and it was decided, reluctantly, to withdraw them. This was successfully done under cover of intense artillery fire in the late afternoon.' It was tempting to think that while Corps HQ were having such a jolly time in Brussels – which they were – 11th Armoured Division was left out on a limb. Eventually on the morning of 7 September Lt General Horrocks came, saw the problem for himself and said: 'You must get them back.' At 0300hrs, in pitch darkness and pouring rain, 3rd Mons was ordered to attack eastward, starting from No. 7 dry docks and crossing the Yserbrug bridge towards Merxem. But they met tough opposition in their efforts to relieve pressure on the KSLI bridgehead.

4th KSLI took 150 casualties including 31 killed, and Colonel Ivor Reeves was seriously wounßded. The Merxem bridgehead at Antwerp is a famous battle honour.

From 6 September onwards Colson's Resistance groups had patrolled across Leopolddok towards Wilmarsdonck and into the north-west corner of Merxem. At Wijnegem, east of Merxem, Pilaet's men held the bridge they had captured on the night of the 5th, which they held until the reinforced Germans counter-attacked on the night of 17 September.

The battle for Antwerp was over, but in a sense it was also starting. The first flying V-1 landed on 12 October, the first V-2 on 23 October, and altogether 1,214 rockets landed in greater Antwerp, with another 302 in the dock area. 15,000 civilians were killed or wounded in these attacks. On 12 December the Rex Cinema was hit, killing 242 soldiers on leave and 250 civilians. But even worse, between 1 October and 8 November the 1st Canadian Army suffered 12,873 casualties (50 per cent Canadian, 50 per cent British and Polish) in the brutal clearance of the river Scheldt.

Nevertheless, the capture of Antwerp was an amazing success. Nearly 9,000 prisoners of war were taken. Almost all of the vital Antwerp dock area with its 30 miles of wharves, 632 cranes and hoists, 186 acres of warehouse storage space and its oil storage facilities (for over 100 million gallons) was safe, thanks mainly to the brave Resistance movement. The Sherman tanks and motorised infantry had cleared the city and the port area and almost immediately RN Port Clearance team No 1572 arrived to inspect and repair port damages.

But Hitler now planned to recapture Antwerp in Operation Wacht am Rhein!

CHAPTER 5

Operation Astonia: Capture of Le Havre

Operation Astonia, which took place on 12–14 September 1944, was probably one of the best-planned and executed battles of the Second World War. Unusually it involved the Royal Navy, the RAF and two British Army divisions. The 49th (West Riding of Yorkshire) Division under Major General E.H. 'Bubbles' Barker was formed in 1907 and earned three Victoria Crosses during the First World War. In 1940 it fought in the ill-fated campaign in Norway before garrisoning Iceland peacefully for two years, earning itself its nickname, the Polar Bears. This became its divisional insignia. In Normandy its three brigades were the 70th Brigade (10th and 11th Durham Light Infantry and 1st Battalion Tyneside Scottish), the 146th Brigade (4th Lincolnshire Regiment, 1/4th Kings Own Yorkshire Light Infantry, and the York and Lancaster Regiment, the Hallamshires), and the 147th Brigade (11th Battalion Royal Scots Fusiliers, and 6th and 7th Battalions the Duke of Wellington's Regiment). The Division landed just west of Arromanches on 11 June and was thrown into the attritional fighting at Audrieu, St Pierre, Cristot and Le Parc de Boislande, all clustered round the killing fields of Fontenay-le-Pesnel and Tessel Wood in Operation Martlet. Rauray in early July was a fine defensive action against the panzer might of 9th SS and 2nd SS Divisions. The 49th Division's losses were so great that on 19 August the 70th Brigade was disbanded and replaced by the 56th (2nd South Wales Borderers, 2nd The Gloucestershire Regiment and 2nd Battalion The Essex Regiment). They were allowed to keep their Egyptian Sphinx emblem as well as that of the Polar Bear.

Then followed two weeks of pushing and shoving to help clear the salient from Flers to Argentan and the north to the river Seine. The RE (sappers) built or rebuilt bridges over seven rivers including the Vie, Tourques, Celonne and the Risle on the way to Rouen.

*   *   *   *

The 51st Highland Division had probably the most dramatic and tragic start to the Second World War, more than any other formation. As part of the British Expeditionary Force (BEF) it came under command of the French 9th

Corps and was penned into a salient around St Valéry and captured. Winston Churchill had to make the terrible decision. He was desperate to keep France and the French Army – still the largest in Europe – fighting the German Wehrmacht. If the 51st Highland Division rejoined the British Army at Dunkirk and was evacuated to England, the French Army and the politicians would say 'Perfidious Albion' and regard it as a betrayal, since technically the Highlanders were under French command. So they were sacrificed. Winston Churchill wrote: 'The fate of the Highland Division was hard, but in after years not unavenged by those Scots who filled their places, re-created the Division by merging with the 9th Scottish [Division] and marched across all the battlefields from Alamein to final victory beyond the Rhine.'

The resurrected 51st Highland Division fought magnificently in General Montgomery's Desert Army. From August 1942 until their return to the UK in November 1943 they were heavily involved in the fighting at Alamein, in the capture of Tripoli and Tunis, and throughout Operation Husky (the Sicilian campaign).

In Normandy Montgomery obviously expected too much of the Division and the GOC was replaced by Major General Tim Rennie. The 51st Highland Division landed on D-Day and was in action immediately around Colville on the right flank of the bridgehead, incurring 307 casualties in the first week. Its brigades were the 152nd Brigade, with 2nd and 5th Seaforth Highlanders and 5th Cameron Highlanders; 153rd Brigade with 5th Black Watch and 1st and 5th/7th Gordon Highlanders; and 154th Brigade with 1st and 7th Black Watch and 7th Battalion Argyll and Sutherland Highlanders.

The triangle around Colombelles, Ranville and Cuverville was the battleground for much of June and July, often under devastating fire from the German minnenwerfer ('moaning minnies') mortar fire. This six-barrel, rocket-propelled mortar caused the most casualties of any German weapon in Normandy. It looked like a Heath Robinson contraption: ugly, cheap to make, very mobile and distinctly lethal.

Lt Colonel Ralph Carr, commander of the Royal Engineers, wrote home: 'At the end of six weeks we were very tired, even the gunners and the sappers. There was no let up. Pinned up in our little corner under steady shellfire by day and air attack by night, every 24 hours brought its trickle of casualties .... After the Caen battle we found ourselves relegated to holding the shattered ruins of villages, splintered leafless woods smashed by six weeks' fighting, reminded at every turn by the sights and smells of our hastily buried dead.'

Next came Operation Totalise under 2nd Canadian Corps, in which the infantry were carried in self-propelled armoured Priests stripped of their 105mm guns towards their objective, Tilly-la-Campagne. Against 12th SS Division and 1055th Infantry Regiment, Scottish casualties were high. In late August during the breakout from the Normandy 'cauldron', the 51st Highland Division, along with many others, was bombed and strafed vigorously and frequently by RAF Spitfires, Lightnings, Typhoons and Lancasters, which caused many 'friendly fire' casualties. In the Division's advance from Tilly to Lisieux, 1,761 casualties were sustained and 1,600 Germans were captured. The High Command ensured that the Highland Division would return to St Valéry. On 3 September General Thomas Rennie moved into the Chateau at Cailleville, where General Fortune and his staff had been forced to surrender in June 1940. The brigade groups went into the same areas in which the 1940 brigades had fought their last battle. In the military cemetery each grave of the '*Ecossais Inconnu*' was scarlet with geraniums in full bloom, contrasting with the white wooden crosses; the massed pipes and drums of the Highland Division played Retreat at Cailleville. General Rennie, dressed in his Black Watch kilt, battledress blouse and tam o'shanter with red hackle, tall, dark, sombre and extremely smart, stood beside the French mayor.

*   *   *   *

There were many reasons why the Allies wanted to capture Le Havre. They knew that when taken and the port facilities repaired, a daily unloading target of 5,000 tons of valuable supplies was feasible. Additionally, the Navy was anxious to change the port's ownership. The heavy gun batteries at Le Havre had a most definite nuisance value, while the E-boat flotillas were an even greater menace. From Le Havre human torpedoes and explosive motor boats had been making determined attacks on the Royal Naval defence lines in the Channel (Trout line) and against anchorages around Mulberry. Radar showed that exceptionally heavy traffic had been moving close inshore towards the end of August, moving reinforcements to the Le Havre garrison from St Valéry-en-Caux (before its capture later by the 51st Highland Division to avenge the tragic defeat in 1940.)

For a week there were ferocious little sea battles off the French coast between Le Havre, Dieppe and Fécamp. On the one side British Hunt-class destroyers and frigates, motor torpedo boats, US motor torpedo boats and a French destroyer took on German destroyers, submarine chasers, armed trawlers, R-boats, E-boats, minesweepers and artillery-ferry barges. The British had air superiority against daytime sorties but the Germans often had protection from their coastal batteries. Enemy losses were so heavy that on 29 August their surviving coastal flotillas were withdrawn from Le Havre. Twenty-one boats of various kinds had been sunk and a further 13 badly damaged out of the original strength of four torpedo boats and 41 other vessels.

Le Havre had been receiving dire treatment from the RAF. On 14 June a daylight raid mainly by 222 Lancasters with Pathfinders dropped 1,230 tons of bombs on E-boat pens and the motor torpedo boats in the harbour. Some 22 12,000-pound Tallboy bombs were dropped, one at least penetrating a pen.

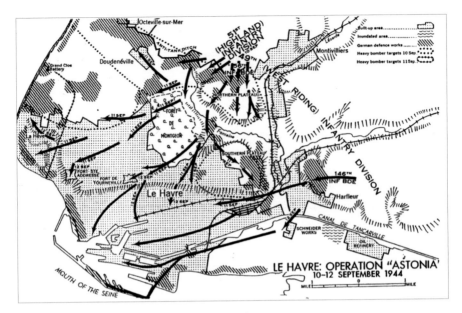

Le Havre: Operation Astonia, 10–12 September 1944.

Further heavy raids followed on 31 July and 2, 5, 6, 8, 9, 10 and 11 September. The bombardments were devastating. On 10 September 992 aircraft bombed eight strongpoints marked by Pathfinders. During the raid of 14 June the German torpedo boats *Falke, Jaguar* and *Moewe*, ten E-boats, two R-boats, and 15 minesweepers and patrol vessels were sunk. Admiral Kranke, the German naval commander, wrote: 'The attack on Havre is catastrophe. Losses are extremely heavy. The loss of the torpedo boats and the H7Bs is especially bitter. Naval situation in Seine Bay has completely altered since yesterday's attack ....'

Unlike the dedicated Nazi fanatics commanding Hitler's fortresses of Cherbourg, St Malo and Brest, Colonel Eberhardt Wildermuth was an extraordinary choice. He had been a banker by profession, not a Nazi, and at the time of the siege – Operation Astonia – was described as being 55, tall, skeletal and balding. He had seen heavy fighting in 1940 in France, then in Russia and Italy, and was given a peaceful coastal sector near Venice to defend. Out of the blue, on 14 August, he was appointed commandant of the bastion of Le Havre.

Wildermuth had nearly 14,000 troops under command: the usual mix of Wehrmacht, coast defence, Luftwaffe ground and anti-aircraft troops, Kriegsmarines, OST battalions and naval maintenance staff for the E-boat flotillas. Besides several powerful batteries of heavy coastal-defence guns, Wildermuth had over 115 guns of all kinds but few anti-tank weapons. The 15 miles of inland defences were interspersed with minefields, anti-tank ditches, barbed-wire entanglements and many substantial and deep strongpoints impervious to RAF bombing. The risk to civilians was obvious, and the original population of 164,000 had had many opportunities to leave. Leaflets in French had been dropped before the siege commenced. By the end of Astonia, 5,000 French civilians were dead, mainly killed by the bombing. Front-line loudspeaker vans exhorted them to leave, but in vain. Hitler's order to Wildermuth on 31 July said: 'Take no account of the fate of the civilians in the city.'

Le Havre ranks with inland Rouen among the leading ports of France, and consists of a series of dock basins excavated in the broad belt of silt which runs along the north shore. As a deep-water port it needs continuous dredging. Before the war the harbour entrance was widened to 820 feet to allow the great French liner *Normandie* to berth, and the Passe du Nord Ouest was dredged to a depth of 35 feet.

Inside the entrance is the Avant Port, beyond that the Arrière Port leading east to the 'wet' docks, which are linked to each other by dock gates, locks and passages. South-east of the Avant Port lies the Bassin Théophile-Ducroq, which can accommodate very large vessels. The Tancarville canal links the Bassin de L'Eure to the river Seine at Tancarville, which links with Rouen 70 miles upstream and inland.

In the town of Le Havre were two forts and many road blocks, pillboxes and fortified houses together with anti-aircraft guns and some anti-tank guns. In theory Le Havre was impregnable although the calibre and morale of the garrison troops were doubtful. It was known afterwards that ammunition was plentiful and sufficient food was available to feed the garrison of 14,000 for three months.

It took ten days of very careful co-ordination and planning to get two infantry divisions, the mass of artillery support and 'Funny' tank support into place. The attack began at 1745hrs on 10 September. The RAF on 10th and 11th dropped 11,000 tons of bombs, mainly on the eight key strongpoints (out of the 400 concrete bunkers in the area). HMS *Warspite* and the monitor *Erebus*, escorted by the destroyers *Grenville* and *Ulysses*, reached their bombardment position 15 miles from Cap de la Hève. HMS *Warspite* fired 353 15-inch shells at four coastal batteries throughout the 10th. Spotting aircraft observed and corrected aim. One German defensive coast battery had four 16-inch guns and another had three 11-inch guns. Once they straddled *Warspite* and forced her back to a 31,000-yard range.

Major Roland Ward of 617th Assault Squadron, Royal Engineers, wrote an account of the plan:

> The attack was to be in four stages – first the attack by the 56th Infantry Brigade [Polar Bears], their objective being the Ardennes plateau which overlooks Le Havre from the north. On this front eight gaps were to be attempted [through the minefields] but only the three middle ones were to cross the [anti-tank] ditch which lay beyond the minefield. The second stage was to be a night attack further to the right [north] by the 51st Highland Division. The third stage was an attack the following morning [11th] through Harfleur by 146th Brigade

[Polar Bears]. The fourth stage would be penetration and exploitation into the heart of the city on the second and third days. The obstacles and defences at Le Havre were remarkably similar to those we had been practising on in Suffolk. A total of 11 gaps had to be made through the deep minefields, six of them to cross the wide anti-tank ditch.

Excellent overprinted maps and air photographs were provided which showed two places in the north-east near Montivilliers where the anti-tank ditch had not been completed. The corps commander, Lt General John Crocker decided to put battalion attacks through those gaps.

The GOC of the Polar Bears, Major General 'Bubbles' Barker, wrote in his diary:

> 4 Sep. I'm fed up learning the Canadians are mopping up the Le Havre peninsula and have asked J.C. [John Crocker] to have it stopped and merely have credit given where due. The 49 Div have done everything and got across the Seine under very difficult circumstances.
>
> 6 Sep. The monks at Fécamp gave us a case of Benedictine, made in the monastery there. They buried all they had, the Boche gave them a large supply of sugar to make more just matured for us! I have just come back from watching the RAF do some very accurate bombing of the Boche positions in front of me. Ammunition dump went up in the Forêt de Mongeon with a lovely mushroom of smoke. It is very galling to hear of the other Armies forging ahead with no opposition and to be left here with the sticky end.
>
> 8 Sep. I only wish we could leave this Canadian Army. They have such an inferiority complex that they concentrate almost entirely on themselves. It's

Polar Bear attack on Le Havre, supported by the 'Funnies', flails and scissor-bridge. (*Imperial War Museum BU-859*)

maddening not to be able to deal with [the investment of Le Havre] any quicker, but it is a tricky undertaking and we cannot chance a reverse at this stage. I want no more casualties than I can help.

The plan of attack was comprehensive and thorough. Models of the town and its pillbox defences were made, and studies by all ranks, plus the corps, divisional, brigade and battalion plans were explained by the COs to their men. In addition to the splendid 'Funnies', 12 field regiments, four medium regiments and two heavy regiments of artillery were in support. RAF Bomber Command raids, Alvis (1645–1745hrs), Bentley (1845–1900hrs), Buick (1900–1930hrs) and Cadillac, D+1, were completed by 0800hrs.

On the 4th and 5th the FFI and patrols brought information of the enemy's strengthened position. Indeed, 'A' Squadron of the Recce Regiment had captured an entire company on the morning of the 3rd. During the next nine days the Recce Regiment provided a Phantom wireless net of 15 stations covering every unit to help the GOC's information network. It rained depressingly as the Polar Bears and the 51st Highland Division tightened the encircling net. Brigadier-Major Paul Crook, 49th Division, recalled:

> The defences were softened up for two days before the assault by shelling from Royal Naval ships at sea and bombing by the RAF. From the Field of the Cloth of Gold we were able to watch with awe and pleasure the massive raids by the air forces on the defences. They were accurately carried out and had a heartening effect on the morale of our troops and consequent disheartening effect on the enemy. Captured prisoners subsequently stated that the bombing was very frightening but there were comparatively few casualties both to the German troops and civilians owing to the excellence of the dugout shelters. The breakdown of communication prevented the German commanders from knowing what was going on and stretching their resources and fire power.

The sheer volume of bombardment from the air, from the sea and from 18 regiments of artillery had certainly softened up the defences before the combined infantry and tank attacks that followed. Crab flail tanks on boggy ground cleared paths through the minefields, AVRE Churchill tanks laid large fascines in the anti-tank ditch south of the Montivilliers-Octeville line. AVRE bombards threw petards at close range at the pillboxes, and Crocodiles, also at short range, flamed defence points. But it was the six brigades of infantry (Gordons, Argylls, Black Watch and Seaforth) in the north, and in the south and east (Gloucesters, South Wales Borderers, Essex, Leicesters, Royal Scots Fusiliers, King's Own Yorkshire Light Infantry, Hallams and Lincolns) who steadfastly winkled out the defenders.

5th Seaforth moved up along the coast through Fécamp to Beaumesnil, 12 miles north of Le Havre, and stayed there a week. Air photographs and information from French civilians showed the exact extent of the problem of the attack in great detail: the gapping (Ale, Rum and Gin) of the very professional defences (wire, minefields, anti-tank ditches and formidable pillboxes). 5th Seaforths would use a 49th Division gap, pass through and turn right (west) to attack and capture the strongpoint 76 on the high ground east of Fontaine-la-Mallet. Captain Alastair Borthwith recalled: 'The usual column trudging along resignedly in the darkness, heads down, steel helmets and rifle muzzles making a frieze against the night sky – a column immensely patient, almost apathetic, storing up nervous energy for the demands of the night. A black night of low cloud, no wind and three searchlights to light us on our way ...' The King's Own Light Infantry took objectives codenamed Eggs, Ham, Sausage, Bacon, Kidney and Marmalade. German envoys came out to treat with Major General Barker and told him that Hitler had personally ordered the defence of Le Havre to the last man and the last round. The general answered, 'I wish you good luck and a Merry Christmas'. Harfleur in the south-east was taken, and the 51st Highlanders captured Octeville, La Hève and Fort Ste Addresse.

The Gloucesters stormed the main fortress and found the garrison well prepared for surrender; they even had their suitcases packed. In one day they captured 1,500 prisoners including the naval admiral and his staff, 30 Algerians, 30 Italians, half a dozen French 'comfort' girls and a fine cellar. The Hallamshires cleared the docks and the main Mole – a strip of land a mile long and 100 yards wide, studded with large concrete pillboxes. They took 1,005 prisoners, three Dornier flying boats and a submarine. Colonel Wildermuth told his captors: 'In my opinion it was futile to fight tanks with bare hands. As early as 9 September I had given orders to all my officers that Allied infantry attacks were to be opposed everywhere even with side arms only. But in the event of an attack by tanks, resistance nests which no longer had any anti-tank weapons were then at liberty to surrender.' There was much evidence that the sight of the fearsome Sherman Crabs flailing noisily away *through* the German minefields broke morale. Over 11,300 prisoners were gathered in against British losses of 1,388 killed in action and 250 wounded. Liddell Hart considered the assault the best planned and the most efficient of all sieges and assaults on the fortress-ports.

Brigade-Major Crook recalled: 'And what a night [10th]. There were flail tanks flashing away detonating some mines and missing others. Armoured assault engineer vehicles were chuntering around and tanks following up. There were the noises and effects of our own supporting fire from a variety of weapons, finally of course there was the din of battle, organised chaos and danger.'

The British Assault Unit 30 led by Captain Huntington-Whiteley were given maps showing that their main target was a bank in the square on the seafront – an important information and communications centre. On their way into the city centre in their scout cars they captured two groups of German sailors, leaving only one team of four Marines to continue. Shortly afterwards this team's scout car was ambushed. The captain and Marine Shaw were killed and Marines Feeley and Livingstone captured. The German admiral used Livingstone as an intermediary to negotiate a surrender. Feeley then signed the Allied leaflets advocating 'surrender' dropped by the RAF on the German garrison. The young entrepreneur charged 100 francs for each signed 'pass'. One assumes he did not sign the leaflets 'Eisenhower' or 'Montgomery'. When members of AU30 went on leave to Paris shortly afterwards, their pockets were bulging with French francs!

By the end of the battle 1st Gordons had suffered 14 casualties but had collected a total of 600 prisoners and much equipment and loot, which was found in the bunkers and coastal defences. Major Lindsay, the second in command, said: 'They lined up in front of me. There you are, the Master Race, help yourselves.' And the Jocks soon had a fine collection of watches, fountain pens, pocket knives and French francs. The 5/7th Gordons got 50 cases of Bollinger '34 or '37 champagne in Fort Ste Addresse, and soon every Jock was smoking a Wehrmacht cigar. The garrison blew up a naval gun, which caused a breach in the walls of the fort and so 250 prisoners were taken. Private Stan Whitehouse, 1st Gordons, was deputed by Sergeant Edmonds to guard a liqueur store, 'a veritable Aladdin's cave' and some time later he had sunk half a bottle of Dutch orange Curaçao and was in a helpless condition. Crafty Sergeant Edmonds had organised a smugglers' run, selling the captured Wehrmacht rum to the local café owners. The spoils were considerable: £25 to each of the 'smugglers', whose pay was 21 shillings per week. Stan was shown the German cemetery containing the 2,000 graves of those killed by the RAF bombers who had dropped bombs with fuel oil around barges of an invasion fleet. The screams of the burning Wehrmacht were heard by the citizens of Le Havre.

After the final surrender Major General Barker wrote in his diary for 12/13 September:

> We have taken some 6–7,000 POW and the Jocks [51st Highland Division] a good many also but old 49 has really done the job. I feel I put the chaps into battle with a good plan and they had been able to do justice to their efforts and their high morale and courage. The show went through like clockwork in spite of the very strong defences. Casualties are remarkably light. My tanks of all sorts co-operated superbly and the gunners were quite excellent. The real cause of the success was that the Boche went down into their deep shelters for the bombing and our artillery, and did not get to their positions till too late. We got into them too quick. We had to outflank every strongpoint before they gave in.

On 13 September General Rennie sent a message to the 51st Highlanders telling them of another important task successfully accomplished in close co-operation with the Polar Bears Division. 51st Highland captured 122 officers and 4,508 other ranks for the loss of 138 casualties. The Polar Bears lost 301 casualties and took nearly 7,000 prisoners. The main losers, apart from the German garrison, were the French civilians who suffered heavily. Astonia was over – a typical well-planned, brutal, set-piece Monty operation – and was very successful. Whilst the Channel ports were being invested and captured, the three armoured divisions, Black Bull, Desert Rats and the Guards had been streaming north to capture Antwerp, Ghent and Brussels. On 17 September Monty's rather optimistic message went out: 'Today the Seine is far behind us. The Allies have removed the enemy from practically the whole of France and Belgium except in a few places and we stand at the door of Germany.'

Royal Navy port clearance team Number 1571 came up from Dieppe to inspect Le Havre, with Commander Walsh, US Navy and Lt Commander Freemantle, Royal Navy. With them was the same US Navy mine disposal party which had operated at Cherbourg in July. They found a wooden case four feet square. Inside was a new demolition mine, RMK, and inside that was an 'O' mine in a unit chamber adapted for electrical firing, suspended from the quayside, resting on the bottom of the seabed. They found 25 surface mines but no mines within the *bassins* or alongside the quays. Three days later the port was declared free of mines but 165 wrecks, wrecked bridges, cranes etc blocked the waterways. It became a valuable base for Allied coastal forces which had been beating up the German E-boats for the last month. The port was open for traffic and cargo on 9 October and 3,650 tons per day were unloaded, rising to 5,000 in November onwards.

CHAPTER 6

The Cinderella Army: Canadians in the Scheldt Campaign

To their everlasting credit Canada sent its army to Britain shortly after the outbreak of war; the 1st Division arrived on 17 December 1939. From Greenock and Glasgow it went initially to Aldershot. It very nearly went to Norway, then landed in France but re-embarked during the BEF retreat. Three battalions were sent to Ireland as part of the garrison in case of invasion. Churchill wrote in October 1940: 'The Canadian Army Corps (two divisions) stood most conveniently posted between London and Dover. Their bayonets were sharp and their hearts were high. Proud would they have been to strike the decisive blow for Britain and Freedom.' In January 1941 Churchill reluctantly sent two Canadian battalions to reinforce the garrison in Hong Kong under Brigadier Lawson. The garrison was later overwhelmed by the Japanese attack in December. In July 1942 Operation Jubilee was planned and Churchill talked to General A.G.L. McNaughton, commander of the Canadian Corps 'Home Forces': 'I thought that this operation would give a glorious opportunity to the Canadian Army, which had now for two years been eating its heart out in Britain awaiting the invader.' Churchill was under pressure from Stalin to open a Second Front, and the Canadian Parliament to make military use of the tough, bored young Canadian soldiers. So the ill-fated one-day raid on the well-defended port of Dieppe, Operation Rutter, then Jubilee, took place on 19 August 1942.

It was a brilliant plan on paper. The Royal Navy, the RAF, the Commandos and above all, the Canadian 2nd Division fought a magnificent, but totally doomed, one-day battle. The Canadians had 2,000 troops taken prisoner, 900 killed and 400 wounded out of the 5,000 who landed. Churchill wrote afterwards: 'The Canadian Army in Britain had long been eager and impatient for action and the main part of the landing force was provided by them ... although the utmost gallantry and devotion were shown by all troops ... and many splendid deeds were done, the results were disappointing and our casualties were very heavy.' The disaster proved what everybody probably suspected beforehand. To attack a well-defended French port with the usual violent, skilled German defenders was nigh impossible. Still it was a sop to Uncle 'Joe' Stalin, and probably hastened the development of the famous Mulberry harbours, vital to the success of Operation Overlord in June 1944. Canadian forces also took part in the Sicilian and Italian campaigns.

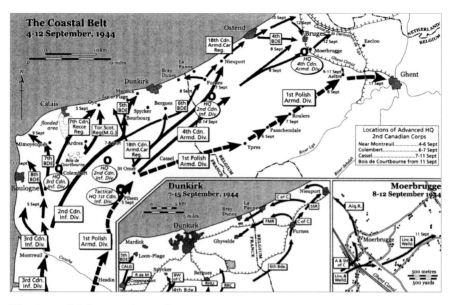

The Coastal Belt, 4–12 September 1944.

In late 1943 the Canadian Defence Minister, Colonel J.L. Ralston, agreed with General Sir Ronald Adam, the adjutant general, to transfer 200 young Canadian officers to the British Army for use as first replacements in 21st Army Group in Operation Overlord. 'Canloan' was a great success. These officers proved to be of such high quality that they were absorbed directly into British units and were taken on the D-Day landings. They mostly went into the infantry divisions. Many subsequently were casualties and many won awards for bravery.

The Canadian 2nd Corps was allocated the dangerous honour of landing on D-Day in the Juno sector, astride the river Seulles. Major General R.F. Keller commanded the 3rd Canadian Infantry Division, backed up by the 2nd Canadian Armoured Brigade. The weather was worse around Juno beach than in any other D-Day sector and many landing craft were sunk by the choppy sea and strong high tide. By mid-morning the Royal Winnipeg Rifles and the Regina Rifles of 7th Brigade were two miles inland. On the eastern side 8th Canadian Brigade had a sharp fight at Bernières and the Queen's Own Rifles and the Régiment de la Chaudière moved inland, but were halted on the way to Bény-sur-Mer. The reserve brigade, the 9th, was ashore by 1230hrs despite the beach and streets being packed with armour and transport. By dark the leading Canadian troops were nearly seven miles inland and their tanks had reached the Caen-Bayeux road. Two battalions reached the environs of Caen, three miles from the city's north-west outskirts. On the right the 7th Brigade linked up with 50th Northumbrian Division, making the common beach-head 12 miles wide and six to seven miles deep. The next day, 7 June, Colonel Kurt

Above and below: Enemy coast artillery in Pas-de-Calais region. Heavy concrete casemate under construction, and labourers at work on casemate.

Meyer, commander of the 12th SS Panzer Division and the fanatical teenagers of the SS Hitler Jugend Division, fought some of the fiercest actions of the campaign against the Canadian 9th Infantry Brigade group, who were forced to retreat for two miles. At one stage the Regina Rifles reported 22 Panther tanks in their area, of which at least six were destroyed. In their first six days ashore the Canadians had 72 officers killed and 124 wounded, and 945 other ranks killed and 1,590 wounded. Lt General Harry Crerar commanded the 1st Canadian Army in Normandy, which had taken over the sector east of the river Orne at the end of July. Lt General G.C. Simonds was the able, forceful commander of 2nd Canadian Corps, with battle experience in Sicily and Italy. During the capture of most of Caen from 18–20 July, Operation Atlantic cost Crerar's men 1,965 casualties.

In Operation Totalise on the night of 7 August 2nd Canadian Corps was launched in a renewed offensive towards Falaise after an advance of six miles, much of it in turretless Canadian-built converted tank-chassis. Their previous nemesis, Colonel Kurt Meyer's 112th SS Panzers, counter-attacked and caused chaos. The British Columbia tank regiment lost 47 Shermans in a day and had 112 casualties; the Algonquins had 128 casualties. Operation Tractable followed on 14 August and got off to a bad start when the RAF 'short-bombed', causing 300 casualties. But Louvières was captured on the way to Trun, and St Lambert was bitterly contested. There had to be a scapegoat for the failure of the Americans, British, Poles and Canadians to close the Argentan-Falaise Gap, through which the German 7th Army was trying desperately to escape. The history books and the Allied commanders pointed their fingers at General Crerar, who promptly fired many officers, including Major General Kitching. Montgomery wrote on 20 August: 'I call on all commanders for a great effort. Let us finish the business in record time ... The first task of the Canadian Army is to keep the Normandy "bottle" securely corked.'

By 17 August the Canadian Army casualties in the Normandy campaign were 76% in the infantry, 7% in the armoured corps and 8% in the artillery. The War Office, using the desert war casualty ratios, predicted 48% infantry, 15% armour and 14% artillery. Every division in Normandy had a light anti-aircraft (LAA) regiment but, with the domination of the RAF and USAAF in the air war, most of the LAA regiments were disbanded and retrained as infantry.

General Harry Crerar had survived the criticism of the Canadians in Normandy and now, in late August, had command of a larger formation: the 1st British Corps, which included the 49th Polar Bears and 51st Highland Division; the 2nd Canadian Corps, which included the 2nd and 3rd Canadian Infantry and 4th Canadian Armoured Divisions; and the 1st Polish Armoured Division – a total of six divisions. Their main task was to chase and defeat as much as they could of General Von Zangen's retreating 15th Army, and to capture the ports of Le Havre, Dieppe, Boulogne, Calais, Dunkirk, Ostend,

Zeebrugge and, with the Navy and Marines, the Scheldt estuary (Flushing, Breskens, Walcheren), and South and North Beveland. The opening and clearance of ports was absolutely vital although neither Eisenhower nor Montgomery put much emphasis on this, nor provided much help. The Canadians were the Cinderella army out in the cold polders, with incessant rain and bitter resistance.

Adolf Hitler had designated the ports of Le Havre, Boulogne, Calais, Dunkirk, Breskens, Flushing and Walcheren Island as *festung* (fortresses), with a dedicated commander and a reasonable garrison. He issued dire threats for failure. Moreover, General Von Zangen, on Hitler's orders, had dropped off several of the 15th Army divisions to help garrison each fortress.

The Canadians left Normandy with sighs of relief and moved north-west to Elbeuf on the Seine. On 26 August Montgomery ordered the 1st Canadian Army to take Le Havre (Operation Astonia), secure the port of Dieppe, and destroy all enemy forces in the coastal belt – at Boulogne, Calais and Dunkirk on the way to Ghent.

Rouen was captured easily on 31 August and, appropriately on 1 September, the Canadians captured Dieppe, this time without a fight. The 2nd Canadian Division spent three sentimental days visiting the cemetery where 800 Canadian officers and men are buried. The Essex Scottish pipers played 'Retreat' at the Place Nationale and memorial services were held under warm, blue skies. One typical episode was when Montgomery summoned Crerar to a meeting to discuss future co-operation between the 2nd British Army and 1st

Calais harbour.

US Army. Crerar's presence was in no sense necessary, so he stayed on a further four hours at Dieppe for the final remembrance service. Monty, a totally unsentimental man, was livid and told Crerar his position was 'untenable'. However, Monty could not fire Crerar; only the Canadian government could do that. In any case, Crerar was waiting for 1,000 reinforcements to arrive at Dieppe and be integrated into the 2nd Canadian Division.

Lieutenant Guy Simonds gave orders to his 2nd Canadian Corps on 4 September for the start of what became known as 'The Cinderella War': the Canadians were rarely in Montgomery or Dempsey's thoughts in September 1944. Simonds' 2nd Division would clear the coast from Dunkirk to the Dutch border. Major General Dan Spry's 3rd Division was to clear the road from Dieppe, capture Boulogne, the coastal batteries at Cap Gris-Nez, and then Calais. Simonds' armoured division, 4th Canadian and 1st Polish were directed inland towards Ghent and Bruges. No one knew whether the Channel ports would be defended or not. Further south, Cherbourg, St Malo and Brest were captured with some difficulty and the harbours were systematically wrecked. Spry's 3rd Division had three major battles and sieges ahead without the support of the RAF and Navy, that had helped the two British divisions capture Le Havre under Crerar's command.

According to the German General Warlimont Lt General Ferdinand Heim, aged 50, looked, 'with his thin pinched face and prominent blue eyes, a larger version of Göbbels'. Heim had been a first-class staff officer on the Russian front and was promoted to command 48th Panzer Corps. He then had the

Boulogne harbour.

misfortune to have two Roumanian divisions under his command over-run by the Russians. Hitler promptly had Heim dismissed and sent to prison for five months, after which he was unexpectedly released and sent to Ulm. Then in August 1944, out of the blue, he was sent to command the fortress-port of Boulogne and told to follow Hitler's usual order: 'defend to the last man and bullet'. The garrison of 10,000 included the 64th Infantry Division, many Kriegsmarines, fortress troops, some Osttruppen (non-German volunteer troops from east European countries), artillery and engineers. General Model had ordered a defensive zone to a depth of six miles to be built around the town. Within this zone he ordered all bridges to be destroyed and minefields to be laid. On 2 September Heim made every officer sign a pledge to hold and defend the strongpoint or sector under command 'to the end of my life and that of the last man under me'.

Operation Wellhit was the codename for the capture of Boulogne. With a population of 45,000 and an unloading capacity of 11,000 tons a day, the city was an important port. It was also scheduled to receive petrol, oil and lubricants (POL) via the secret pipeline under the sea (PLUTO). Defensively, Boulogne is a natural fortress nestled beneath a ring of surrounding hills that guards all the approaches and roads into the town. The defences ran from the coast to the west side of the town through the hills of Ecault, St Etienne-au-Mont to Mont-de-Thune and then north through the heavily defended Mont Lambert. The harbour lies at the entrance of the river Liane, with the Bassins Napoleon, Loubet, Darse Sarraz-Bourne, and Gambetta and Chanzy quays.

The RAF was invited to help in the attack, and on 17 September 370 heavy bombers, mainly Lancasters, dropped 1,463 tons of explosives on the port area, sinking 31 R-boats. At the same time 351 Halifaxes and 41 Mosquitoes dropped the same amount of bombs on the Mont Lambert defences. The Canadians were also helped by a strong contingent of 'Funnies': 141st RAC (the Buffs) with two squadrons of Crocodile flame-throwers, the Lothians Sherman mine-flails with two squadrons, plus the 81st and 87th Assault Squadrons RE with their bombard-firing Churchill AVREs – all were carefully co-ordinated with Spry's 8th and 9th Brigades. For three days the battle raged, and eventually 9,500 German defenders were captured including General Heim. Mopping up went on for several days in the dock area and in many forts with underground cellars. Heim and the RAF combined had caused considerable damage to the port facilities: no fewer than 25 wrecks fouled the harbour and 26 blockships closed the entrance. Using the US 'Tombola' mooring, successful on the Normandy beaches, PLUTO was pumping oil in mid-October, and on 18 November the port was back in business.

Montgomery and Eisenhower's staff criticised Crerar for taking so long to capture Boulogne, comparing it to Operation Astonia!

General von Trestkow was the German commander of the important port of Dunkirk. The town and harbour were strongly held with a garrison of

12   DUNKERQUE. — La Place du Mink. — Mink Place. — LL.

Dunkirk, Mink square.

about 12,000 men. The 18th Luftwaffen-Feld Division, 1st Festa (Garrison) 82nd, 1244th Artillery Group, a Flak-AA Group and Marine Regiment 618 all combined to put up a ferocious defence. There were strong points sited at Mardick, Loon Plage, Spycker, Bergues and Bray Dunes. Much of the area had been flooded and roads and tracks above the level of the muddy fields were targeted by artillery and mortar fire. Air reconnaissance reported that the Dunkirk, Boulogne and Calais areas were 'deserted', but as at Le Havre, the defenders were deep inside their Todt-built strongpoints, bunkers, pillboxes and casemented coastal batteries.

For the week of 7–15 September the 4th, 5th and 6th Brigades of Major General C. Foulkes' 2nd Canadian Division tried everything. They surrounded the ten-mile perimeter of the outer defences some three miles from the town centre. Artillery support was now rationed to three rounds per gun per day and supply of heavy mortar bombs to five. What was really needed was a repeat of Operation Astonia, with massive artillery programmes, RAF deluge bombing, and Royal Naval monitors firing heavy shells. The Canadians missed the deadly support from Crocodile flame-throwers, AVREs and Flails: indeed a minimum of two infantry divisions were essential.

On 13 September Monty wrote to General Crerar: 'The things that are now very important are (a) Capture of Boulogne and Dunkirk and Calais, (b) The setting in action of operations designed to enable us to use the port of Antwerp.' A kind view would be to say that obviously Monty had not looked at a map of the coastal area, had not looked at any current Ultra reports about the German forces in the region, had not realised that Crerar had not got the support needed (from the RAF and Royal Navy in particular), and was too busy thinking about his thrust towards Berlin, i.e. Market Garden.

On 17 September Crerar was told to halt further attacks on Dunkirk while the British 4th Special Service Brigade and the Czech Armoured Brigade arrived to invest (i.e. surround but not attack) Dunkirk. Eventually, in May 1945, General von Trestkow surrendered, appropriately to the Belgian 'White' Brigade.

David Bercusson, the Calgary Highlanders' historian, wrote: 'We fought an unknown, undramatic, dirty little war in water-logged country on the approaches to Dunkirk under almost constant shelling fire from the heavy guns in the German-held enclave. The Highlanders slugged it out with an enemy determined to follow Hitler's orders to the last man.'

Lt Colonel Ludwig Schroeder, aged 43, with a tired, resigned face, was the commandant of the Calais garrison of 9,000 troops. There was the usual mix of second-grade coastal units, Kriegsmarines, Ost battalions and Luftwaffe Flak units. Schroeder had had an unimpressive military career on the Eastern front, before being posted to the 59th Infantry Division. Half-way between Boulogne and Calais were sited the ten substantial coast batteries with four guns each, usually of 38cm calibre. Each casement gun crew was about 175 strong. Many guns had a 120-degree traverse, but some had all-round traverses. On the inland side there were minefields, barbed wire entanglements and pillboxes. Half of Schroeder's defenders held the strongpoints of Noires Mottes, Bellevue Ridge, Coquelles and Vieux Coquelles, as well as the coastal batteries.

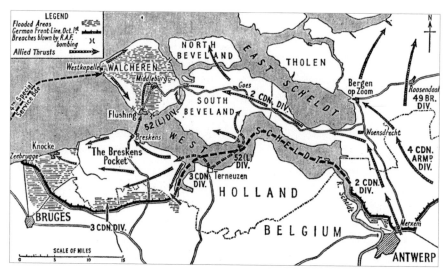

Opening of the Scheldt Estuary, October–November 1944.

Major General Spry directed his three brigades to tackle all the coastal batteries with great help from the RAF and the British Funnies of 79th Armoured Division. They also had a bit of help from the Dover guns 'Winnie' and 'Pooh', one with 14-inch shells, the other with 15-inch shells, which at 20-miles range knocked out two batteries. The Canadians attacked on 25 September and, after an immense four-day bombardment, eventually captured all batteries and the town of Calais by 0900hrs on 31 September.

*   *   *   *

It took all of October for the Canadians, the 52nd Lowland Scottish Division, in action for the first time, the Royal Navy and a Marine Commando Brigade to capture Walcheren and the Bevelands. Lt General Wilhelm Daser, with his small peaked nose, horn-rimmed glasses and pink bald head, seemed an unlikely commandant of Walcheren Island and the Beveland isthmus. His 70th Infantry Division, known as 'White Bread' due to all the Wehrmacht soldiers in it having gastric problems, held out from 24 October to 9 November. Lt General Knut Eberding and his 65th Infantry (Leave) Division, with 1,400 troops, garrisoned Zeebrugge, Cadzand, Breskens and Terneuzen along the south side of the 'Scheldt Fortress South'. The operations Angle, Switchback, Vitality 1, Vitality 2, Infatuate 1 and Infatuate 2 went on into early November. The Royal Navy completed the

82nd Assault Squadron RE LVT park, loading for assault on S. Beveland, 25 October 1944. (*Birkin Haward*)

Night assault on S. Beveland (Operation Vitality), 25 October 1944. (*Birkin Haward*)

final task of reopening Antwerp harbour with fleets of minesweepers in Operation Calendar.

It took 85 days to clear the Scheldt and open the vital harbour, which soon was unloading 10,000 tons of supplies a day. Eventually, when the four million square yards of harbour quays and *bassins* had been swept and cleared, 40,000 tons *per day* were achieved.

The Canadians, at great cost and in appalling polder country, had won their Cinderella war.

CHAPTER 7

The *Verdronken* Land of polders and Peel country

Holland had endured over four years of Nazi tyranny. On 10 May 1940 Winston Churchill wrote: 'The Dutch Ministers were in my room. Haggard and worn with horror in their eyes, they had just flown over from Amsterdam. Their country had been attacked without the slightest pretext or warning.' An avalanche of fire and steel had rolled across the frontiers and when Dutch resistance broke out and the frontier guards fired, an overwhelming onslaught was made from the air. The whole country was in a state of wild turmoil. The long-prepared defence scheme had been put into operation. The dykes were opened, the waters spread far and wide, but the Germans had already crossed the outer lines through the inner Gravelines defences and threatened the causeway enclosing the Zuyder Zee. They broke through, bridging the canals or seizing the locks and water sluices. The Luftwaffe bombed Rotterdam into a blazing ruin and threatened Amsterdam, The Hague and Utrecht with the same fate. Queen Wilhelmina, her family and the Dutch government sought safety in England.

In September 1944 Holland was again in a state of utmost confusion as remnants of the Wehrmacht streamed back towards Germany from their defeat in Normandy. The notorious Dr Arthur Seyss-Inquart, the German Reichskommissar for Holland, and the brutal Dutch Nazi Party leader, Anton Mussert, fled from The Hague to a vast concrete and brick bunker in Apeldoorn, 15 miles north of Arnhem.

In a radio broadcast from London Queen Wilhelmina announced that liberation was at hand as Brussels and Antwerp were captured. Her son-in-law, Prince Bernhard, became commander in chief of the Netherlands forces and the leader of all underground resistance groups. These, with a wide range of political views, were to be grouped together as *Binnenlandse Strijdkrachten* (Forces of the Interior). Prince Bernhard warned the underground resistance not to take premature and independent action. General Eisenhower made a special broadcast confirming that freedom was imminent, as did Pieter Gerbrandy, the exiled Dutch prime minister. With all these messages and with the Allied armies on their doorstep, the Dutch people went wild. All the Dutch Nazis fled and trains leaving for Germany were crammed full. Dutch collaborators fled too, and even German soldiers panicked, stole horses, wagons, cars and bicycles, which often they piled high with loot from France

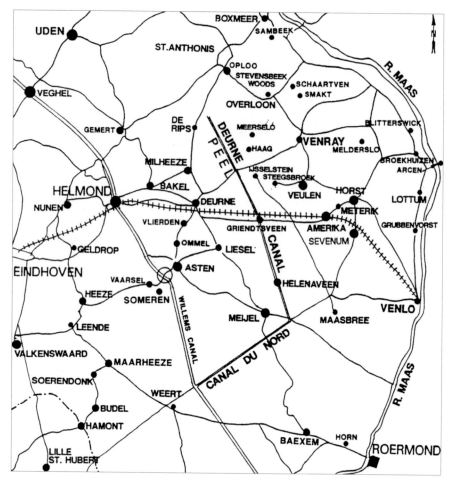

South-east Holland.

and Belgium. Walter Goerlitz, the German historian, wrote in his *History of the German General Staff* (translated): 'Naval troops marched northwards without weapons, selling their spare uniforms ... They told people that the war was over and they were going home. Lorries loaded with officers, their mistresses and large quantities of champagne and brandy contrived to get back as far as the Rhineland. It was necessary to set up special courts martial to deal with such cases.' Dutch flags appeared; orange ribbons, bows and buttons were proudly worn. Radios were fetched from their hiding places and tuned into the BBC 'Radio Orange' programme. Schools closed. Offices closed. Trams stopped running in The Hague.

The Dutch population of about ten million was crammed into a small country just over half the size of Eire. There were underground resistance cells in every town and village, and rumours and news spread rapidly. There was an excellent telephone service which continued functioning all the time

Eindhoven crowd – sombre and worried in case the dreaded 'moffen' (German jerries) return. They didn't! (*Imperial War Museum B-10125*)

with mainly Dutch operators, but also some Germans. BBC Radio Orange in London on 4 and 5 September had broadcast that Antwerp and Brussels had been captured by the Allied Army (true) and that the Dutch fortress town of Breda, seven miles from the frontier, had also been liberated (false). Nevertheless the 5th became known as *Dolle Dinsdag* or Mad Tuesday as the Germans panicked and the Dutch public celebrated the forthcoming liberation. Prince Bernhard arrived from London via Paris and he met Field Marshal Montgomery and General Horrocks on 7 September at the royal palace of Laeken in Brussels. Bernhard's news and information about German troop movements and resistance plans were dismissed rather brusquely. Probably Monty knew some of the details of Operation North Pole.

There is a large plaque on the wall of a parliamentary building in The Hague outlining the tragic operation called (translated) the North Pole, or more colloquially *Der Englander Spiel* (the English game). It was a tragedy for the Special Operations Executive (SOE) in London, whose task, according to Winston Churchill, was 'to set Europe alight'. SOE had many successes in France and other countries, but Holland was a disaster. All 60 SOE agents were captured by Dutch SS troops and imprisoned under guard in a Catholic theological college at Haaren in southern Holland.

Towards the end of 1941 the German Abwehr, the military intelligence department of the OKW (*Oberkommando der Wehrmacht*), headed by Wilhelm Canaris; Major, later Oberstleutnant, Herman Giskes of the Abwehr; and SS Sturmbannführer Josef Schreieder of the Sicherheitspolizei, set up the plan

'Dolle Dinstag' or 'Mad Tuesday' – newspaper news of possible freedom. (*Imperial War Museum BU-10279*)

Operation North Pole. A Dutch traitor betrayed a fellow Dutch radio operator named Hubertus Lauwers who had been dropped into Holland by parachute by SOE on 7 November. Lauwers was arrested and after 'so-called' interrogation was coerced into continuing to communicate with the Dutch section of SOE, probably located in Baker Street, London, under very close German supervision. Lauwers was a brave man and on several occasions tried to omit, on purpose, prearranged security checks on each message. It was incredible that SOE London ignored his warnings and continued to send agents and radio operators into Holland and into the hands of the North Pole organisers. Most of the 60 operatives who were dropped were forced to reveal their codes and security checks and continue to work their radio sets, sending reports back to London.

From early 1942 to early 1944, a period of 20 months, *Der Englander Spiel* continued. Altogether 50 radio sets, 15 tons of supplies, 500,000 guilders in cash, 900 Sten guns, and huge amounts of explosives, ammunition, grenades, pistols and revolvers were dropped and captured. Even worse, 12 RAF bombers and 83 aircrew of the RAF Special Duties Squadron were shot down by Luftwaffe night-fighter planes after they had made their drops.

Eventually, on 31 August 1943 Pieter Dourlein and Ben Ubbink succeeded in escaping from Haaren and reached the Dutch Legation in Berne, Switzerland, three months later. At the end of November 1943 they wrote a detailed report for SOE HQ exposing North Pole and the penetration of Dutch resistance. SOE deliberately continued to transmit messages to Holland giving the impression that nothing had changed. The Giskes and Schreieder team were not duped and closed down *Der Englander Spiel* appropriately on 1 April 1944. Giskes sent a cheeky message in clear: 'To Messrs Hunt, Bingham & Co, Successors Ltd, London. We understand you have been endeavouring for some time to do business in Holland without our assistance. We regret this since we have acted for so long as your sole representative in this country. Nevertheless should you be thinking of paying us a visit on the Continent on an extensive scale we shall give your emissaries the same attention as we have hitherto.'

SOE immediately revamped their intelligence networks. Although the mainstream Dutch Resistance groups were separate from the covert radio networks, British Intelligence remained extremely cautious when dealing with their Dutch operations. Another Dutch traitor, the huge, young and ugly Christiaan Lindemans, known as King Kong, was a double agent, reporting in 1943 and 1944 to Lt Colonel Herman Giskes. Lindemans penetrated and betrayed a number of Dutch resistance cells and the Gestapo arrested and executed many Dutch patriots as a result.

When Prince Bernhard heard on 21 September that the Guards Armoured tanks had been stopped at Elst and the Polish Brigade dropped near Driel rather than the southern side of the Arnhem bridge as originally planned,

ARNHEM

Regional emblem of Arnhem. (*Market Garden Veterans Association*)

THE BRIDGE INTO ARNHEM
FROM THE 'ISLAND.'

A V.2. FOR ANTWERP SEEN RISING FROM
NORTH HOLLAND OVER THE NIJMEGEN BRIDGE.

A HALT BEFORE CROSSING THE
RHINE AT WESEL.

NIJMEGEN RAILWAY BRIDGE FROM THE ROAD ONE.

Sketches of Verdronken land by Michael Bayley, 2 Kensingtons.

he demanded of his chief staff officer, Major General 'Pete' Dorman: 'Why wouldn't the British listen to us? Why?' When the Dutch generals had learned of the route that Horrocks' 30th Corps proposed to take they wanted to warn them of the dangers of using exposed dyke roads. Bernhard said: 'In our military staff colleges we had run countless studies on the problem. We knew tanks simply could not operate along these roads without infantry.' General Dorman had personally held trials with armour in that precise area before the war.

Prince Bernhard was even more apprehensive about the fate of Holland. 'If the British were driven back at Arnhem, I knew the repressions against the Dutch people in the winter ahead would be frightful.' He was right – they were frightful.

Holland's notorious police chief, SS Lt General Hans Albin Rauter, who reported to General Friedrich Christiansen, the armed forces commander in the Netherlands, declared an emergency after Mad Tuesday. His police took a bitter revenge on anyone suspected of belonging to a resistance cell. Men and women were arrested, shot, or sent off into concentration camps. A strict curfew was ordered. Rauter put up posters saying 'Where more than five persons are seen together they will be fired on by the Wehrmacht'. During the fighting in Arnhem and Oosterbeek Dutch resistance fighters wearing orange armbands, captured alongside regular Allied forces, were executed out of hand by SS troops. Rauter's reign of terror lasted eight months; after the war he was executed on 25 March 1949.

The Netherlands had the highest per capita death rate of all Nazi-occupied countries in Western Europe: 2.36% of the population. The winter of 1944–45 was very severe and there were 30,000 deaths, mainly due to starvation or disease. It was known as *Hongerwinter* (hunger winter), or the Dutch famine.

The Dutch government in exile in London stated that: 'the large cities were already without meat and it was expected that supplies of bread, butter, sugar and potatoes would run out by the end of October. Occupied Holland was also short of fuel and light. In the major cities, sewerage and mains drinking water would soon cease.' Anne Frank's diary described the 'food cycles, by which I mean periods in which one has nothing to eat but one particular dish or kind of vegetable. We had nothing but endives for a long time, day in, day out, endive with sand, endive without sand, stew with endive, boiled or "en casserole". Then it was spinach, after that followed swedes, salisfy, cucumbers, tomatoes, sauerkraut, etc.'

The polders and Peel country

For centuries the Dutch had been fighting a battle with the North Sea to reclaim, drain and make use of land thus rescued. It was the *verdronken* (drowned) land, and eventually became rich agricultural land requiring an elaborate network of dykes to keep the small fields adequately drained. The fields, called polders, were usually about 400–500 metres square, and sometimes up to 1,000 metres. They were either saturated in thick mud or, at worst, several feet of icy water covering a glutinous bed, which made every pace forward an immense effort. The polders were found in river deltas, former fenlands and coastal areas. The low-lying land was enclosed by dyke embankments usually about four metres high. Muskrats often caused leaks in the dykes and heavy rain had to be pumped out or drained by opening sluices. Dykes would not be made of sand or dry peat but of the most solid earth possible, sometimes reinforced. Often the dykes draining the polders were criss-crossed with cuttings called *kreeks* or *vliets*, some almost as wide as the Leopold canal. These served as minor 'highways' or tracks between various hamlets and farms. The total absence of cover for attacking troops meant that if the enemy zeroed his artillery or mortars onto the top of dyked roads movement became impossible. The Netherlands had 20 polder areas.

The British Army had no experience of fighting in the polders where the digging of slit trenches, waterlogged before they were dug, became a grim shivering joke. A leading tank was virtually certain to encounter a mine or a well-sited anti-tank gun.

At the end of September 1944 and for the next four months the greater part of the British Front were the Peel marshes around the river Maas salient, which stretched 20 miles on either side of Venlo.

4 Lincolns flood patrol, Autumn 1944. (*Imperial War Museum B-15001*)

A 'peel' is a flat, heather-covered peat bog in which trees crowd together in any small piece of land above the average elevation. In 1944 the whole area was comprised of reclaimed land, usually under water throughout late autumn and winter. Every field was surrounded by a large dyke. The few roads were liable to rapid disintegration under any heavy vehicles. The 8th Corps historian referred to the Peel country as a 'quagmire', totally unsuitable for the two Allied armoured divisions guarding most of that front: 'It is perhaps the worst country in the world for armoured fighting for no tank or SP dare leave the track and one cleverly placed mine field can cause enormous delay.'

This author, a troop leader in 13th RHA, was leading his troop of four Sexton SP 25-pdrs, each weighing over 30 tons, very, very slowly along a track in the Peel country near Amerika. The divisional sappers had brought in from far away hundreds of cut-down trees and railway sleepers to give substance to the track. There was light snow on the ground. On both sides were lying the dead bodies of the 9th SS Hohenstauffen Division. Rather naively, the 20-year-old asked the sapper/engineers why the corpses had not been buried. The answer was, 'Oh, Jerry has booby trapped most of them'. The German Schu mine is made almost entirely of wood. When trodden on, a spring ejects a small explosive which detonates at knee height, blowing off a leg or both. A month later in Operation Aintree the author's OP Bren gun carrier went up on a double Teller mine reserved for 33-ton tanks. His driver was blown to pieces and the author was in Eindhoven hospital that night.

South Lancashires advance on Venray during 'Operation Aintree', November 1944. (*Imperial War Museum BU-1212*)

Divisional Sappers and Flail tank advance through Overloon. (*Imperial War Museum B-10818*)

The small towns, villages and hamlets in the Peel country were Venray, Veulen, Overloon and Oploo. One infantry officer with 1st South Lancashires recalled: 'the fighting around Overloon and Venray marked a return to the utter devastation of the Normandy battlefields. Dead cattle strewed the landscape. The trees were stripped bare and the rain had reduced everything to black slimy mud. Hardly a human soul was to be seen. Once more it was war stripped of any softer tones – naked and beastly.'

No wonder that the German Field Marshal von Manstein, Chief of Staff, wrote of their blitzkrieg attack in 1940: 'The flat land of Holland was crossed by innumerable canals and rivers, making difficult the deployment of large armoured forces.' So the panzer attack was shifted to the Ardennes to get behind the French Maginot Line.

Detail from picture on p. 69 with destroyed telegraph pole. (*Imperial War Museum B-10818*)

CHAPTER 8

Dilemma of the Allied Airborne Army

In May 1940 Adolf Hitler had deployed his paratroop detachments that seized Belgian river crossings and neutralised the fortress of Eben Emael. Two divisions had also been dropped into 'Fortress Holland' around Rotterdam. They were assisted by the noisy Stuka dive-bombers and Rommel's panzers. In the violent attack on Crete in May 1941 Hermann Göring's 7th Airborne Division under General Kurt Student lost over 5,000 paratroops drowned or killed on land, and many more were wounded. As a result the Führer forbade any more parachute operations. In 1944 Student's Parachute Army were exceptionally tough PBI (poor bloody infantry).

However, the Allied High Command still had great confidence in the concept of airborne landings to ensure the capture of vital bridgeheads. It is true that Sicily was not a success, and on D-Day the American air landings were initially inaccurate, but Major General Richard Gale's 6th Airborne had undoubtedly helped by seizing the left flank of the bridgehead near Caen in a brilliant *coup de main* on vital bridges.

SHAEF had created a major reserve, the First Allied Airborne Army. General Marshal, the Chairman of the Combined Services in the USA, and General Hap Arnold, Chief of the USAAF, were anxious to use this formation for a *major* strategic deployment. The two British divisions were 1st and 6th and the two American divisions were the 82nd and 101st, with the 17th Division still in training. In September 1944 the Allied Airborne Army (AAA) was commanded by Lt General Lewis Brereton. Lt General Frederick Browning was Deputy to Brereton and commanded 1st Airborne Corps, plus Major General Sosabowski's Polish Brigade. After the Normandy breakout, Eisenhower offered the AAA to both Bradley and Montgomery. Bradley was not interested so Monty 'jumped' at the opportunity. There were no fewer than 17 planned drops, all of which were aborted for various reasons. They included Operations Tuxedo, Wastage, X, Wild Oats, Beneficiary, Y, Swordhilt, Hands Up, Transfigure, Boxer, Axehead, Linnet 1, Linnet 2, Infatuate and Comet. Major General Roy Urquhart, GOC British 1st Airborne, wrote: 'By September 1944 my division was battle-hungry to a degree which only those who have commanded large forces of trained soldiers can fully comprehend. In fact there were already signs of that dangerous mixture of boredom and cynicism creeping into our daily lives. We were ready for anything.' Parts of the division had fought in North Africa, Sicily and Italy in 1942 and 1943, but had been inactive and restless since then.

Comet, Montgomery's plan, evolved on 2 September and Eisenhower gave it his approval. It was an audacious plan to drop 1st Airborne with 1st Polish Brigade attached and try to achieve what Market Garden failed to do two weeks later, with two superb US airborne divisions plus the full might of Monty's armies. Comet was extremely rash, conceived in the euphoria of success even before Brussels and Antwerp were captured. The way to Berlin was open – except for Model, Student, Von Zangen, Hermann Göring, Josef Göbbels and Adolf Hitler's sheer domination and determination! The start date for Comet was planned for 9 September. Brigadier 'Shan' Hackett, whose 4th Parachute Brigade was to capture the bridge at Grave, wrote: 'The airborne movement was very naïve. It was very good on getting airborne troops to battle, but they were innocents when it came to fighting the Germans when we arrived. They used to make a beautiful airborne plan and then add the fighting-the-Germans bit afterwards ... Thank goodness Comet was cancelled, it would have been a disaster. But the same attitude persisted with the eventual Arnhem plan.'

So Montgomery produced a brilliant, unrealistic plan for Comet, and shortly after, a more elaborate, equally doomed plan for Market Garden. Nevertheless, Comet's planning had involved several key principles that long experience had taught (some of) the airborne commanders, which unfortunately were not adhered to in Operation Market. Comet involved using glider-borne troops landing close to the bridge in *coup de main* attacks, similar to 6th Airborne landings on Pegasus bridge at Bénouville on D-Day. Once the bridges were seized the parachute brigades would land on nearby drop zones (DZs) and join up with the glider troops to hold the bridges until ground forces arrived. The Comet plan adhered to the important basic airborne rule: land as close to the objective as possible and capture *both ends of any bridge at once.* The other key point was that of surprise: land the vast bulk of the airborne armada on the first day, come what may. Lightly armed parachute troops lack mobility and need to consolidate quickly before enemy counter-attacks and fire power can be organised.

As in any military high command since wars started, and SHAEF was an excellent example, there was constant dissension, dislike, rivalries, PR tactics and perhaps a bit of double dealing! The teams of Brereton and Browning detested each other. Urquhart was an excellent soldier, liked by everyone, but he had no experience of airborne warfare. The main transport commander, Air Vice-Marshal Leslie Hollinghurst of 38th Group RAF, could not agree on key policy with Major General Paul Williams of US 9th Troop Carrier Command. Lt General Browning was a charming, distinguished Grenadier Guards officer with an excellent First World War record. But although in the Second World War he had risen in the ranks of the airborne formations, he had seen no active service and had made only two practice jumps, injuring himself both times. Now he was determined – this was his last chance to get into battle. Regrettably he used guile and deceit to ensure that Market (and of course Garden on the ground) went ahead. He was Montgomery's trusted adviser on air warfare – almost an Iago-type confidant.

His first mistake was to mislead his divisional commanders about the Ultra and other information sources, which reported that Field Marshal Model and active remnants of two superb panzer divisions were recuperating in the Arnhem area. This knowledge would have meant that portable anti-tank guns and many more PIATs, with their bombs, should have been loaded for the first drop. Also the troops should have rehearsed their tactics against armour. In the decision about sorties, Major General Williams vetoed Air Vice-Marshal Hollinghurst, who was prepared to allow his aircraft to make *two* lifts on D-Day (17 September), and Brereton and Browning *backed* Williams' decision to go for one drop only.

The next mistake was the decision not to have a *coup de main* dropping on the vital Arnhem bridge, allegedly because of the presence of heavy German flak guarding the bridge and the neighbouring Deelen airfield. In fact, RAF bombers had dropped bombs on Deelen to put it out of action, but Browning still went along with Brereton and Williams. Colonel George Chatterton, CO of the Glider Pilot Regiment, appealed personally to Browning: 'We were landing too far away [six miles to the west of the bridge]. He replied it was an RAF decision because of the bridge defences by AA guns. I nevertheless suggested that my pilots could land their gliders near the bridge and although there would be more casualties on landing due to the size and unevenness of the enclosures, it would surely be preferable to landing miles away.' Browning said there was nothing he could do but he did discuss the matter of the *coup de main* with Major General Richard Gale who had led the British 6th Airborne in Normandy. Gale confirmed that the bridge at Arnhem *should* be seized by the *coup de main*, followed by at least a brigade landing adjacent to it. Browning kept this sound advice to himself!

The most experienced airborne warrior was the US Lt General Matthew Ridgeway who commanded US 18th Corps, which comprised the three US airborne divisions. Ridgeway perforce reported to Browning. The pair detested each other. Ridgeway was scornful of Browning's lack of battle experience in the Second World War and of his poor leadership. In Operation Market Ridgeway was isolated and resentful. But Major Generals Gavin and Taylor both performed magnificently in the field under immense pressure and with negligible help or advice from Browning.

So all prospects of surprise were lost before Market got under way. If the weather broke, as it did, there would be a disaster. Many of the drops after D-Day fell into enemy hands, for which they were rather grateful. Now Browning produced his real *folie de grandeur*. He pulled rank and decreed that he would command the Allied Airborne Army on the ground, although it had been made clear that 30th Corps under General Horrocks would take control of Major General Taylor's 101st Airborne, dropping in the Eindhoven/Grave area. Browning hijacked 38 Horsa gliders from Urquhart's D-Day plan and deployed himself and his HQ staff to fly into the Nijmegen area and sit on top of the Groesbeek Heights. Those 38 Horsas could have carried the rest of the powerful 1st Airborne landing brigade, or Sosabowski's tough, brave Poles, to alter the balance of power on D-Day.

Browning only had one major command decision to make during the first week of the operation. Back in England was the 52nd Lowland Division, which was earmarked to fly in to Deelen airfield on Thursday. Major General Hakewill Smith sent a signal to Browning offering to fly in a brigade of the Division by glider on Wednesday 20th, and land them as close as possible to 1st Airborne. It was a generous offer; such a landing near the south end of the Arnhem bridge, for example, might have transformed the situation there. It would have been a risky venture but John Frost's men were still holding out there at that time. Or the brigade could have been landed somewhere north of the Rhine where it could have reinforced the Oosterbeek perimeter and provided Urquhart with sufficient reserves to defend the Westerbouwing height properly. But Browning sent back this answer: 'Thanks for your message, but offer not – repeat not – required as situation better than you think. We want lifts as already planned including Poles. Second Army definitely requires your party and intend to fly you to Deelen airfield.' Browning clearly showed in that signal a lack of awareness of the situation at Arnhem and Oosterbeek. Hakewill Smith's proposed operation would have required a reallocation of gliders and transport aircraft, but that was the type of reorganisation that Browning could have handled better if he had remained in England. The only radio links to Urquhart were by 21st Army Group HQ or by Phantom, and by the 20th September 1st Airborne was already in serious trouble.

Almost single-handedly Browning wrecked Urquhart's chances – Monty's 'Forlorn Hope' was soon to be surrounded by Model's panzer troops. It was a terrible start for Market.

CHAPTER 9

War of the Generals

Bernard Montgomery and Bill Slim were the outstanding British generals during 1939–45. The history books state that Montgomery never lost a battle apart from being in the BEF retreat to Dunkirk in 1940. Nevertheless, there were many battles that he did not win, particularly in Normandy in the summer of 1944. Operations Charnwood, Epsom, Jupiter, Goodwood, Totalise and half a dozen others were at best painful, attritional 'draws'. Monty was a deeply self-centred character, complex with no sense of a reciprocal personal relationship. Ungenerous in spirit and irascible, he had a scarcely veiled contempt for the non-British legions in his huge armies.

Unfortunately, Montgomery's arrogance and confidence that he was the master of the battlefield made him many enemies. Even in SHAEF there was a powerful minority, including British senior officers, who thought that he should be fired and that somebody less abrasive, Alexander perhaps, should replace him. The war of the generals!

Ascetic, humourless, and domineering in public, Montgomery had an enormous flair for publicity. It is safe to say that the vast majority of his troops (including this author) thought that Monty would take them, rather painfully, to eventual victory. His command of the battlefield was superb, with a great deal of help from Dempsey; from his small inner circle of young officers (Poston, Henderson, Mather and others) who acted as his battlefield scouts; from, although he never admitted it, Ultra at Bletchley Park; and from the RAF whose Typhoon 'cab ranks' so often blasted the way ahead. The only time he admitted to a mistake was for the apparent slowness to clear the Scheldt to get Antwerp open for business, although, even in this case, he adroitly shifted the blame to the Canadian Army! Often he gave outrageous hostages to fortune. On D-Day he expected Caen to be captured. In Epsom he expected to capture and hold Hill 112. In Goodwood he expected to get to Falaise, and in Market Garden he expected his troops to get to the Rhine in two days. All these expectations were made public at the time.

For the capture of Berlin Stalin deployed 2.5 million men and 6,250 tanks under Generals Zhukov and Konev. In the final assault on the city 464,000 soldiers were in action with 12,700 guns, 1,500 tanks and 21,000 *katyushi* (SP mortars). Between 16 April and 8 May 1945 almost 300,000 Russian casualties were incurred (Konev 113,825 and Zhukov 178,490), including

100,000 killed in action. The Berliners suffered terribly with 125,000 killed in the siege. Montgomery's establishment of a bridgehead over the Rhine in Market Garden in the hope of advancing and presumably capturing Berlin with 21st Army Group was a delusion.

Montgomery worked closely with Dwight (Ike) Eisenhower although it is clear that he had contempt for Ike's battlefield experience. But Eisenhower was a superb and ideal political soldier: courteous, long-suffering, with a committee approach to a military problem. Instead of a crisp, logical Monty-style series of commands, Ike would usually pass down a 'project' to the next rank of officer, who in turn would pass down a project, and so on. The Americans had a classic, democratic army, and that was the way they made war. The only exception was General George Patton, who was a law unto himself and was rated by the German high command as the Allies' best armour commander. 'Old Blood and Guts' Patton hated Montgomery, who didn't even notice the fact!

Towards the end of Operation Overlord and the closing of the Argentan-Falaise Gap Monty was already making detailed plans for the next stage – an advance to the Rhine: the Rhine endeavour.

Eisenhower's American football style was for the whole of his command, including the British, Canadians and Poles, to advance steadily more or less in a straight line, with no dangerous salients, putting constant pressure on the German front lines. Monty and General Erwin Rommel both believed in the *schwerpunkt* method of a strong, concentrated narrow advance with co-ordinated armour and infantry and appropriate flank protection.

So there was a complete clash, not only of personality but also of military strategy. After a traditional set-piece of artillery and RAF bombing, Monty would plan for a precise breakthrough as he did, eventually, in the famous Alamein battle. Monty was not too concerned about the logistics behind him; in all his campaigns his advances had never been rapid enough to warrant anxiety. After the 300-mile armoured gallop from the Seine to the Dutch border, POL, ammunition and transport were rationed and Eisenhower eventually actually had to *order* Montgomery to pull out all the stops to open Antwerp docks and clear the Scheldt for supplies. In a message on 9 October he said: 'I must emphasize that I consider Antwerp of first importance to all our endeavors on entire front from Switzerland to Channel. I believe your personal attention is required in operation to clear entrance.' It was a difficult relationship, handled with the utmost tact, and possibly respect by Ike for his difficult Limey general.

Nigel Hamilton, one of Montgomery's biographers, asserted: 'Montgomery viewed himself as the natural twentieth-century heir apparent to the legacy of Marlborough and Wellington.' And that is what – despite the obvious faults – he was.

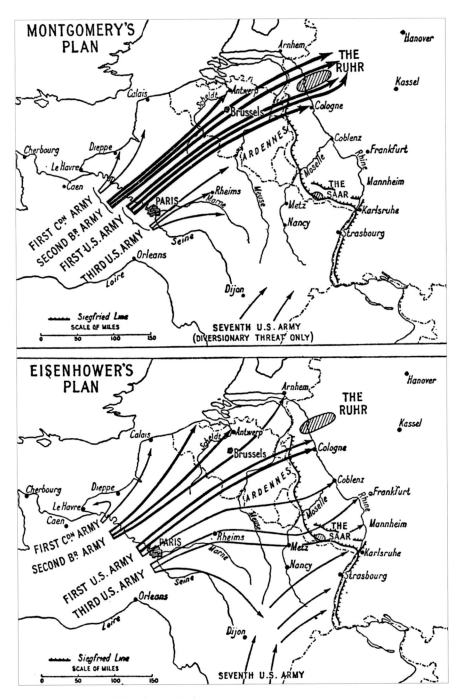

Montgomery's and Eisenhower's plans.

CHAPTER 10

Monty's Greatest Gamble

Operation Comet (originally code-named Fifteen) was first planned for 2 September, before the capture of Brussels and Antwerp. With limited airborne resources available, Montgomery had been planning ahead to seize and hold key bridges up to the Lower Rhine. But on 4 September, when he was presented with the addition of 82nd and 101st US Airborne Divisions, plus the Polish Brigade, he was determined, as was clear to Bill Williams, his Chief Information Officer, to use these 'spare' divisions as his *schwerpunkt* into a massive development of Comet. However, the key point of Comet – for the three small *coups de main* battle groups to be landed *before first light* in the Arnhem, Nijmegen and Grave bridge areas – was not included in the new Market and Garden plans. Comet had been cancelled because there were no airborne forces available to land between Grave and the ground forces start line. Now these forces were available.

Monty's plan for Garden was as follows:

101st US Airborne Division would seize the bridges and crossings between Eindhoven and Grave.

82nd US Airborne Division would capture the two major bridges at Nijmegen and Grave, and would take and hold the high ground between Nijmegen and Groesbeek.

1st Airborne Division, with 1st Polish Independent Parachute Brigade under command, would capture the bridges at Arnhem and establish a bridgehead in preparation for a further advance northwards by 2nd British Army.

52nd Lowland Division, which had seen little action, was a reserve infantry unit that could be landed by glider, or preferably by transport aircraft, at a captured airport or major airstrip, probably north of Arnhem. As it happened, even when Major General Urquhart's 1st Airborne was *in extremis*, he decided not to bring the 52nd into battle. The division was sent to help clear up the Walcheren Island operation.

The plan was that 2nd British Army, spearheaded by 30th Corps with 8th and 12th Corps on its flanks in echelon, would break out of its bridgehead on the Meuse-Escaut canal and advance as rapidly as possible along the

'Monty' and his generals: Dempsey (on his left), Crerar (on his right), Thomas (on his far right) and 'Pip' Roberts (behind his right shoulder). Behind Monty are Scottish generals wearing tam o'shanters.

road through Valkenswaard to Eindhoven and thereafter through Son, St Oedenrode, Veghel, Uden, Grave, Nijmegen and Elst to Arnhem, joining up with the airborne forces. Finally it was to secure and dominate the country northwards to the Zuyder Zee, cutting off the line of communications between Germany and its forces in the Low Countries. 30th Corps' flanks would be protected on the right by 8th Corps, which would capture the towns of Weert and secure as far north as Helmond, and on the left by 12th Corps, which would take Rethy, Arendonck and Turnhout before advancing to the river Maas. Responsibility for protection of the line of communication along the corridor was allotted to 8th Corps.

A considerable amount of information was arriving every day about the German recovery, and was being ignored at the highest level of command. On 5 September an Ultra decrypt revealed that 2nd SS Panzer Corps was to take two further armoured divisions under command and move to the Venlo-Arnhem-s'Hertogenbosch area.

Montgomery's trusted Army Group commander, Lt General Miles Dempsey, was worried by the Ultra news and the fact that 11th Armoured Division was fighting fiercely in the suburbs of Antwerp against determined enemy. He wrote in his diary on 9 September:

> It is clear that the enemy is bringing up all the reinforcements he can lay hands on for the defence of the Albert Canal, and that he appreciates the importance of the area of Arnhem-Nijmegen. It looks as though he is going to do all he can to hold it. This being the case, any question of a rapid advance

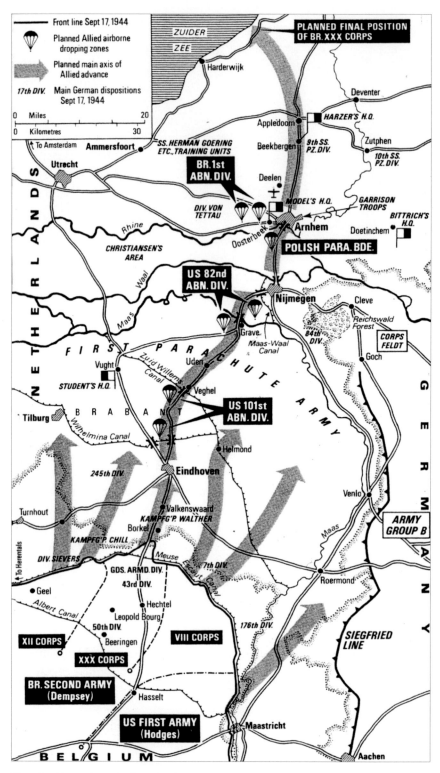

Plan for Operation Market Garden.

to the north-east seems unlikely. Owing to our maintenance situation, we will not be in a position to fight a real battle for perhaps ten days to a fortnight. Are we right to direct 2nd Army to Arnhem, or would it be better to hold a left flank along the Albert Canal, and strike due east towards Cologne in conjunction with 1st Army?

Dempsey proposed a different axis of advance eastwards towards the town of Wesel on the Rhine. When Montgomery showed him the signal from London about the first attacks by V-2 missiles and the new and urgent need to over-run their bases, he kept his misgivings about Market Garden to himself.

On 10 September 21st Army Group issued an intelligence summary that referred to the presence of 9th and 10th Panzer Divisions in the Arnhem area. Ultra produced evidence that Oosterbeek/Arnhem was now Field Marshal Model's HQ. The red warning bells should have been sounding the alarm loud and clear. The Intelligence Officer (G-2) of the British 1st Airborne Corps, Major Brian Urquhart, had received the Army Group summary, the result of interrogations of German prisoners and reports from the Dutch Resistance (tainted unfortunately by North Pole). All indicated that 9th SS Hohenstaufen Division and probably 2nd SS Panzer Corps were in the Arnhem area.

On the 16th a SHAEF intelligence summary stated that the 9th and 10th SS Panzers were withdrawing to the Arnhem area to be equipped with new tanks from a depot in Cleves. Eisenhower ordered his Chief of Staff, Walter Bedell Smith, to fly to Montgomery's HQ the same day, suggesting an extra airborne division or that urgent consideration should be given to shifting the drop zone of 82nd Airborne further north. Monty simply ignored the proposals, saying that the panzer tanks were not battleworthy. Wing Commander Lee, Lt General Brereton's Air Intelligence Officer, dug further into Ultra data and was so alarmed that he flew to 21st Army Group in Brussels – and was effectively ignored.

But the worst fate awaited the next 'messenger'. On 12 September Major Urquhart briefed a Spitfire reconnaissance squadron based at RAF Benson in Oxfordshire to overfly the Arnhem area. Aerial photographs available three days later clearly showed tanks and armoured vehicles parked under trees close to the proposed 1st Airborne drop. When Browning was given this news he threatened Urquhart with a court martial or immediate sick leave 'suffering from stress and exhaustion'. Shakespeare could not have written a more sinister scenario. Certainly the messengers were shot! Browning was Iago, who urgently wanted fame on the battlefield once again. He proceeded *not* to pass on the information to the three divisional commanders, Urquhart, Gavin and Taylor, that there would be a disturbingly strong enemy armoured presence in the Arnhem area.

*   *   *   *

'Monty' (second from right) and his aides in front of three war caravans.

Montgomery presumably made the final choice of his *schwerpunkt* commanders and units. Brian Horrocks was by far the best and most daring of his corps commanders, albeit a very sick man from time to time, and almost certainly in awe of the Guards Armoured 'mafia' – his friends and colleagues.

Montgomery made a poor choice of the Guards. They were undoubtedly extremely brave, but were dilatory in getting going each morning. Moreover, Adair was a competent but uninspiring commander. A far better choice would have been Brigadier Michael Carver, a brilliant armoured leader with 4th Armoured Brigade. Alternatively, a good choice would have been the 11th Armoured Division who still had plenty of thrust and would have advanced during the night if Horrocks had so ordered. The choices of 43rd Wessex and 50th Northumbrian Divisions, who had a background of appalling losses in Normandy, were debatable. Better would have been the 52nd Lowland Scottish Division, who had never been in action before, were trained in air landing operations and would have gone hell for leather to link up with the airborne. They would have needed a more dynamic GOC: Brigadier Churcher, commanding the infantry brigade in 11th Armoured Division, would have been ideal. He subsequently became GOC of 3rd British Division.

It is easy to be wise after the event. There has been endless conjecture why Montgomery masterminded such a daring and complex operation and then failed to insist on what he knew was needed from the AAA and the RAF. He knew little about airborne warfare and he relied too heavily on Browning for

Field Marshal Bernard Montgomery with Major-General Adair (Guards Armoured) left, Lt General Horrocks (30 Corps Commander) right and Major-General 'Pip' Roberts (11th Black Bull Armoured) extreme right. (*Imperial War Museum B-9973*)

advice and guidance. Both, for different reasons, were determined, come what may, for Market and Garden to go ahead.

Monty had been privy to the many aborted AAA drops over the last few months and thought that Market and Garden had a reasonable chance of success. Another Epsom, Goodwood or Jupiter on his track record. The official British history of the Second World War noted: 'Operation Market Garden accomplished much of what it had been designed to accomplish. Nevertheless by the merciless logic of war, Market Garden was a failure.'

There is, of course, another viewpoint. There was no question of Montgomery waiting unnecessarily in order to build up a vast administrative reserve. He launched the offensive into Holland with nothing in hand at all, except what was immediately necessary to take 30th Corps to the Zuyder Zee, and to support limited advances by the corps on either flank. He was not able even to establish those corps in position to render the maximum assistance. Owing to the shortage of transport for troops and ammunition, 12th Corps could secure only one small bridgehead beyond the Meuse-Escaut canal before 17 September, and 8th Corps could not join the offensive until the 19th. Even then this corps had only two divisions, for the 51st Highland was grounded throughout the Arnhem operation so that its transport could be used to supply the forward troops. On the first two days of Market Garden, Dempsey was able to employ offensively only three of the nine British divisions available. The actual breakout was made by two battalions advancing along one narrow road. This was the direct result of Eisenhower's policy. If he had kept Patton halted on the Meuse, and had given full logistic support to Hodges and Dempsey after the capture of Brussels, the operations in Holland could have been an overwhelming triumph; 1st US Army could have mounted a formidable diversion, if not a successful offensive, at Aachen; and 2nd British Army could have attacked sooner, on a wider front and in much greater strength. This hypothesis puts the blame, rather unfairly perhaps, on Eisenhower.

The Rhine endeavour was a great gamble and to Ike's eternal credit he claims in his memoirs that he had no regrets at all in approving the launch of Market Garden.

Detail from picture on p. 93. (*Imperial War Museum K-7586*)

CHAPTER 11

The Bitter Triangle

Compromises have to be made in war, and if three services are involved even more compromises are required.

The Allied Airborne Army was thirsting for action, and Montgomery was thirsting to get across the Rhine and deep into the Fatherland. The RAF in Operation Market had to achieve miracles to accommodate the other two services. To get some idea of the scale of the whole airborne operation, Eisenhower quoted these figures in his D-Day to VE Day report:

> Between 17 and 30 September 20,190 troops were dropped from aircraft by parachute, 13,781 landed in gliders, 905 were air lands on a strip made ready by preceding airborne troops; in addition to this total of 34,876 troops, 5,230 tons of equipment and supplies, 1927 vehicles and 568 artillery pieces were transported by air; and the supporting airforces flew over 7,800 sorties to the isolated forces.

During the planning for this huge complex operation the RAF planners had always been worried about the possibility of heavy plane losses to German flak anti-aircraft guns. Lt General Brereton was later blamed for various mistakes, but his emphasis on the wrecking of most of the German AA sites by 400 RAF and USAAF heavy bombers before 17 September paid off.

The RAF only had sufficient aircraft to carry 16,500 out of the total of 35,000 troops for the three divisional drops. The total aircraft required for 1st Airborne Corps was 3,790 – 2,495 for the paratroops, 1,295 to tow gliders. The combined resources of 38th and 46th Groups RAF and 9th US Troop Carrier Command were insufficient. The eventual allocation was as follows:

HQ 1st Airborne Corps (Browning's unnecessary *folie de grandeur*), 38 glider tugs (British); 101st US Airborne, 424 paratroop and 70 glider tugs (USAAF); 82nd US Airborne, 482 paratroop and 50 glider tugs (USAAF); and 1st Airborne Division, 161 paratroop (USAAF) and 320 glider tugs (RAF).

A total of 1,534 aircraft and 491 gliders, the largest single concentration of transport aircraft ever gathered (up to mid-September 1944) waited in 23 separate airfields to carry the first lift to their drop and landing zones in Holland. The air plan was extremely complex and a masterpiece of staff work.

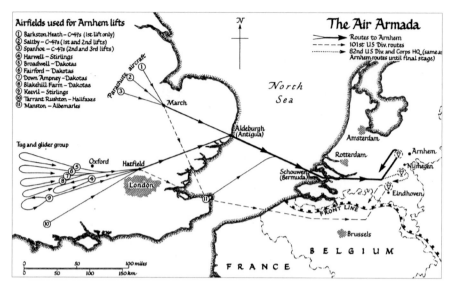

Airfields used for Arnhem lifts.

The two air corridors were designed to take the troop carriers between the densest concentrations of German AA and flak batteries. The northern route was for British 1st and US 82nd Airborne Divisions, and the southern route for US 101st Airborne. About one thousand Allied fighters were in the air to protect Market's first lift, led by Pathfinders whose task was to locate the landing zones or dropping zones and drop coloured smoke canisters, Eureka electronic homing beacons, and 'day-glo' marker panels.

The 'bitter triangle' was caused by the decisions that had been taken by the RAF planners:

(a) There should be no *coups de main* landing on, or very close to the target bridges.

(b) 1st Airborne would be dropped six miles from their main objective – the Arnhem bridge.

(c) Instead of having two flights on the first day to achieve the maximum surprise, flights would be scheduled over three days (giving the Germans sufficient time to surround 1st Airborne).

(d) There should be no extra drops at night.

(e) There should be no drops south of the Lower Rhine near the bridges.

(f) The 82nd US Airborne drops and objectives were so many that the capture of Nijmegen bridge was the last.

All the protests by the airborne divisional commanders were ignored by Browning, Brereton and Major General Paul Williams. Air Vice-Marshal Hollinghurst, who commanded 38th Group RAF, was prepared to make two sorties on the first day, the first taking off before dawn, but this was refused.

Lt General 'Boy' Browning, commander of the Allied 1st Airborne Corps.

General Horrocks and 30th Corps desperately needed close air support (CAS) from cab ranks of Typhoons and Tempests to take out panzers, SPs, road blocks and other key targets. For a variety of reasons the RAF's record was adequate, brave, but not sufficient: D+1 97 CAS strikes for 82nd Airborne; D+4 119 for 101st Airborne; D+5 a few for 1st Airborne; D+6 22 for 1st Airborne; D+7 81 for 1st Airborne. The weather was the main problem, but 2nd Tactical Air Force was prohibited from entering airspace over ground operations when an air lift or supply drop was scheduled.

*   *   *   *

The chain of command was very complicated: US and British alternated at all senior levels as SHAEF policy, which did not help on this occasion. It is surprising that Montgomery did not play his usual shrewd dominant role, but trusted Browning implicitly. In any case, Montgomery could not influence the RAF planners, even though the army had spelt out very clearly what their objectives were and the shortage of battle time involved.

So the magnificent disaster got under way. It was doomed now. Field Marshal Model and General Student, with the Führer on their back, had plenty of time to block Monty's extreme gamble.

CHAPTER 12

Monty's Forlorn Hope: 1st Airborne Division

In the desperate sieges of the Indian and Peninsular Wars the 'Iron Duke', Wellington, had recourse to invite a very brave group of soldiers to storm the breaches of a fortress or city under strong resistance. They were called the 'forlorn hope' and they were usually killed in action, wounded unto death, or taken prisoner.

*   *   *   *

Major General Robert 'Roy' Urquhart, the 42-year-old commander of 1st British Airborne Division, was a tall, burly Scotsman with long combat experience in North Africa, Sicily and Italy, but no airborne warfare experience. He regarded his men as 'very highly trained infantry troops'. Urquhart confessed to air sickness, and had never parachuted, nor been in a glider. His 'Red Devils (*roten teufel*) were hungering for a fight', but cynics called them the 'stillborn Division'.

The Red Devils had arrived back in the UK from the Mediterranean theatre of war, mainly in Sicily and southern Italy, in December 1943. Since Overlord and D-Day 15–17 drop missions had been aborted and the Allied armies seemed to be winning the war in north-west Europe without airborne assistance. Urquhart was fortunate in having three experienced brigadier commanders. Brigadier Philip 'Pip' Hicks, senior in rank and designated as Urquhart's No. 2, commanded the powerful 1st Air Landing Brigade composed of 7th King's Own Scottish Borderers (KOSB), the 2nd South Staffordshires, and the Border Regiment. Brigadier John 'Shan' Hackett commanded 4th Parachute Brigade with 10th, 11th and 156th (Para) Battalions of lightly armed desperadoes. Brigadier Gerald Lathbury commanded 1st, 2nd and 3rd Parachute (Para) Battalions.

The glider troops had a less glamorous image than the parachute troops, but it was more dangerous for them because a glider landing was a controlled crash, even under ideal conditions, and they suffered a higher level of injuries and fatalities than the paratroops. In the air a 'tug' towing a glider was an easier target for flak, and there was also the risk of the tow breaking in mid-air.

Major General Roy Urquart, GOC
1st British Airborne Division.
(*Imperial War Museum H-40947*)

A parachute battalion was a lightly armed, lean unit, nearly all of whom were volunteers and many of whom came from Guards regiments, encouraged by Lt General Browning. Its entire purpose was to get to its target by swift air transport and to drop *immediately* into action. There were three rifle companies instead of the four in a normal infantry battalion. The fittest, keenest soldiers, many not more than 19 or 20 years old, were in the rifle companies. The three sections in a platoon were each commanded by a sergeant or a lance sergeant instead of the usual corporal. The few heavy weapons were the 3-inch mortar and Vickers machine-gun platoons. Otherwise it was the rifle, or a Sten gun, or the PIAT (Projector infantry anti-tank). British parachute troops did not have a reserve parachute as had the Americans! Qualified parachutists received *extra* pay: two shillings a day for other ranks, and four (later reduced to two) shillings for officers. Their red berets were in fact maroon.

The Royal Artillery had a significant presence with Lt Colonel Robert Loder-Symonds, RHA, commanding 800 gunners arriving in 170 gliders. They had 24 American-made 75mm guns firing 14.7-pound shells up to a five-mile range. The gun, its towing jeep and a trailer with ammunition could fit into one glider. There were also two anti-tank batteries in the Division. Each battery had four troops, each with four 6-pdr guns, and three extra troops had the powerful new 17-pdr gun, capable of destroying any panzer tank or SP. There were key Forward (Airborne) Observation Officers (FOOs) with signallers and jeeps to give fire support to any divisional unit as well as any 30th Corps artillery that came in range. Eventually 64th Medium Regiment, based near Nijmegen, brought down barrages and stonks towards the end of the airborne battle.

Lt Colonel Edmund Myers, Commander Royal Engineers (CRE), had 500 sappers under his command, many of whom had fought in Norway and Sicily. 9th Field Company was a glider unit and carried out engineer duties for the whole Division. The 1st and 4th Parachute (RE) Squadrons were attached to those brigades. The 261st (Airborne) Field Park Company provided a detachment. All the men were fully trained infantry and were useful additions to the Division's rifle strength.

✻   ✻   ✻   ✻

The British Army in 1944 mainly used two standard radio sets: the No. 19, a large set with a range of 12 miles in good conditions, but requiring a heavy battery charger and a jeep (or truck or tank); the 22 set, a medium size with a smaller battery charger, also needing a jeep with a maximum range of six miles. The portable 68 set used by infantry signallers had replaceable dry batteries and a range of up to three miles. The Airborne Division used the 68 set, carried in a kit bag attached to the operator's leg, which was immediately usable on landing. The artillery had the 19 sets and the divisional command net was the 22 set.

If battalions were separated by more than three miles, or if brigades by more than six miles, or in local conditions such as built-up areas in towns and villages or woods, then radio contact would be lost. So for the 350 signallers who went to Arnhem it was totally frustrating. The town of Arnhem blocked off communication and the eventual town fighting blocked everything off. In January 1944 the Airborne Division ruled that the maximum diameter of the 'goose-egg' (slang for the oval shape on planning maps to show unit locations), would not be more than three miles. One would have thought that Brereton, Browning, Urquhart and all the senior planners would have realised that radio communications in the Arnhem area would be difficult, even impossible. And they were!

✻   ✻   ✻   ✻

The Royal Army Medical Corps mustered 400 men with Nos 16 and 133 Parachute Field Ambulance attached to the 1st and 4th Parachute Brigades respectively. No. 181 Air Landing Field Ambulance would fly in with the Air Landing Brigade.

✻   ✻   ✻   ✻

Other support services were 69 Military Police for traffic control and guarding of prisoners. 70th REME (Royal Electrical & Mechanical Engineers) were also present, mostly on radio and weapon repairs. Sixteen Intelligence Corps members were fluent in various languages, all except Dutch of course! There were also a number of intrepid media reporters including Jack Smyth (Reuters), Stanley Maxtead and Guy Byam (BBC), Alan Wood (*Daily Express*), Marek Swiecik, a Polish journalist, plus army photographers, censors, and a public relations officer. They were limited to bulletins of a few hundred words per day. The well-known Walter Cronkite was with 101st US Airborne Division.

*   *   *   *

The total war establishment for 1st Airborne was 12,215 men. The number dispatched by air to Arnhem was just over 8,900.

The Glider Pilot Regiment was not part of 1st Airborne. It was part of the Army Air Corps and was available to whichever airborne division needed it. It was trained to fight on the ground, unlike its American counterparts.

General Browning's 'Operational Instruction No. 1' of 13 September to Urquhart gave him the primary task of capturing one or more of the Arnhem bridges; secondly to establish a 'sufficient bridgehead' for 30th Corps to deploy north of the Lower Rhine. Thirdly he was to make every effort to destroy the flak in the area of the dropping and landing zones and Arnhem to ensure the safe passage of subsequent air lifts.

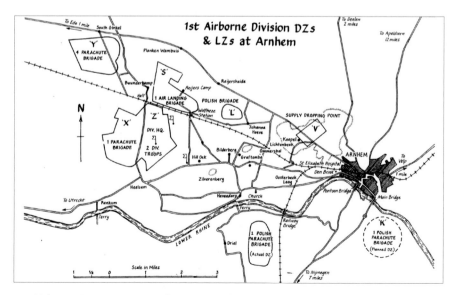

1st Airborne Division DZs and LZs at Arnhem.

The Division's objective was Arnhem's two bridges. The main road bridge was made of concrete and steel and with its elevated approaches was nearly two kilometres long. The double track railway bridge was less important. And there was also a very small chain ferry at Heveadorp.

Urquhart studied the plans for Operation Market allotted to his division and quickly found serious flaws in it:

> The operation was not planned for one major drop on the first day, which would have needed the RAF and USAF to start very early in the morning. His division would drop over three days, giving the Germans ample time to destroy the second and third drops.
>
> No *coup de main* of a brigade dropping *on* the main road bridge and preferably at *both* ends.
>
> All the drops were scheduled to be in the Oosterbeek and Wolfheze area about 6–8 miles away from the vital bridge.
>
> This probably meant severe street fighting, for which his troops were ill prepared, in the clearance of Arnhem, a substantial town, and Oosterbeek, a considerable suburb.
>
> There was distinct lack of information about the enemy and their dispositions.
>
> The radios used by the airborne had a limited range of three miles and they were easily blocked by high buildings.

1st Airborne Paratroops in a C-47 Dakota on their way to Arnhem. (*Imperial War Museum* K-7586)

General Browning brushed aside all these objections, pleading lack of time to alter the complicated schedules. Urquhart as a regular soldier did not have the courage (if not for himself but for his 12,000 men) to take his immense worries higher up the line to General Dempsey, or even to Field Marshal Montgomery.

By meekly accepting these terrible conditions, Operation Market was doomed before it started. Browning, as Monty's airborne 'expert', was completely to blame, and he then added salt to the wound. He reduced 1st Airborne's quota of air transport by 38 Horsa gliders, which he needed for his *folie de grandeur*, ie. taking the Allied Airborne Army HQ to land near Nijmegen at Groesbeek Heights. This lift should have taken most of 1st Air Landing Brigade or the Polish Independent Brigade into battle on D-Day. It was one of the vainglorious episodes of the Second World War. In the event US 101st Airborne Division, once landed, came under General Horrocks' 30th Corps command and, because of the radio problem, Urquhart's command was out of reach, thus Browning would have no effective authority. He and his huge HQ staff should have remained in the UK.

As a result of all these appalling planning errors Monty's 'Forlorn Hope' went to war without a hope in hell.

*   *   *   *

The RAF and USAAF performed bravely and efficiently on D-Day, 17 September, and by 1420hrs 5,191 troops had been landed safely in their 320 gliders, although 36 failed to arrive.

Brigadier Lathbury sent his three parachute regiments off on three parallel routes east towards the Arnhem bridge. Lt Colonel John Frost's 2nd Parachute Regiment (2 Para) on the lower river route was successful in reaching the bridge at dark and by the next morning had over 750 men guarding the north side of the road bridge. Most of the 1st Air Landing Brigade under Brigadier P.W.H. Hicks remained to guard the dropping zones.

Field Marshal Walther Model, commander of Army Group B, was having lunch with his staff in the Hotel Tafelberg in Arnhem when the airborne avalanche descended a few miles away to the west. Model immediately moved to Terborg, thence to the HQ of General Wilhelm Bittrich, commander of 2nd SS Panzer Corps, at Doetinchem. They ordered Obersturmbannführer Walther Harzer, GOC 9th SS Hohenstauffen Panzer Division (what was left of it), to secure the Arnhem road bridge, defeat the airborne landing near Oosterbeek, and send his recce troops south to Nijmegen to find out the situation there. They also ordered Brigadeführer Heinz Harmel, commanding 10th Frundsberg Panzer Division, to secure the Nijmegen bridges as quickly as

British carrier knocked out in Oosterbeek on 17 September.

Walther Harzer's panzers of 9th SS Panzer division enter Arnhem.

possible and form a defensive bridgehead at their south end. By 1440hrs these orders had been transmitted and acknowledged. The 'Führer's Fireman' had quickly and efficiently got his panzers and panzer grenadiers on the move. The SS Training Battalion No. 16, under Captain Sepp Krafft, was on an exercise in the woods near Wolfheze, a mile north-west of Oosterbeek and close to the dropping zone. He shrewdly positioned his companies astride the two main roads into Arnhem and blocked Lathbury's 1st Parachute Brigade, inflicting considerable casualties on 1st and 2nd Battalions. By 1530hrs Krafft had 400 troops deployed in action.

Thanks to the steadfastness of the vast RAF armada zeroing in on the Pathfinder beacon, the Operation Market drop achieved almost complete success. Field Marshal Model and General Bittrich reacted quickly and vigorously and alarm bells rang, figuratively, up to Adolf Hitler and from him to Göring and Himmler. Reinforcements started to pour in to the Arnhem area from the east, north and west.

Kampfgruppen (impromptu battle groups) were formed instantly: Spindler to the west of Arnhem, Moeller in the centre, Krafft in Arnhem, Knaust, Brinkmann, and many others. Kampfgruppe von Allworden's Panzerjaeger and Kampfgruppe Bruhns blocked 1 and 3 Para Battalions who were struggling to get through Oosterbeek and the outskirts of Arnhem; General Kussin, the Stadtkommandant, was killed by 3 Para at 1730hrs. The writing was on the wall. The *schwerpunkt* of 1st Airborne's advance, the near-impossible trek of eight miles, was comprehensively blocked within 12 hours of dropping near Wolfheze.

House clearance and street fighting are a corporal's job – it is nasty and brutal 'mouse-holing' at close quarters. The generals and the colonels lose control almost immediately. Tough, ruthless 'squaddies' with grenades, machine-guns and lots of guts are needed. And in the week to come the airborne troops became not the hunters but the hunted. German SPs prowled the streets. Mortars rained down incessantly and skilled snipers took their toll. Perhaps rashly, General Urquhart tried to move closer into the town with Brigadier Lathbury and they had to take refuge in a house where they were holed up for 40 hours. Lathbury was wounded and paralysed.

There was then a leadership crisis. Urquhart was missing so Brigadier Philip Hicks assumed acting division commander responsibility. Brigadier John Hackett reached Divisional HQ at 2300hrs and made it clear that 'it was a grossly untidy situation', and questioned Hicks' authority and competence to command the Division in Urquhart's absence, since he, Hackett was senior to Hicks! Urquhart had made Lathbury his official second-in-command and he was out of action.

The second lift, on Monday D+1, arrived late because of mist over the airfields in England. By 1500hrs nearly 2,000 airborne troops were delivered. 4th Parachute Brigade was in 126 USAAF transports and the RAF aircraft

Brigadier Lathbury, commander
of the British 1st Parachute
Brigade.

German defenders prepare an ambush for British paratroops. (*Imperial War Museum MH-3956*)

towed 296 gliders with the balance of 1st Air Landing Brigade and 1st Airborne divisional units. Light flak shot down six aircraft and many more were hit; 22 gliders failed to arrive at landing or dropping zones. The main landing and dropping zones were concentrated in the Heelsum-Wolfheze-Ede triangle covering the Renkum and Ginkel heaths. Corporal Thomas Smithson recalled seeing the RAF drop: 'We did everything we could, like waving, but it didn't do any good. One afternoon seven Dakotas came in slow and low. And the Germans had God knows how many 88mm guns and they shot the first five down – bang, bang, bang. Down they came. Missed the sixth one and shot the seventh one down. They were all dropping their stuff but you just couldn't get it. So we had no supplies whatsoever.'

✢   ✢   ✢   ✢

SS Corporal Alfred Ziegler, a dispatch rider with the Von Allworden Kampfgruppe blocking 1 and 3 Para, wrote: 'Do you remember the famous photographs of the dead paratroops by the six-kilometre Arnhem stone? We were told first of all to let the British through and then we opened up from all directions and cut the first lot down. There must have been 30 to 40 prisoners. They were so beaten and submissive that it only needed one man to march them off to the rear … They were completely surprised … They came marching straight down the road in company file … They should have taken a route through the trees because it was a truly macabre mistake. Perhaps they were too arrogant or cocksure ….'

✳   ✳   ✳   ✳

The most important British attack during Operation Market started at 0400hrs on 19 September. It was so disastrous that it was later called Black Tuesday. The purpose, of course, was to break through the German defences in Arnhem and reach and reinforce Lt Colonel John Frost and the indomitable men of 2 Para guarding the north end of the road bridge. But the Kampfgruppe Spindler was the most important German battle group that influenced the eventual defeat of 1st Airborne Division. At 34, Lt Colonel Ludwig Spindler was commander of the 9th SS Hohenstauffen's armoured artillery regiment. He had been decorated with the Iron Cross in the Polish and the Russian campaigns and was awarded the German Gold Cross in Normandy. His battle group was assembled during the afternoon of the airborne landing on 17 September. At one stage no fewer than 16 other units came under his command. On the 19th the Spindler group had its *sperrlinie* (blocking lines) in an L-shape running west–east and north–south. The railway station and its

20mm flak gun is set up on the German barrier defence in Arnhem.

yards on high ground in central Arnhem formed the west–east axis. And SS Kampfgruppe Harder (under Spindler) formed the north–south axis from the railway lines and deep cuttings south through streets to the water's edge of the Lower Rhine. The *sperrlinie* also blocked off any contact with the Frost battle group of 2 Para, which was totally surrounded.

The 1st Parachute Brigade's attack was directed down two parallel roads emerging from a Y junction fork just south of St Elizabeth Hospital. The upper road was Utrechtsweg, which ran past the Arnhem Municipal Museum on the top of a scrub-covered incline. The Onderlangs, two parallel roads running along the northern side of the Rhine, formed the lower road.

The 2nd South Staffs led along the Utrechtsweg followed by 11 Para, and their advance went well for about 600 yards just past the museum, under intense fire from the newly arrived Sturmgeschutz Brigade who were defending the buildings ahead with many mortars and assault guns. The Staffs survivors took up positions in and around the museum. When their PIAT anti-tank bombs ran out the German assault guns just battered and shelled them. Their CO, Lt Colonel McCardie, was captured, together with most of the survivors. But Major Robert Cain took command of a separated group and managed to escape to the west. He was a PIAT specialist and died later in Operation Market in a valiant shoot-out, for which he was awarded a posthumous VC. 11 Para moved up to support the Staffs and their leading company was also overwhelmed. Major General Urquhart, now back in command after 40 hours of 'captivity', ordered the rest of 11 Para back towards Oosterbeek. At Heijenoord Diependal they were caught in the open by heavy mortar fire and virtually destroyed.

SS Captain Hans Moeller's Engineer Kampfgruppe was part of the Spindler defences. He wrote:

> … again and again the enemy tried with great determination to break through our lines. His desperate attacks were repelled time after time with the same resolution that characterised the fighting that raged from house to house – from garden to garden, yes, even from flat to flat, man against man. The engineer group stood firm against all attacks. Around 1000hrs [on the 19th] the paratroopers slackened the momentum. They had suffered great losses in men and material and we had been shown we were up against a very strong and determined opponent. We permitted them the chance to recover their wounded as well as dead and wounded civilians.

Concurrently, 1 Para followed by 3 Para were tasked with reaching Frost's 2 Para on the southern axis along the two parallel Onderlangs. Ahead of them was the ubiquitous Kampfgruppe, and to the south across the river was a huge brickworks mainly occupied by part of Hauptsturmführer Viktor Gräbner's well-equipped SS Panzer Aufklarungs Abteilung 9. He had 30 armoured half-tracks and ten eight-wheeled armoured cars, many of which mounted 75mm guns. Lt Colonel David Dobie's 1 Para over-ran their initial outposts but were soon under intense flanking fire from automatic light cannon from the brickworks across the river, and from the Spindler defenders ahead and to the left. After two hours Dobie called off the attack after losing 100 out of his 140-strong battalion. The 40 wounded survivors took shelter in houses but by 0730hrs were forced to surrender. Lt Colonel John Fitch, CO of 3 Para, tried to support 1 Para but met exactly the same fate from intense fire from three flanks. Fitch was killed by a mortar bomb and the survivors were forced back to the Rhine Pavilion restaurant position where they were over-run and captured.

* * * *

In three hours early on Tuesday morning Major General Urquhart's fine brave division had had 1 Para, 3 Para, part of 11 Para and 2nd South Staffordshires all killed, wounded or taken prisoner. It was a total disaster for the 1st Parachute Brigade.

Model and Bittrich had achieved defensive miracles. Kampfgruppe von Tettau had six battalions from west of Oosterbeek with four more on their way. Bittrich's 2nd SS Corps, mainly 9th SS Hohenstauffen and part of 10th SS Frundsberg, had the equivalent of eight battalions sealing off the airborne salient to the north and the east. On Black Tuesday, the 19th, Model's forces had over 14 battalions surrounding six Allied battalions, as 1st Air Landing Brigade was still defending the drop zones for possible reinforcements. Moreover, a number of Tiger tanks, many Panthers and SP guns, Nebelwerfer 'moaning minny' mortars and some flame-throwers put their iron ring around the doomed Red Devils. Corporal Thomas Smithson recalled:

> Towards the end of the battle their plan was to systematically destroy every house by putting a shell into it. They were moving forward wiping them out one at a time up the road. You can't fight tanks with rifle and bayonet. So you just moved back until there was nowhere to go back. Towards the end there was hardly anything that wasn't burning or smoking or collapsing or falling down. There were so many casualties they were wheeling them in all the time. They'd got nowhere to put them, so they were lying outside and getting wounded again by shellfire. It was always a question of: 'Any news of 30th Corps? No news.' During the night you'd hear the clanking and movement of armour and you'd think, oh, it's 30th Corps, but when it got light – no 30th Corps. It was German armour.

The third lift in late afternoon of the 19th was a disaster. The parachute drop for the Poles was cancelled due to poor weather. Warned by the previous two lifts, German flak batteries were on the alert and brought down 20 planes. Thus only 29 aircraft reached the release point at 1600hrs. Not only was 10 Para on the landing zone and blocking it, but the Luftwaffe Messerschmidt fighter planes tore into the defenceless transports and gliders containing the (non-parachutist) Poles.

Marek Swieciki, a Polish war correspondent, wrote: 'It grew hot and horrible in the air. Several gliders caught fire and rolling over from wing to wing, dived in a mad flight to the ground. Several others landed helplessly with shattered undercarriages. Even from the distance we could see the torn walls and hanging rudders. One of the gliders broke up in the air like a child's toy, and a jeep, an anti-tank gun and people flew out of it.' SS Captain Sepp Krafft and his SS panzer grenadiers could hardly believe their luck: '4 and 9 Company cross the [Arnhem-Ede] road and inflict considerable losses again on the British [gliders].' Generalleutnant Hans von Tettau, who commanded the German force to the west of Wolfheze, noted: 'Approximately 50 [Luftwaffe] fighters attacked Wolfheze, unfortunately our own reconnaissance unit was already there.' Friendly fire, German on German. Also unfortunately, the Poles and the Paras were exchanging gunfire in the heat of the battle.

Urquhart had sent the recently landed 4th Parachute Brigade to occupy the high ground of Arnhem, north of Oosterbeek. They had been guarding the landing zones and then spent the 19th and 20th penned into a large rectangle with Wolfheze to the west and the Spindler blocking line to the east. The newcomers, Kampfgruppe Krafft, were attacking from the north near the pumping station, and von Tettau from the west. It was very confused fighting for 10 Para, 156 Para and 'Lonsdale Force', commanded by Major Dickie Lonsdale, 2i/c of 11 Para, which was composed of the remnants of stragglers from the massacre of 1 and 3 Para in the Onderlangs, and the Staffs and 11 Para from the Utrechtseweg. Lonsdale Force numbered just over 400 men with some anti-tank guns.

*   *   *   *

'Phantom' sent a message on the 20th to 21st Army Group, which was passed on to Browning and Horrocks: 'senior formation still in vicinity north end of main bridge [Frost's 2 Para], but not in touch and unable supply. Arnhem completely in enemy hands. Request all possible steps expedite relief. Fighting intense and opposition extremely strong. Position not too good.'

During the 20th, Brigadier Hackett's 4th Brigade fought a series of bloody little actions through the woods from Wolfheze to Bilderberg, the north-

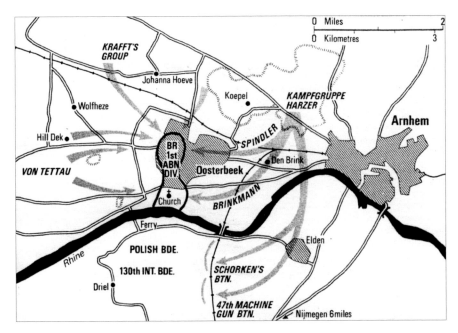

German counter-attacks against British 1st Airborne Division.

west suburb of Oosterbeek. The German battle groups of Bruhns and Krafft captured Wolfheze, and Urquhart's battered divisional survivors were penned into a defensive rectangle. SS Battalion Commander Eberwein's Kampfgruppe captured 100 British at Wolfheze station and later another 578 at Koude Herberg. General von Tettau then misread the battle. He had 4th Parachute Brigade by the throat having captured altogether 800 prisoners, 20 mortars, 18 jeeps, 15 anti-tank guns and 44 motorcycles, but he simply waited and waited for other battle groups to get into position!

Ironically the British radio communications were almost nil. The Germans simply used the excellent Dutch telephone network to communicate.

Field Marshal Model orchestrated the final five days. Coastal Machine-gun Battalions 37 and 41 arrived; ammunition in large quantities was being delivered *direct* to the mortar, artillery and flak units; flame-throwers were brought to the battlefield to scorch strongpoints and buildings; Pioneer-Lehr Battalion 9, an assault-pioneer school trained for street fighting, landed at Deelen airfield. Model visited most of his many kampfgruppe commanders, listened to their requests, and urged them on, and on.

After three or four days of intensive street fighting and house to house clearance the Germans called the small town of Oosterbeek *Der hexenkessel*, the 'witches' cauldron'. The several thousand Dutch inhabitants were crowded into cellars without water, electricity or gas – refugees as the mortar bombs, artillery and tank fire from Bittrich's panzers battered the serene, pretty houses into a shambles of rubble. Burned-out jeeps, civilian vehicles and an

German troops in Arnhem.

occasional German SP gun littered the streets. A few surviving hotels were turned into impromptu field hospitals. Many wounded paratroopers were in cellars, being tended by Dutch civilians. Cornelius Ryan called it 'a ravished landscape pitted by shell craters, scarred by slit trenches, littered with splinters of wood and steel and thick with red brick dust and ashes'. Sergeant Louis Hagen, in his memoir *Arnhem Lift*, recorded:

> The life we had led at Arnhem was nearer an animal existence than anything we could have conceived, and yet the more savage the fighting got, the more civilised the men seemed to become ...There was such gentleness and friendship among them as would have made any of them almost uncomfortable back on station. Although they were fighting like tigers, and in that fight had to be completely ruthless, there was no tough behaviour or coarseness of speech. It was almost uncanny.

SS Captain Hans Moeller, commanding a battle group of 9th SS Hohenstauffen Panzer Division, wrote that there was 'bitter isolated and hand-to-hand fighting as my men fought their way from room to room, from the ground floor up, from garden to garden and from tree to tree. One tank and one armoured halftrack were knocked out by anti-tank fire. Schmatz and the second company had kicked off their attack at the same time to cover the right flank of third company. He attacked the surprised paratroopers from the rear with flame-throwers, which enabled SS Lieutenant Linker to catch his breath and retain and consolidate the new position. The Red Devils still fought back and battled ... like cornered tigers.' One of the cornered tigers was Captain Lionel Queripol commanding 'A' Company of 10 Para, who covered the retreat from Wolfheze early on the 20th, throwing hand grenades and shooting with his pistol. He was awarded a posthumous Victoria Cross for gallantry.

By Thursday 21 September the final thumb-shaped pocket, half a mile wide and a mile and a quarter deep, was crowded with 3,600 airborne and 2,500 Dutch civilians, according to Martin Middelbrook's excellent book *Arnhem 1944: The Airborne Battle*. Brigadier Hicks commanded the western and northern sides and Brigadier Hackett the western side. Urquhart's divisional HQ was in the Hartenstein Hotel. There were about 1,200 infantry survivors augmented by 2,300 gunners, signallers and glider pilots – a fighting hotchpotch.

At long last help arrived from the outside world in the form of the Polish paratroopers who had been dropped, not at Elden as originally planned (which might have helped both 30th Corps and Colonel Frost's 2 Para), but at Driel, almost due south of the 'cauldron'. As both the railway bridge and the Heveadorp were out of action, for different reasons, the Poles were stranded until 30th Corps arrived. The Poles were ferried across in small boats: 250 crossed and 200 reached the Airborne pocket.

The other bit of good news was that 64th Medium Artillery Regiment firing pinpoint salvoes from near Nijmegen smashed up some German attacks. The British FOO had a powerful 19 set and then made radio map reference on 160 different targets. The hell continued on that Saturday, the 23rd. In the week of fighting the defenders had knocked out roughly half of the panzer tanks and SP assault guns with their anti-tank guns and PIATs. LanceSergeant J. D. Baskeyfield knocked out at least three. When his original gun crew of South Staffs was killed, he crawled to another, despite a wounded leg, and manned the gun until he too was killed. For this he was awarded a posthumous VC.

Lonsdale Force was defending the perimeter near Oosterbeek Laag church. In spite of being wounded Major Lonsdale delivered an encouraging speech from the pulpit, whilst his men ate, drank, cleaned their weapons or slept. The Brigade Major RA, Philip Tower, whose gunners' 75mm pack howitzers had done yeoman service, noted:

> It must never be forgotten that on the 1st Air Landing Light Regiment during those last days, fell much of the glory of Arnhem. They were mortared almost continuously, the whole gun area was under observation and swept by machine-gun fire. They were subject to attacks, usually backed with tanks, at least twice a day. Finally their troop positions were over-run and the whole regiment concentrated in 3rd Light Battery's area around Oosterbeek church. They fought as gunners, normal field gunners firing indirectly in support of the whole division, though ammo was very short. They fought as anti-tank gunners over open sights at ranges down to 50 yards, manhandling their 75mm guns ... They fought as infantry in defence from gunpits and command posts – and in attack and counter-attack led by battery commanders and troop commanders alike.

The decision to operate the 'Berlin' evacuation from Oosterbeek was a rather sad and botched affair. On Saturday 23rd Urquhart's two emissaries, Lt Colonel Mackenzie, 1st Airborne Chief of Staff, and the CRE Lt Colonel Edmund Myers made their way across the Lower Rhine in a rubber dinghy to Sosabowski's Polish Brigade HQ. From there Mackenzie radioed a detailed report on the plight of his division to 30th Corps HQ. The intrepid pair reached Nijmegen and talked to Generals Browning and Horrocks, and on their way back they visited Major General Ivo Thomas's 43rd Division HQ. Both men noticed a distinct lack of urgency all round. The generals all thought that Mackenzie and Myers were exaggerating their case. The next day, the 24th, Horrocks, Browning, Thomas and Sosabowski met at Thomas's HQ at Valburg. The day before at 2000hrs, British 2nd Army HQ (Lt General Dempsey, after conferring with the Field Marshal) had authorised Operation Berlin, the evacuation plan, if the *local commanders thought it necessary!* Browning, as usual, ducked out of any responsibility. Urquhart and the fate of the beleaguered 1st Airborne Division were in Browning's hands. If he had had the courage, perhaps he should have accompanied Mackenzie and Myers back to the 'witches' cauldron' and seen for himself how truly desperate the battle situation was.

William Buckingham's book *Arnhem 1944* makes the point: 'It is therefore difficult to avoid the conclusion that Horrocks, Browning and Thomas kept the evacuation decision to themselves for 36 hours while they went through the motions to avoid being blamed for the failure of Market Garden. This suggestion is supported by discrepancies between Horrocks' and Thomas's recollections of events (related in Major Geoffrey Powell's book *The Devil's Birthday: The Bridges to Arnhem*) and the shameful subsequent blame from the Field Marshal on Major General Sosabowski.'

The unceasing bombardment of 1st Airborne Division was claiming more and more casualties, and the overstretched medical units, assisted by Dutch doctors and nurses, worked non-stop to cope with the unending flow of wounded. At 0930hrs on Sunday 24 September, Colonel Graeme Warrack, the Assistant Director Medical Services of the Division, told Major General Urquhart that all the dressing stations were under fire and that he wished to arrange a truce with the Germans for the evacuation of all the wounded. Urquhart agreed but emphasised that Warrack must make it clear to the Germans that the approach was being made purely on humanitarian grounds. The truce was subsequently effected through the senior German medical officer at the Schoonoord Hotel dressing station, which by now was being manned by both German and British medical staff.

The German High Commander, General Bittrich, agreed, and by 1500hrs that afternoon the truce and the evacuation began. An unearthly hush settled over the area as the firing stopped. Convoys of vehicles arrived and the wounded were loaded aboard them. During the next two hours the convoys drove out of Oosterbeek towards Arnhem, carrying more than 250 men, and more than 200 walking wounded were led out of the area to St Elizabeth Hospital in Arnhem.

*   *   *   *

The rest is history. Urquhart's evacuation plan went like clockwork under an immense covering artillery barrage. The fire plan began at 2050hrs and took six hours to complete. In strong wind and rain the survivors played follow-my-leader, holding the shirt tail of the Dennison smock of the man in front. The last positions were abandoned by 0230hrs on the morning of 26 September. The glider pilots were the guides from Oosterbeek church to the river's edge, following a white tape. Some 200 men were left behind but 2,398 were rescued including 160 Poles, 75 Dorsets from 43rd Wessex Division and some shot-down RAF aircrew. On the last day in the 'witches' cauldron' about 258 Airborne and friends were killed in action, the second highest total in the entire battle. About 450 Dutch civilians were killed and many more wounded, and severe German 'punishments' followed. Altogether 1st Airborne Division had 1,485 killed in action and 6,500 taken prisoner, a third of them wounded.

Major General Roy Urquhart apparently did little of note during Operation Berlin; he was taken by jeep to Browning's Advanced Airborne HQ in Nijmegen. Perhaps Browning should have had the courtesy to welcome the survivors as they stepped ashore on the southern banks of the Lower Rhine. He was considered to be the 'Father of the Airborne Movement' and as such was praised in Lt Colonel John Frost's autobiography *A Drop too Many*. However, at the end of the book (p. 246) the 'Corps Commander' (General Browning) was tersely, but strongly, criticised.

Detail from picture on p. 68. (*Imperial War Museum B-15001*)

CHAPTER 13

Frost's War

John Frost was a real warrior. Just before the start of the Second World War he had been seconded from his regiment, the Cameronians, to the Iraq levies, a force of Assyrian, Kurdish and Arab tribesmen. Their main base was the RAF station and airfields at Habbaniya on the river Euphrates, 80 miles north-west of Baghdad. Frost's biggest problem was varying the diet of bully beef and biscuit. He chased and shot gazelle and bustard and hunted jackal with imported hounds; he played polo and flew Audax and Moth planes. The hunt committee presented him with a copper hunting horn with which he rallied his troops after he joined the Parachute Regiment. As a company commander, in February 1941 he jumped from a Whitley bomber with his stick of 2 Para on to Bruneval, north of Le Havre. They briefly captured a secret radar station, dismantled the essential parts and photographed the immovable parts. All went well despite German resistance, and Winston Churchill was very pleased.

The unpleasant Tunisian campaign followed in December 1942 with difficult jumps and actions around Depienne Oudna, Sidi Hadjeba and Happy Valley near Bou Arada. Frost commanded 2 Para, which was cut to pieces in abortive operations by 10th Panzer Division and the Luftwaffe. One legacy of Tunisia was the adoption by 2 Para of the Arab cry of *Waho Mahommed* – a happy, noisy greeting and custom!

During the extended battles around Tamera in March 1943, Frost's men and all of 1st Airborne Brigade were first called the 'Red Devils' (translated) by the Germans.

Frost's two battlefield worries were ammunition supplies, as flying and dropping mean limited ammo supplies; and caring for the wounded, as the nearest RAP or hospital could be a huge distance away. He also developed a system whereby weapons – not only pistols and Sten guns, but also the heavier and unwieldy Bren guns and rifles – were *attached to the parachutists' legs* as they dropped from their plane.

In Sicily in July 1943 Operation Fustian, the Airborne capture of the vital Primosole bridge over the river Simeto south of Catania, took place.

When the 1st Airborne Brigade returned to the UK and prepared and trained for Operation Overlord, Lt Colonel Frost noted his training essentials for his airborne troops. Skill at arms came first: the ability to shoot a variety of weapons and shoot well, without using too much ammunition. Secondly,

Lt Colonel Frost.

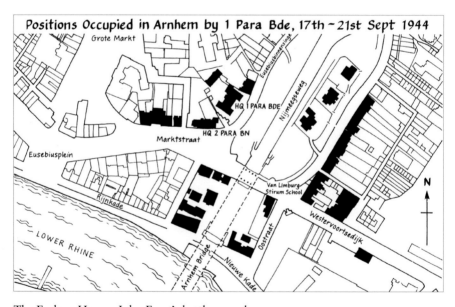

The Forlorn Hope – John Frost's battleground.

Arnhem Bridge on the first day of Operation Market. The Recce Squadron of 9th SS Panzer Division had been almost completely destroyed whilst trying to cross from the south.

'immaculate communications': wireless links had to work whenever they were required. And thirdly, physical fitness: PT for *everyone* before breakfast each day. The required marching standard was 30 miles a day carrying 'half a hundredweight' (approximately 60 pounds)!

Frost and his men, after fighting the Germans over a period of about two years, 'had acquired a wholesome respect for German soldiery: mutual sufferings and memories of being close to them on rain-soaked tops of lonely hills persisted ... stretcher bearers of both nations could move the wounded unharmed ....'

When, on 15 September, Brigadier Gerald Lathbury briefed his key officers of 1st Parachute Brigade about Operation Market, they were all delighted that at long last they were being 'given a really worthwhile task'. But Frost immediately found the 'glaring snags. The dropping zones selected by the Air Forces were several miles from the objectives and on the north side of the great main river *only*. This entailed a long approach on foot, through enclosed country and built up areas, surprise would be lost and the enemy would have plenty of time and opportunity to destroy the bridges [road and railway]. Just as bad the bridge or bridges should be seized on *both* sides if you hope to capture it without heavy casualties.' Frost realised that enemy AA guns and the airfield at Deelen could be the reasons for the 'unreasonable attitude' of the Air Forces concerned. He was in no doubt at all that the AA guns could and should be destroyed or neutralised. It would be better for the airborne troops directly to access and drop near their objectives rather than have a long, arduous and doubtful approach on foot – but this had to be accepted. The Air Force planners assumed that the farmland south of the river was unusable for gliders and not suitable for paratroops. But the original plan showed the Polish Brigade dropping near Elden, south of the bridge. Frost wrote all this in his memoirs, *A Drop too Many,* and then made the telling point that the Air Forces could have made two sorties on D-Day: 'with good staff work aircraft would not have needed more than five hours from take-off to landing, if the first sortie left at dawn'.

All these valid reservations were made known to Major General Urquhart, the new divisional commander, but they were blocked. Frost's 2 Para was tasked with seizing the railway and the main bridge over the Rhine on the most southerly route near the river. Major Digby Tatham-Warter, OC 'A' Company, led with instructions on arrival to put one platoon across and south of the bridge. Frost and 2 Para HQ would follow. Major Victor Dover, OC 'C' Company, was next tasked with the capture of the railway bridge near Oosterbeek, to pass across it and then move to reach the south end of the main bridge. Major Douglas Cranley, OC 'B' Company, was Frost's reserve 'for any eventuality'. It was a very good plan in the circumstances. The landing on D-Day was almost perfect and at 1500hrs Tatham-Warter marched briskly towards the bridge, leaving a trail of German dead, wounded and prisoners. 'Digby was a thruster', Frost wrote later. His group followed and passed through the village of Heveadorp where the Dutch gave the paratroops a great welcome: apples, pears, jugs of milk and orange flowers (the Dutch national colour). Nobody checked to see if the little, but useful, ferry was available. They went through Oosterbeek and Major Dover took 'C' Company down to the river to capture the railway bridge over the Lek. Frost watched his men surge onto the bridge, which was then blown up with a mighty explosion, leaving the southern span lying in the water. Although 'A' Company was held up by an enemy post at Den Brink, the 'thruster' led his men through the gardens of the houses, bypassing the post. The pontoon bridge was reached, but the Germans had dismantled the centre portion and rendered it useless. Two of Frost's companies reached the main bridge soon after dark and by the morning of the 18th the bridgehead garrison numbered 750, including Brigade HQ, some engineers, RASC and a lorry-load of ammunition from the dropping zone. Major Freddie Gough, OC the Recce Squadron, arrived with some jeeps, as did Major Dennis Munford, OC the Light Regiment (RA), with his signallers.

Captain Eric Mackay's sappers from 1st Parachute Squadron proved to be invaluable, strengthening the defences in the 18 buildings clustered around the north end of the bridge. Soon Frost discovered from captured prisoners

The great road bridge in Arnhem over the Lower Rhine, the paramount objective
of Market Garden. Frost's paratroops guarded the north bank (left) and destroyed
many German armoured vehicles burnt out on the bridge (right).

that several of them came from 9th SS Panzer Division. As he said: 'We
had been given absolutely no inkling of this possibility. The odds against
an outcome in our favour were heavy indeed.' Quite quickly Frost's battle
group was assailed from three directions, north, east and south, by two
kampfgruppen, Knaust and Brinkmann. SS grenadiers dug in on the south
bank, engaging Frost's outposts from across the river, and soon a battery
of Nebelwerfers ('moaning minnie' mortars) and artillery stonks ensued.
Squads of SS troopers would slip into buildings and throw demolition
charges in to drive the British out. SS Section Commander, Alfred Ringsdorf
summed up the cruel and bitter fighting: 'This was a harder battle than any
I had fought in Russia. It was constant, close range, hand-to-hand fighting.
The English were everywhere. The streets were narrow, not more than five
metres wide and we fired at each other from only yards away. We fought to
gain millimetres, cleaning out one room after the other. It was absolute hell.'
One attack from SS troopers hidden inside an ambulance, who tumbled out
wildly firing their Schmeisser machine-guns from the hip, was smashed up
outside Frost's HQ. Two six-pdr British anti-tank guns were sited to fire
across the bridge and under the bridge ramps. Private James Sims, in his book
Arnhem Spearhead, quotes a young mortar crewman who observed the light

Ruins of battle HQ of British 1st Parachute Brigade. This building was in a key position near the bridge; its destruction by the Germans precipitated the loss of the north end.

tanks, armoured cars and half-tracks of Brinkmann's recce battalion making a determined attack: 'Black smoke belched from the leading tank, now well ablaze, but it still brought a stream of well-aimed machine-gun fire from the turret guns. The gunner went on firing until the flames got him. He died with screams of agony.'

SS Captain Graebner's strong armoured force was returning from Nijmegen and attempted to force its way through Frost's anti-tank screen. Five Puma eight-wheeled armoured cars, nine half-tracks and eight fortified truck transports rushed the bridge on 18 September at 0930hrs. A furious battle ensued; altogether Graebner lost 12 of his 22 armoured vehicles. The battle raged for two hours as the paratroopers used PIATs, machine-guns, 3-inch mortars and anti-tank guns, but the five Pumas that sped across to safety caused much havoc in the next few days.

The terrible war of attrition continued and by the 19th Frost's citadel had dwindled from the original 18 hours to ten. From the north heavy artillery was brought to bear on the facades of houses and on strong points, reducing them to rubble. Infantry closed in from the west and tank guns and panzer grenadiers from the east. A pair of huge Tiger tanks nosed their way through the wreckage of Graebner's failed attack on the bridge, as described by Frost: 'They looked incredibly sinister in the half light, like some prehistoric monsters, as their great guns swung from side to side breathing flame.' SS Grenadier Private Horst Weber recalled: 'starting from the roof tops, buildings collapsed like dolls' houses. I did not see how anyone could live through this inferno. I felt truly sorry for the British.' The cellars were filled with the wounded. The houses above them were ablaze. The anti-tank ammunition was almost spent and by Tuesday night, the 19th, the garrison was reduced to 400 men fit to fight.

On Wednesday morning, 20 September, Frost's signallers got through to Major General Urquhart by using the Arnhem telephone exchange, and Frost was told that the rest of the Division could not help him. The Polish Brigade had been redirected from the drop originally planned for them near Elden, south of the bridge, which would have greatly helped Frost's defenders, to Driel, which would help Urquhart's survivors in the Oosterbeek pocket.

Digby Tatham-Warter, carrying his comic umbrella, was wounded, as was Father Egan the chaplain. Frost wrote: 'We prepared for yet another night; Arnhem was burning. Two great churches were flaming fiercely … it was like daylight in the streets.' Shortly afterwards Frost was wounded in both of his feet and the RMO, Jimmy Logan, gave him morphia. He and Major Douglas Crawley, OC 'B' Company, were carried out on stretchers from the blazing HQ and were taken prisoner. Lieutenant John Grayburn, a platoon commander, though wounded several times, fought to the last on 20 September until he was killed. He was later awarded a posthumous VC. By dawn only 150 men were left, all the rest had been killed, wounded or taken prisoner. Frost later wrote:

> The SS men were very polite and complimentary about the battle we had fought, but the bitterness I felt was unassuaged. No living enemy had beaten us. The battalion was unbeaten yet, but they could not have much chance with no ammunition, no rest and with no position from which to fight. No body of men could have fought more courageously and tenaciously than the officers and men of the 1st Parachute Brigade at Arnhem bridge.

Frost's war was over.

CHAPTER 14

Taylor's 101st US Airborne Division: The Screaming Eagles

By Christmas 1944 the US 101st 'Screaming Eagles' Division had become the most famous unit in the American Army due to their heroic defence of the key town of Bastogne. But their arrival in Normandy on D-Day, 6 June, was distinctly unhappy, almost disastrous. Tasked with drops, mainly during the night, to protect the perimeters of the Utah Beach assault, the 805 American planes carrying 6,600 parachutists were rudely disturbed by German flak guns. The wild, inexperienced glider pilots took violent evasive action. By dawn on the 6th, Major General Maxwell Taylor had only 1,100 combat-worthy men at the divisional HQ; the rest were scattered over a huge area 25 miles by 15. Many drowned in the swamps and floods of the Cotentin. Twenty-four hours later Taylor still only had fewer than 3,000 men. Nevertheless, in the next ten weeks the Screaming Eagles gave a good account of themselves.

There followed a three-week period when a dozen or more drops were planned for the Allied Airborne. When Taylor and his staff were given their dropping plans and schedules in Operation Market, they were most unhappy; by guile and persuasion (something Major General Urquhart should have done) they convinced Lt General Brereton and the airborne planners that 101st should have one large and two small drops just north of Eindhoven. Taylor's task was very difficult. His division had to drop and then seize *seven* separate bridges and a further four within Eindhoven if possible. From south to north these were the road and rail bridges over the Wilhelmina canal near Son and Best, about seven miles north of Eindhoven; the road bridge over the river Dommel at St Oedenrode; and the road and rail bridges over the Willems canal and river Aa near and in Veghel. Three separate landing areas had been chosen; two of them in a triangle between St Oedenrode, Son and Best were parachute jumps. A glider landing lay neatly between two of the parachute zones. It was a complicated plan for the 506th, 502nd and 501st Parachute Infantry Regiments (PIR). From airfields around Basingstoke and Reading 585 C-47 Dakotas flew the 'southern' route, led by General Taylor in person. Between 1300 and 1330hrs on the 17th, 6,769 men were dropped with minimum casualties and loss of equipment. The glider landings an hour later were less successful but landed 252 men, 32 jeeps and Walter Cronkite, the American journalist. However, the signal units never arrived, so Maxwell Taylor was out of touch with Browning's HQ at Nijmegen, although 101st on

Major General Maxwell D.
Taylor.

the ground reported to General Horrocks' 30th Corps. Taylor entrusted his
502nd PIR with objectives in Best and St Oedenrode; the 506th with Son and
Eindhoven; and the 501st around Veghel. He had the largest area to seize and
the least time to do it, so his first lift consisted largely of infantry and jeeps,
with supporting elements to follow in the second and third lifts.

Within 45 minutes of landing General Taylor personally led the 1st
Battalion 506th PIR through the Zonsche Forest towards the bridge over the
Wilhelmina canal at Son. 88mm flak guns soon caused casualties and, despite
a valiant bayonet charge by the paratroops, the bridge was blown. One way or
another 506th PIR got across the Wilhelmina canal and set up a bridgehead.
Veghel, with its four crossings, the rail and highway bridges over the river
Aa, and the Willems canal, were captured within two hours. In the south, St
Oedenrode and the Dommel river highway bridge were also taken. Colonel
Robert Sink's other two battalions found Eindhoven and its bridges lightly
defended on the 18th, and General Taylor managed to radio 30th Corps to
warn them of the destruction of the Son bridge and that bridging material was
urgently required. The Guards Armoured arrived about 20 hours late. It took
them the whole day on the 18th to cover the six miles from Valkenswaard into
Eindhoven. By the time a Class 40 Bailey Bridge was erected at Son, Operation
Garden was 30 hours late.

The second lift arrived just in time with 428 gliders carrying 2,579 men,
146 jeeps and 109 trailers. The main task for the Screaming Eagles was to
keep open the 15-mile-long stretch of road north of Eindhoven, north-east of
Grave, which soon became known as 'Hell's Highway'. General Kurt Student

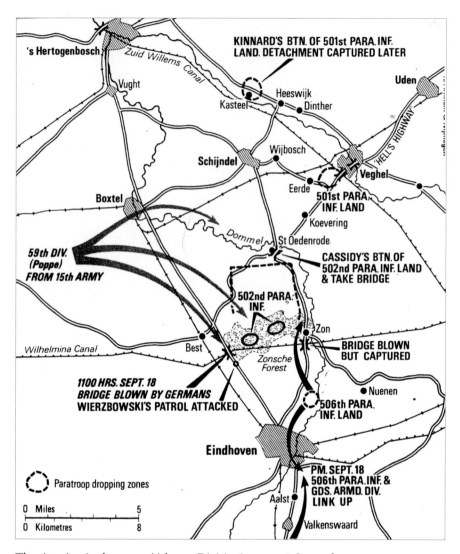

The situation in the 101st Airborne Division's area, 18 September 1944.

sent kampfgruppe after kampfgruppe to attack the lightly armed parachutists from the west flank and from the east flank. Indeed the Germans recaptured Best and the bridges over the Wilhelmina canal late on the 18th. Taylor desperately needed armoured support as the Guards, eventually, came through Eindhoven and up to Grave on their way to Nijmegen.

The journalist Alan Moorehead arrived in Eindhoven shortly after the Guards Armoured. He wrote:

> Suburbia, rich, lush suburbia, opened up before the British tanks. Fine allotments, garden villas with council's light, heat and water. Central heating. Sewerage. A

General Taylor's Screaming Eagles US 101st Airborne Division: wrecked glider with its crew near Eindhoven.

district noted for its civic pride, its attractive shopping centres, its charming gardens. We were in Holland. The war flowed between neat privet hedges and mown lawns. The Dutch, plump and homely and jolly flowed out into the streets and danced ring-a-ring a-roses. Everyone wore something orange: orange aprons and ribbons for the little boys and girls, orange paper caps for the grown-up boys and girls. They smiled and smiled. And from every shop window a fine big lithographed portrait of Princess Juliana smiled back at them.

As the armoured column rolled on towards the first great bridge across the Maas at Grave, all Eindhoven gave itself up to holiday. The streets were one long blaze of orange. All the Phillips [Electrical] workers were out with their wives and children. They blew tin whistles and banged toy drums. They made noises with rattles, joined hands and danced in circles… sang part-songs and national hymns. They shook hands with all the soldiers. Liberation had come to Holland – parts of it!

So Horrocks sent 44th Royal Tank Regiment and the 15/19th Hussars, both excellent formations, to help the Screaming Eagles keep the vital highway open. General Maxwell Taylor described it as like 'the situation in the early American West where small garrisons had to fend off Indian attacks along great stretches of road'.

Eindhoven, Holland, 19 September 1944. A Challenger tank of 2nd Troop, 'A' Squadron 15/19th Hussars, who linked up with the American 101st Airborne Division.

In *A Full Life* General Horrocks wrote:

...a German armoured formation had succeeded in cutting our road to the rear. So in addition to making no progress in front, we were now cut off as well. This was no fault of the 101st US Airborne Division, who had been fighting a series of difficult battles to keep our lines of communication open. But it was no easy matter to defend some 25 miles of road with a resolute enemy pressing in on both sides. In fact, many stretches of the road were constantly under shell fire, and at times the banks on either side became the actual front lines facing outwards. As might be expected, this slowed up the traffic moving along the road considerably. Indeed for 25 fateful hours the road was closed to all traffic.

There is no doubt at all that the Screaming Eagles, who suffered 2,118 casualties in Operation Garden, and 3,792 casualties by the time they were withdrawn from the front line at the end of November, played a major role in making Monty's greatest gamble almost viable. Taylor led from the front, and was the only general wounded during Market Garden.

CHAPTER 15

Gavin's 82nd US Airborne Division: The All American

The 'All American' 82nd US Airborne Division was a veteran unit after the Sicily and Anzio campaigns. In the Cotentin peninsula in June 1944 they had initially lost many men in the boggy terrain but recovered well with successes at St Mère Eglise and the capture of Mont Castre. Brigadier Gavin had taken over as GOC when Matthew Ridgeway was promoted to Major General and commander of the three-division US 18th Airborne Corps.

General James Gavin, aged 37, was the youngest general in the US Army. His athletic build and charm earned him the affectionate nickname of 'Slim Jim'. He was immensely popular with his division – they thought him to be bold, fair, 'smart as hell', and a trusted, beloved leader. When he landed near Nijmegen he damaged his back, and, in obvious pain, slung his M-1 carbine over his shoulder and moved off to his command post.

Gavin rather tamely accepted the plan for 82nd Airborne in Operation Market. The Division was assigned the central section of the corridor in a large 25-mile circular area south-west-south-east of Nijmegen. The river Maas crossings were allotted to 504th PIR under Colonel Reuben Tucker, with two dropping zones on the west and north-east of Grave. The airforce planners, for various unsatisfactory reasons, chose 508th PIR under Colonel Roy Lindquist to drop just north-east of Groesbeek, and 505th PIR under Colonel William Ekman to drop between Groesbeek and Mook to the south-west.

There were immediately two important mistakes. Lt General 'Boy' Browning decided arbitrarily to join the fight, and his 38-glider team of rather useless staff dropped on the Groesbeek Heights, a heavily wooded ridge 300 feet above polder level, eight miles long, south-east of Nijmegen. Browning's fears about 'here be dragons' or scores of panzer tanks lurking in the Reichswald Forest, south-east of Mook, and the need to control his airborne divisions, meant problems for Gavin and for the success of Market Garden. Since, on landing, 101st US Airborne reverted to General Horrocks' 30th Corps, and 1st Airborne in Oosterbeek and Arnhem were not in radio communication, Browning was reduced to 'helping' Gavin.

The second important mistake, which none of the generals (Montgomery, Dempsey, Brereton and Horrocks) spotted, was that not only were the key Nijmegen road and rail bridges several miles away from the various dropping zones, but also that there was absolutely no plan or time schedule for their

Major General James M. Gavin.

capture. Gavin, still a brigadier, was too overawed by the top brass during the briefing session and kept quiet. The two 'popular' reasons given were the need to protect the LVs for future drops after the Grave and Hernen bridges were captured, and the 'dragons' lurking in the Reichswald! The strictures by Montgomery, Brereton and Horrocks to capture the bridges with violence and great speed were simply ignored.

When Field Marshal Model realised that a substantial Allied airborne operation was under way to capture Arnhem and its vital bridges, he knew that his key objective was to retain control of the main road bridge, south, in Nijmegen. One way or another, despite Colonel Frost's brilliant *coup de main* at the Arnhem bridge, Model rushed reinforcements into Nijmegen.

On 17 September the Kampfgruppe Henke established a line of defensive posts based on the two traffic circles south of the road and rail bridges. Kampfgruppe Reinhold arrived the following day and a triangular defence was swiftly organised: Reinhold in the village of Lent just north of both bridges; Kampfgruppe Euling 10th SS around Hunner Park and the Valkhof, just south-east of the road bridge; and Henke 10th SS defending the rail bridge.

In and around the German Reichswald there were no 'dragons'. General Kurt Feldt, CO of 406th Wehrmacht Infantry Division, a low-grade training and replacement division, had responsibility for the region east and south-east of Nijmegen.

The All Americans' landings on D-Day went like clockwork: 482 gliders landed 7,467 troops safely in the three landing zones, and 504th PIR captured the Grave and Moelenhoek bridges within a few hours. The two canal bridges to the north at Malden and Hatert were destroyed by the Germans. To his

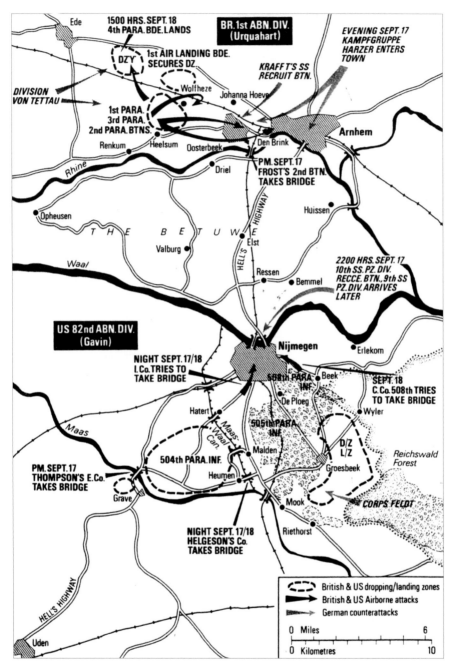

British and US dropping zones and airborne attacks, and German counter-attacks, 17–18 September 1944.

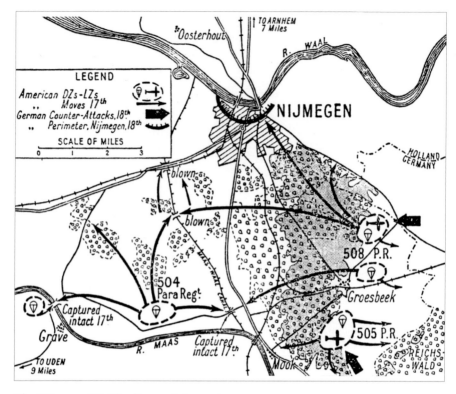

The Nijmegen 'Air-Head', 17–18 September 1944.

credit, in the late afternoon, Gavin sent probing patrols at company level towards the Nijmegen bridges, but they were sharply stopped by 10th SS troops.

Early in the morning on D+1, the 18th, General Feldt sent four small kampfgruppen (Stargaard, Fuerstenberg, Greschick and Goebel) to attack 505th and 508th PIR on the Groesbeek Heights. They had no 'dragons', only a motley force of 2,300 men, and the attacks fizzled out. In mid-afternoon Gavin's second drop of 450 gliders and tugs landed with the 82nd Airborne's artillery, anti-tank guns, engineer signals and medical units. This was followed by 135 B-24s laden with supplies. On Browning's orders the 82nd spent the day consolidating the gains made, with no further probes, let alone attacks on the vital bridge.

General Horrocks wrote in *A Full Life*:

By 10 am on 19 September the Grenadier Guards Group (1st Motor Battalion and 2nd Tank Battalion), now in the lead, made contact with the second strip of our aerial carpet – the 82nd US Airborne Division, who, to our great joy, had captured intact the road bridge over the Meuse at Grave. Had the Germans succeeded in destroying this bridge our advance might

Major General 'Slim' Jim Gavin's All American 82nd Airborne dropping around Nijmegen. (*Imperial War Museum EA-39925*)

easily have been delayed for several days, for the broad river would have proved a formidable obstacle.

In addition to this success the 82nd, having captured another important bridge over the Maas-Waal canal at Heumen, were holding the high ground about Berg en Dal to the east of the main road, and had penetrated to within 400 yards of the road bridge over the Waal in Nijmegen itself. At this point they had encountered stubborn resistance from the 10th SS German Division.

The town of Nijmegen is completely dominated by these two immense bridges over the river Waal, by the road bridge on the east and by the railway bridge on the west. To capture one of these, or if possible, both, was vital to our plan, and the fighting which now developed in Nijmegen was bitter in the extreme. Indeed there was a desperate urgency about this battle which I rarely experienced before or after.

Horrocks was, of course, writing after the event. He was, however, right about Colonel Tucker's river battle that followed.

Model sent more troops south to reinforce the Nijmegen garrison: Kampfgruppen Becker and Hermann from his parachute troops, and more Frundsberg 10th SS via the Pannerden ferry. No panzers yet, but four lethal

Captured German kampfgruppen troops. (*Imperial War Museum B-10170*)

Jagdpanzer IV tank destroyers arrived on the scene. Gavin too was reinforced on D+2 by a drop that was severely diminished by the bad weather. 221 out of 385 gliders reached their landing zones, but Gavin's glider infantry regiment in 258 gliders failed to take off. At long last Browning ordered Gavin to take the main road bridge, the longest in Europe, either that day or the next, D+3. The first major attack against massed and ferocious defence failed, as General Horrocks related:

> The Grenadier Guards Group and a battalion of the 505th US Parachute Regiment combined in an immediate attack on the road bridge, which to our astonishment, was still intact; but in spite of the utmost bravery little progress was made. The Germans had fortified the open squares and had constructed a tight perimeter of defences around the southern end of both the vital bridges. Hunner Park, which dominated the southern edge of the road bridge, was particularly strongly held.
>
> They also set fire to every fifth building until some 500 houses were blazing fiercely. Into this hell plunged tanks, Guards and US paratroopers, but all to no avail. By midnight it was obvious that the bridges could not be captured by direct assault.
>
> During the afternoon I met General Browning, who had landed with the airborne corps which he was commanding. From then on we co-operated

closely and took all the major decisions together. We now decided to outflank the bridges from the west by carrying out an assault crossing over the broad river Waal near the power station, some 800 yards downstream from the railway bridge. This was a most hazardous operation but here lay the only chance of capturing the bridges intact. It is to the credit of General Jim Gavin, the commander of the 82nd US Airborne Division, that this appallingly difficult task was accepted without the slightest hesitation.

At first light on 20th September, the 504th US Parachute Regiment and the 2nd Battalion Irish Guards (Tanks) started clearing the western suburbs of the town and by midday they arrived on the river bank. Now took place what many of us consider to have been one of the finest attacks ever carried out during the last war.

It was a sunny afternoon with clear visibility, and the Germans were holding the far bank of the swiftly running river which at this point was quite 400 yards wide. Yet at 3 pm the leading US paratroopers entered the river in British assault boats which they had never seen till that moment. Supported though they were by fire from the tanks of the Irish Guards, and approximately 100 guns, they nevertheless suffered heavily and only half the leading wave, some in boats, some swimming, succeeded in reaching the far bank. Yet this mere handful of men charged up the steep embankment and secured a small bridgehead a couple of hundred yards deep. Gradually more and more troops were ferried across until by evening they had penetrated a mile inland to the village of Lent, where the railway crosses the main road. They had thus cut off both bridges from the rear, a truly amazing achievement.

Engineers remove the charges from Nijmegen bridge.

Gavin's paratroops in Nijmegen.

Guards Armoured Cromwell tanks cross Nijmegen Bridge. (*Imperial War Museum B-10172*)

The brave attack was made by Colonel Reuben Tucker's 3rd Battalion of 504th PIR, commanded by Major Julian Cook. They had a fast-flowing, 400-yard wide river to cross in 26 boats, each 19 feet long with flat reinforced plywood bottoms. There were eight four-foot paddles for each boat, which carried a total of ten men. Cornelius Ryan, in his book *A Bridge Too Far*, gives an intensely vivid description of the full horrors of the river attack, which caused 134 casualties. By 1700hrs the gallant All Americans had captured the rail bridge and by 1915hrs had joined up with the few Grenadier Guards' Shermans that had crossed the great multi-spanned Nijmegen road bridge.

Colonel Tucker was incandescent with rage about the Grenadier and Irish battle groups who had been ordered to halt for the night instead of pushing on over the final 11 miles to Arnhem. There were extenuating circumstances: heavy casualties; house clearing still proceeding in Nijmegen town; the Coldstream group on the right flank guarding the American perimeter to the east were not available; the lack of ammunition, and so on. But still ... The Wessex Wyvern 130th Infantry Brigade had arrived south of Grave and halted there for the night ....

*   *   *   *

When the Guards' Irish group set off at 1230hrs on D+4, 21 September, from Lent towards Elst and Arnhem, 19 hours had elapsed since the capture of the main road bridge. Model would have taken violent action. Horrocks, Browning and Adair sanctioned the delay.

The battles continued less severely on the Island and in the Reichswald-Groesbeek sector south of the Rhine – a long, dreary catalogue of rain and squalor, water-logged trenches, constant mortaring, perpetual exhaustion and often, hard fighting.

Gavin's All American Division stayed in the line around Nijmegen until 11 November when it reassembled near Paris. In the nine days of fighting during Market Garden the Division had 215 killed in action, 790 wounded and 427 missing. They had been magnificent.

CHAPTER 16

Guards Armoured:
'Ever open eye'

The Brigade of Guards has been the heartbeat of the British Army since its first regiment was founded in 1661. Its emblazoned Battle Honours feature the Defence of Tangier, War of Austrian Succession, Seven Years War, French Revolutionary Wars, Indian Mutiny, Crimean War, Second China War and another dozen, including Third Afghan War, leading up to The Great War. A magnificent record in defence of King (or Queen) and country.

In 1941 General Sir Alan Brooke, then Commander-in-Chief Home Forces, decided that the defence of the realm against a possible German invasion urgently needed two infantry divisions to be converted to armour. So approval was given by the War Office, the Major General commanding the Brigade of Guards, and King George VI for the formation of the Guards Armoured Division. The famous Eye insignia, used by the Guards Division in the 1914–18 War, was enhanced by Rex Whistler, the distinguished artist, then a lieutenant in the Welsh Guards.

Major General Sir Oliver Leese was the first commanding officer of the 5th Guards Armoured Brigade, the 6th Guards Armoured Brigade and the Guards Support Group. On 30 May 1942 the 32nd Guards Brigade, with three infantry battalions, replaced the 6th Guards Armoured Brigade, who became independent.

All over the UK military exercises were honing every unit into a more menacing proposition. So Operations Cheddar, Lilo, Pegasus, Sarum, Ebor, Redlynch, Sun Chariot, Spartan and Eagle followed as the new formation became part of 8th Corps. The choice of tanks started from a rather plebeian level – rejects from the Royal Tank Regiment – but progressed through Crusaders and Centaurs to Shermans (and Cromwells for the Recce Regiment). Spit and polish was of course still vital for inspections by the King, Winston Churchill, American CCCS General Marshall and Generals Bernard Montgomery, Alan Brooke and Eisenhower.

For Operation Overlord in June 1944 Montgomery chose his desert favourite, the Desert Rats (7th Armoured) to be first ashore. 11th Armoured Division came next, followed by the Guards, under Major General Allan Adair, by the end of June, thus missing Operation Epsom but in time for Operation Goodwood. The Guards were confronted by 1st SS Panzer Division at Le Poirier and 12th SS at Frénouville. The village of Cagny was a thorn in the flesh, where some Tiger tanks and 88mm anti-tank guns had survived the horrendous bombing barrage and caused much trouble.

8 Corps suffered 1,020 casualties during Goodwood on 18 and 19 June, 11th Armoured had 735, Guards 170, and 7th Armoured 115. The huge loss of Sherman tanks was quickly made up, but the loss of brave young 'tankies' was not so easy to replace.

Operation Spring with the Canadians came next, followed by Operation Bluecoat, where some serious fighting took place in the Caumont offensive in thick *bocage* country against 21st Panzer Division, 3rd Parachute Division, 9th SS Panzer Division, and finally 10th SS Panzer Division. Field Marshal von Kluge had sent his best formations to block off Bluecoat and almost succeeded.

The Guards Armoured Division went into Army Reserve for ten days, and then came under command of Lt General Brian Horrocks, 30th Corps. His order was: 'The 11th Armoured Division directed on Amiens, 8th Armoured Brigade on Beauvais. You will come on as quickly as you can, moving by night if necessary and pass through the 8th Armoured Brigade to seize the crossings over the [river] Somme at Corbie.'

General Adair wrote in the history of the Division, which was out of the line around Condé sur Noireau: 'We were fairly concentrated so that everybody could visit their friends and partake together of any of the amusements provided of which there were quite a few ... for the first time we had the opportunity of meeting French people in normal surroundings. They too were mostly meeting British soldiers for the first time and on the whole both parties were pleased with the encounter ... While we were experiencing this carefree, pastoral existence the Seventh Army was meeting its doom in the "Falaise" pocket.' The Secretary of State (Grigg) and General Montgomery visited on 16 August and four days later Montgomery dispensed medals at an investiture.

The Guards Armoured was the last division into Normandy and, in effect, was the first out of the actual fighting. It is curious that Brian Horrocks did not give Adair a direct order. He meant, 'when you feel like it, come along and join in the fun [you are going to have in Brussels]'. At the end of August Horrocks was seriously ill.

On the journey north Adair did give great credit to the French Forces of the Interior (FFI). For the first time Adair had realised that 'under European conditions, tanks and infantry needed to work in close co-operation down to the lowest level if the best results were to be achieved'. For the record, 11th Armoured had spent two years practising armour/infantry joint co-operation in attack and defence. The new groups were Grenadier, Coldstream, Welsh and Irish, and remained thus until the end of the war.

From 3 September 5th Guards Brigade mustered 1st (Motor) Battalion Grenadier Guards with armoured cars, and 2nd Grenadiers, 1st Coldstream and 2nd Irish Guards with Sherman tanks. 32nd Guards Brigade consisted of

A happy Guards sergeant gives a regal wave to the Brussels crowd. (*Imperial War Museum BU-480*)

Jubilation in Brussels. (*Imperial War Museum BU-505*)

Lt Colonel J. O. E. Vandeleur's 3rd Irish Guards captured this vital bridge at De Grote Bareel – hence 'Joe's Bridge'. (*Imperial War Museum B-9981*)

5th Coldstream, 3rd Irish and 1st Welsh. They were backed by four artillery units: 55th and 153rd Field, 21st Anti-tank and 94th Light Ack-Ack. Despite the enforced stop on 2 September west of Douai for an airborne drop, which was aborted, the Division in effect had a 'point-to-point meeting' between the two brigades with Brussels as the prize. There were two centre lines, each of about 75 miles. The 5th Guards Brigade had a difficult start (Pont-à-Marcq and Leuze), then a straight main road, which was quicker but more likely to be defended. The Welsh Guards' Cromwell tanks and their 'rival' 2nd Grenadiers with Sherman tanks arrived in Brussels at about 2000hrs to a tumultuous welcome. The 1st Belgian Brigade, after a four-year absence, arrived shortly afterwards.

Soon orders came to continue east to capture Louvain and then for 5th Guards Brigade to make for the Albert canal bridge south-west of Oostham, and for 32nd Guards Brigade to make for the Beeringen bridge. The Welsh group forced a bridgehead at Beeringen and seized Helchteren, but were repulsed at Hechtel. The Irish group had to capture the town of Beeringen, in a mining district with many black slag heaps, which were very useful for the German artillery observers. The German 719th Infantry Division put up a spirited defence at Beeringen and Beverloo, and the Irish were beaten back at Heppen by Panther tanks and the boggy ground, which claimed four Shermans. Enemy counter-attacks came in from Bourg-Leopold in the north, particularly on 9 September. 11th Armoured Division, after its dramatic capture of Antwerp, had moved east and cleared the Guards' right flank. General Horrocks now ordered the Guards to capture a bridge over the Escaut canal, ten miles north of Hechtel, come what may! The Household Cavalry led the Grenadier and Irish battle groups by a rough track through sand dunes across the Zwarte Beek, around Hechtel to Exel (Eksel), Lindel and Overpelt in difficult wooded country, approaching the bridge at De Groote Barrier (Grote Bareel) between Lommel and Neerpelt. Lt Colonel J.O.E. Vandeleur's 3rd battalion Irish Guards distinguished itself by capturing the bridge and cutting all wires, fuses and electric circuits. The Neerpelt bridge became the launching point for Operation Garden.

On the morning of 16 September in a cinema opposite the railway station in Bourg-Leopold, ten miles behind the front, Lt General Horrocks outlined the plan for Market Garden to a colourful group of all the senior officers of 30th Corps. They were responsible for leading a dramatic attack, most of it along a single highway of 64 miles through the towns of Valkenswaard, Eindhoven, Veghel, Uden and Nijmegen, to the bridges at Arnhem. If all went well the airborne 'carpet' would drop in the right places at the right time and a vital bridgehead would be established over the river Rhine. The optimists vied with each other. Monty said that he now hoped the war 'could be won reasonably quickly'. SHAEF and the generals all said something similar.

Horrocks established the principle of 'day movement only', and night moves were allowed only in the event of operational necessity, or if the movement could be completed within two hours of darkness. This meant that a divisional commander *could order a night attack if the opportunity arose 'of operational necessity'*. For the 20,000 vehicles involved, including 2,300 (with 9,000 sappers and pioneers) for bridging the many canals and rivers, no unit could overtake another, and there would be 'no turning back'. If a bridge was reported blown the road would be cleared of all traffic and the Royal Engineers earmarked for the bridge would be rushed up. Speed was vital as the 1st Airborne dropping zone in the Arnhem area would have to be reached 'if possible within 48 hours'. This was Mongomery's statement of intent.

The Guards would lead until Arnhem, after which 43rd Wessex Wyverns would move up and occupy the area around Apeldoorn. Once Arnhem was secured, 50th Northumbrian Division would move across the Lower Rhine and form a link between 1st Airborne and the 43rd around Apeldoorn. Behind the 50th would be 8th Armoured Brigade (Red Fox's Mask) and the Dutch Princess Irene Brigade. Wherever possible the advance would be two abreast and at an average rate of 35 vehicles per hour.

Horrocks expected the Guards to be in Eindhoven just after 1700hrs on D-Day, 17 September, after a bombardment by 250 guns and waves of rocket-firing Typhoons had blasted a path for them. The history books later rewrote this fact. In General Adair's history of the Division, completed in 1951 and

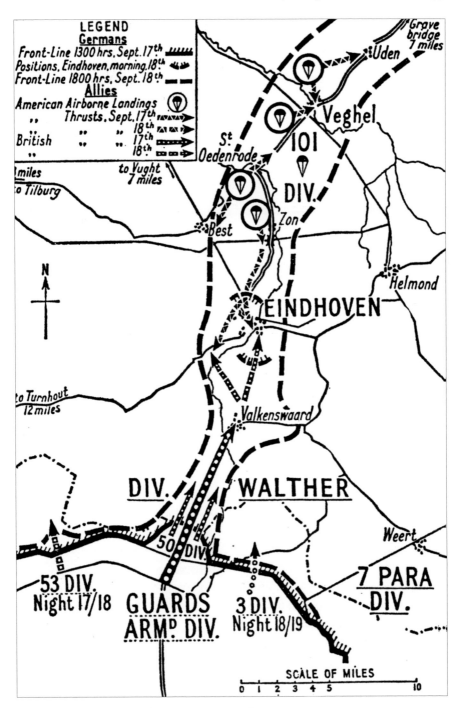

Market Garden: The Breakout, 17–18 September 1944.

published in 1956, he said on page 125: 'The 5th Guards Brigade was to lead and capture Valkenswaard the same evening, at first light on the 18th the advance was to continue and carry straight through. From Valkenswaard the 32nd Guards Brigade would take a subsidiary route through Helmond as far as Grave where the lead would be taken by whichever brigade arrived first.'

William Buckingham in *Arnhem 1944* shrewdly makes the point that the ground assault plan incorporated 11 squadrons of ground-attack aircraft based on the Continent (i.e. *not* in the UK) from RAF No. 83 Group (British 2nd Tactical Air Force) to operate in direct support of 30th Corps. To minimise the risk of collision, 2nd TAF was forbidden to venture within 20 miles of the operational area until well after the transporting planes of paratroops and gliders had delivered their loads and cleared the area. So Horrocks had to fret and dither until the Irish Guards' advance began at 1435hrs. The 101st US Airborne drop around Son was more than 20 miles from the start point, and their main drop finished at 1330hrs.

In Chapter 11, 'Bitter Triangle', Buckingham is quoted as saying that the lack of co-operation in certain vital matters between the RAF, the Airborne and the Army caused most of the problems with Market Garden. If Horrocks and Dempsey had insisted on an earlier start – even two hours earlier – the Guards' task would have been easier and they should have reached Eindhoven as planned.

Major General Adair, the 46-year-old GOC of Guards Armoured, thought that Operation Garden was a bold plan but 'it might be tricky'. He expected the worst moment to be the breakout from the Meuse-Escaut canal bridgehead. Once through that he thought 'the going would not be too difficult'. The two Vandeleur cousins, 'Joe' and Giles, didn't like the 'one-tank front' and the lack of time for planning, as the Irish Guards groups were to lead the attack.

Cornelius Ryan in *A Bridge too Far* recounts how the senior officers of the Dutch Princess Irene Brigade, Colonel Albert de Ruyter, Lt Colonel Charles de Mortanges and Major Jonkheer Jan van Blokland, were dubious about the plan for Operation Garden. 'It was made to seem quite elementary. First we'll take this bridge: then that one and hop this river .... The terrain ahead with its rivers, marshes, dikes and lowlands, was extremely difficult – as the British well knew from our many presentations.'

Field Marshal Model and Generals Bittrich and Student had positioned an arc of troops under Kampfgruppe Walther around the Neerpelt bridgehead, expecting a probable breakout. The German defenders had counter-attacked the Neerpelt bridgehead on 15 September with Kampfgruppen Von der Heydte, Kerutt and Segler. Their attack on the La Kolonie area failed, mainly due to heavy artillery defensive fire targets.

When the Guards attacked on the 17th the Walther group had the equivalent of ten weak infantry battalions, and the Roester Panzer group had ten tanks plus tank destroyers and considerable artillery. On Walther's right, the western side of the centre line, was Lt General Kurt Chill's 85th Infantry Division, and on his left was the Parachute Division Erdmann.

The Irish Guards group lost nine tanks quite quickly; Lt Colonel 'Joe' Vandeleur called in Typhoons and deployed infantry on both sides of the road, some of whom had been riding on the Shermans. Major Kerutt's 1st Battalion of the Parachute Training Regiment von Hoffman bore the brunt of the Guards' attack, which reached Valkenswaard by 1700hrs, but only entered the town unopposed *two and a half hours* later. Brigadier Gwatkin visited Vandeleur in Valkenswaard. There are various versions of the meeting (see David Bennett's *A Magnificent Disaster*), but Gwatkin said: 'Push on to Eindhoven tomorrow, old boy, but take your time. We've lost a bridge.' Gwatkin actually gave the order to Vandeleur to halt at 2200hrs.

General Adair's official history states on page 129 that the crucial bridge just south of Valkenswaard was reached at *half-past seven* (1930hrs).

David Bennett's book states on page 68 that the 2nd Household Cavalry Regiment's armoured cars met the Americans *north* of Eindhoven on D-Day, reported the destruction of the Son bridge, and returned from Best with this news. 'The result is that the Irish Guards did not go forward on D-Day evening. Had the Guards grasped the urgency of the situation they would have advanced to the edge of Eindhoven to await further instructions.' By the next morning the Germans had established two sets of blocking lines on the Eindhoven road.

By the evening of D-Day Horrocks said in his memoirs that he was disappointed that Eindhoven had not been reached. He should have been hounding Adair, who should have been hounding Gwatkin and chivvying the gallant Irish to get a move on. Horrocks would have acted more vigorously had he had Major General 'Pip' Roberts, GOC 11th Armoured (of Amiens and Antwerp fame) under command.

On the second day, 18 September, 2nd Household Cavalry Regiment left Valkenswaard at 0530hrs on the central Club route, followed at 0645hrs by the Grenadier Guards group. The 50th Tyne Tees sent a battalion, which arrived in Valkenswaard at 0900hrs. The Irish Guards started their advance at 1000hrs; they were then held up south of Aalst and again on the Dommel river. When the Welsh Guards on the right flank, taking the Heart route, were told by Dutch civilians that Geldrop and Helmond, east of Eindhoven, were strongly defended, they abandoned their flanking advance and, perhaps a little tamely, rejoined the main axis. By dusk they had cleared Leende and Heeze, south-east of Eindhoven, after several actions. Eventually the Irish group reached Eindhoven, occupied by the US 101st Airborne, and followed the Household Cavalry past six abandoned 88mm anti-tank guns to the Son bridge. The 14th Field Squadron built on the work of the American engineers and by dawn a 40-ton bridge was built. (A Sherman weighs 33 tons!)

The two Guards' Brigade HQs moved to Eindhoven and Valkenswaard respectively. At 0645hrs the Grenadier group sped over the new bridge at

Son and by 0700hrs were through Veghel and Uden. By 0830hrs they had crossed the river Maas at Grave and made their HQ in the monastery at Marienboom.

In the late afternoon the generals were at a command post in Malden, two miles south of Nijmegen. Horrocks and Adair were representing the British Army and Browning and Brigadier General James Gavin were representing the Airborne Army. Technically speaking, once the airborne troops had dropped and were in action they conformed to the 30th Corps command. But 'Boy' Browning, and his extensive 37-glider HQ staff, insisted on continuing to give orders to Gavin. He was told, in front of an audience of the 5th Guards Armoured Brigade, to capture the Nijmegen bridge that day (D+2) or the next.

The road and railway bridges of Nijmegen lie to the north-east and north-west of the town and form the only crossings for 20 miles. The huge 12-span road bridge was the priority target. It is built on high ground and dominates the town and river Waal. The smaller railway bridge could take one-way traffic.

On reaching the 82nd US Airborne HQ Adair remarked: 'I was surprised to discover upon arrival that we did not have the Nijmegen bridge. I assumed it would be in airborne hands by the time we reached it and we'd simply sweep on through.' Eleven miles of corridor remained to be forced open. No one had given any thought to what 'dragons' lay ahead. An amazing degree of thought had been given to the key drop zones, but no thought or plan at all had been made for securing the last 11-mile lap. Montgomery, Dempsey and Horrocks should have made specific plans, and, of course, in the original plan Browning should have insisted that the Polish Brigade be dropped between Elst and south of the Arnhem bridge.

Colonel Henke was Kampfgruppe Commander Nijmegen, and on the 17th he was ordered to co-ordinate defences in the town with a rag-bag assortment of 750 men – three companies of the ersatz Battalion 6 from Wehrkreis VI, a company of the Hermann Göring Training Regiment, and a NCO school. Defending a city with 5–6 km of urban sprawl was difficult, so Henke concentrated his forces south of the road and rail bridges. They were not easy to safeguard because the river Waal is 300 metres across at those points. The 82nd US Airborne sent a patrol into the city at dusk on the 17th, but SS General Wilhelm Bittrich, commanding II SS Panzer Corps, realised the importance of holding Nijmegen and sent the bulk of Kampfgruppe Grundsberg (10th SS Panzer Division), a brigade-strength battle group, to defend the town. Kampfgruppe Reinhold, under SS Kapitan Leo Hermann Reinhold, with 10th SS Engineer Battalion and SS Kapitan Euling's Battalion, was the spearhead. They quickly got enmeshed in fighting Lt Colonel Frost's group, who were defending the north side of Arnhem bridge. Nevertheless, another SS captain, Viktor Graebner, took his reconnaissance battalion east out of Arnhem and managed to reach Elst via Pannerden at 1900hrs. However, finding Henke in control and not attacked, he returned north to try and force the Arnhem bridge from the south side. The post office in Nijmegen held the demolition mechanism for the road bridge. In the darkness Gavin's paratroopers stormed the building and ejected or killed Henke's little garrison, but a fresh SS attack surrounded the building and trapped the paratroops, putting them under siege for the next three days.

SS Kapitan Euling and his artillery commander Sonnenstahl of the Frundsberg had amassed over 70 guns including 29 88mm guns on the north side of the river for the defence of the bridges, with forward observers on the south side and prearranged fire plans.

So, when on the afternoon of D+2, before the top brass conference began, three separate attacks by the Americans, with British infantry, tanks, artillery and air support, were launched against Euling and Henke's defences of the rail bridge, the post office in the centre and towards the road bridge, they all failed. The 5th Guards Brigade Grenadier team, working with Gavin's 2nd Battalion 505th Parachute Regiment, were guided by men from the Dutch resistance, but enemy shelling was intense and several Shermans were destroyed.

However, at 0800hrs on the 20th, D+3, the Grenadier group started on the laborious task of clearing the town as a prelude to a major assault on the bridge by Gavin's paratroops. The King's Company of 1st Battalion (Motor) Grenadier Guards had managed to get into the Valkof, the old fortress on the river's edge, by climbing the embankment and cutting a hole through the barbed wire on top. The Corps Commander, General Horrocks, later wrote:

Meanwhile the Grenadier Guards and the 505th US Parachute Regiment had been busy. In accordance with fresh orders issued the night before by Brigadier Gwatkin, commander of the 5th Guards Brigade, the Grenadiers had developed another attack on the southern end of the road bridge, this time approaching from the west. All day they fought their way forward literally yard by yard and house by house, until in the late afternoon they captured Hunner Park and the Valkof, a large, wooded mound that dominates the southern end of the bridge. In the words of the Grenadier Guards regimental history: 'Capturing a well-fortified mound like the Valkhof would be an operation fraught with incalculable dangers in any circumstances. It was exceptionally difficult in this case because the Germans had had time to surround it with a network of barbed-wire entanglements, slit trenches and dug-outs, all of which were fully manned, but as one company commander later wrote "From the first few moments the fighting did not conform in any way to my original plan. But once we got our teeth into the enemy the men's spirit was so terrific – even laughing and joking – that nothing could have stopped us." Of the many battle honours that the Grenadier Guards can claim, none can have been more richly deserved than Nijmegen.'

Sherman tanks of the Guards Armoured cross Nijmegen bridge.

Euling had fortified the edges of the Hunner Park, which was dominated by a lookout point, the Belvedere, and further to the west by the Valkof. SS troops continued to arrive throughout D+2. The corps commander related:

> At 7 p.m. it was decided to try and rush the bridgehead, and a troop of tanks commanded by Sergeant Robinson advanced rapidly with guns blazing to the bridge which is approximately 400 yards in width with an embankment of equal length on both sides. While travelling these 1200 yards the tanks were easy targets, not only to the enemy anti-tank guns, but also to those Germans who were firing bazookas from positions in the girders above the bridge. Two tanks were hit, but somehow the troop got over, skidded broadside through a road-block at the far end and knocked out two anti-tank guns on the road. The attack finally came to a halt a mile farther on where the guardsmen met the remnants of their gallant American allies who had crossed the river lower down. Perhaps the bravest of all these brave men was the young sapper officer, Lieutenant Jones, who ran on foot behind the tanks, cutting the wires and removing the demolition charges – though we now know that in spite of Bittrich's protest General Model had refused to allow this bridge to be blown as he wanted to use it for subsequent counter-attacks by the Germans.

Many defenders were under the bridge or in the demolition chambers and eventually 80 were winkled out in the darkness, but the German commanders, Euling, Kreuger and Schwappacher, and the survivors of Kampfgruppe Henke, continued fighting into the night and many made their escape through the suburb of Lent.

The rail bridge had been bravely captured by the American 3rd Battalion of 504th Parachute Regiment in a waterborne assault with 26 boats and rafts provided by Lt Colonel C.P. Jones, the Guards chief engineer who had supervised the rebuilding of the Son bridge. The southern half of the bridge was captured at 0900hrs on D+4.

Generals Horrocks and Browning together with Lt Colonel Giles Vandeleur, CO 2nd Battalion Irish Guards, watched the river assault from the top of the massive PGEM electrical power plant overlooking the river. 'It was a horrible, horrible sight,' recalled Vandeleur, 'Boats were literally blown out of the water. Huge geysers shot up as shells hit and small arms fire from the northern bank made the river look like a seething cauldron.' His two squadrons, under command of Majors Tyler and Fitzgerald, had fired smoke shells for a ten-minute cover. 'I saw one or two boats hit the beach, followed immediately by 3 or 4. Nobody paused. Men got out and began running towards the embankment. My God what a courageous sight it was.'

Now for a controversial moment. Lt Colonel Reuben Tucker was outraged that Guards Armoured did not push their armour and motorised infantry behind Sergeant Robinson's troop of Shermans once they were over the huge road bridge. The rest of Robinson's squadron, led by Captain Lord Carrington, established a defensive position and halted. At that moment there was no significant German force between the Nijmegen bridgehead and Colonel Frost's men, who were still holding on to the northern end of the Arnhem road bridge.

An hour after Robinson's troop had got across, two companies of Irish Guards, along with two troops of engineers, four 17-pdr anti-tank guns and more Shermans arrived. Sergeants Robinson, Pacey and Knight had got as far as Lent, a mile beyond the bridge, and were halted by two anti-tank guns. SS Colonel Heinz Harmel, commander of the Frundsberg 10th SS, said later: 'The four panzers [Shermans] who crossed the bridge made a mistake when they stayed in Lent. If they had carried on their advance it would have been all over with us.'

Both the Generals, Horrocks and Adair, simply got it wrong. The urgency demanded by Montgomery was rarely displayed. Adair has been described as a 'plodder' and this seems appropriate, but Horrocks had no excuse at all. He was a sensitive and imaginative officer. He had commanded a corps in fast, mobile warfare in North African desert, and had devised a single sledgehammer tactic for crushing the strong defences round Tunis and Bizerta. His resulting serious wounds kept him out of action for a year, until Montgomery vetted him and brought him into Normandy to take command of 30th Corps in August 1944. Then his handling of his three armoured divisions in the Great Swan north was exemplary. Now he seemed to have lost his sparkle and confidence.

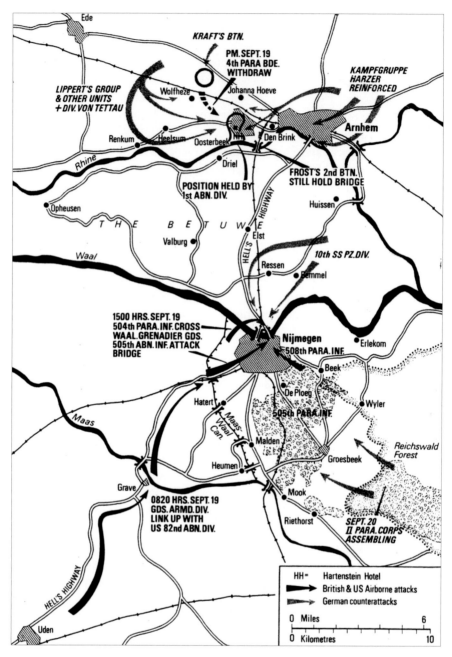

British and US airborne attacks and German counterattacks, 19–20 September 1944.

Or perhaps he was overwhelmed by efforts to spur on his many friends in the Guards Armoured Division. In his autobiography *A Full Life* he wrote:

> Thus, by the evening of the 21st, almost a miracle had been achieved. Thanks to some very hard fighting by British and American troops, whose co-operation on this occasion should be an object lesson to all allies in the future, these two important bridges had fallen into our hands intact. Another hurdle had been overcome and I went to bed a happy man – almost the last time, incidentally, that I was to do so in this battle.

Very strange indeed!

Nor does General Adair's history of the Division show any real urgency. The adjutant of the 1st Airborne Division Royal Engineers group had crossed the Lower Rhine on the evening of 20 September and reached the Guards Armoured bridgehead in Nijmegen. He brought the news of the first four days fighting in Oosterbeek, but nothing of Frost's holding of the north end of the Arnhem bridge. So Adair wrote: 'This information was disquieting enough to provide an additional spur, had any been needed, to our determination to push through at once to Arnhem if humanly possible.' Very strange indeed!

There was a clear window of opportunity of at least five hours during the night of the 20th when the road to Arnhem from Nijmegen was substantially free of German blocking troops. Adair could at least have ordered his excellent Household Cavalry armoured car unit to push, chivvy, explore and radio back. In fact, at 0700hrs on the 22nd, they drove in the mist through Oosterhout, north-west, at 0700hrs to meet the Polish drop at Driel.

Adair recalled: 'When I saw that island [the dead straight dyke road ahead between Nijmegen and Arnhem looked like an island] my heart sank. You can't imagine anything more unsuitable for tanks: steep banks with ditches on each side that could easily be covered by German guns ... they would have to have a shot at it – to get along that road was obviously first a job for infantry.' Every armoured division in the British Army had three battalions of lorried infantry and a battalion of motorised infantry, in carriers or half-tracks. Adair had 5th Coldstream, 2nd Scots Guards, 3rd Irish Guards in the first category and 1st Grenadiers as the Motor battalion. But it was not to be. Neither Adair nor Horrocks was sufficiently motivated, so everybody waited for Major General G.I. Thomas, 43rd Wessex Wyverns, to appear to do the dirty work. The Wyverns had not even reached the Grave bridge eight miles to the south.

The next day (the 21st), during this hiatus, Lt Colonel Frost's gallant defenders at the Arnhem bridge were over-run at mid-day. When the Nijmegen road bridge was secured, after five days, the Guards Armoured Division had only lost 130 men killed, wounded or missing, since the beginning of Operation Garden. In Colonel Tucker's brave river assault crossing, the 3rd

Battalion 504th Parachute Infantry Regiment had suffered 134 casualties, including 28 killed.

There were four possible routes out of Nijmegen towards Arnhem: north-east via Lent, due north, north-west towards Elst, and west-north-west through Oosterhout by minor roads and tracks towards Driel.

On the 21st the Guards tried hard, although they only started moving at mid-day. Captain Langton, who navigated using a captured map, led the Irish group. Lt Colonel 'Joe' Vandeleur told him to 'go like hell and get on up to Arnhem', whilst asserting to his second in command, 'We've got to try. We've got to chance that bloody road.' So the Irish passed the village of Oosterhout off to the left and the hamlets of Rissen and Bemmel on the right. Then suddenly a German SP gun near Elst knocked out the four leading Shermans. The Typhoon cab rank was overhead but the RAF ground-to-air radio was not working! The Irish Guards infantry moved up into orchards on both sides of the road and were unable to do anything to deal with the single SP gun which had halted the entire relief column only six miles from Arnhem. So the Welsh Guards group tried next. They passed Fort Lent and their leading troop encountered three German tanks and knocked them out. Their official history says: 'By then it was growing dark. The Higher Command had decided that before any further advance could be made the bridgehead must be enlarged so that more troops could be brought into the Island. The Welsh Guards were ordered to withdraw to harbour near the bridge.' Without Typhoon cab rank close support it was impossible to break through the blocking lines the Germans had put in place south of Elst. The dashing Household Cavalry armoured cars managed to sneak through lanes and tracks in the mist and joined up with the Poles early on the 22nd.

SS Lt Colonel Walther Harzer had by now set up a *sperrverband*, or blocking line, running from Elst north up to the Rhine, partly to fend off the Poles and partly to fend off the Guards and any reinforcements they might bring up. The Kampfgruppen Knaust and Brinkmann were in Elst, under command of the Frundsberg (10th Waffen SS Division), and another *sperrverband* Gerhard was blocking 30th Corps. It was strange that Horrocks was still under the impression that the Polish Brigade had been dropped at the *original* dropping zone of Elden, south of the Arnhem bridge, instead of Driel.

Finally, General Thomas's Wyverns 129th Brigade took over the lead and found progress very slow. On D+5 at 1430hrs the Grenadiers, who had been resting in Nijmegen, moved back towards Veghel, and the Coldstreamers moved towards Voekel. For three days the 5th Guards Brigade had the task of protecting the right flank of the Wyverns as far as the Waal, while keeping one tank regiment in reserve for a counter-attack. On the 23rd the Welsh Guards attempted to capture Bemmel, north-east of Lent, but failed on the 24th. On the 26th the Welsh occupied Aam. The 32nd Guards Brigade was urgently needed to clear the 'Hell's Highway' between Veghel and Uden, south-west of

Grave, which had been cut by a strong German thrust. Parachute Regiment 6 under Colonel von de Heydte, arriving from Boxtel, was met by Guards tanks and 501st Parachute Infantry Regiment of 101st US Airborne, and was halted near Eerde. Eventually the Coldstreamers captured Volkel town and airfield, before moving on to Erp and Boekel, and the key 30th Corps highway was cleared again.

The Coldstream group following behind the Grenadiers occupied the very important food dump at Oss, which contained plentiful, but unusual German rations. These operations took place over the 23 and 24 September. The Grenadiers had a successful action on 27th and 28th around the Heesch crossroads, backed by a Leicester Yeomanry barrage; over 200 German troops were captured or killed. The next day another 68 Germans were captured, mainly from the 712th Infantry Division, one of General von Zangen's escapees.

The Guards Division then spent about two weeks on the Island, fending off vigorous counter-attacks around Aam, a mile east of Elst, which was now held by the Wyverns. The 9th and 116th Panzer Divisions attacked with Panther tanks and infantry armed with flame-throwers. The Irish group bore the brunt and suffered 170 casualties before being relieved by the Coldstreams. 32nd Guards Brigade was in reserve around Ressen. It was unpleasant and dangerous fighting in mud and rain until the Division came out of the line from the Island on 6 October.

Sherman tanks with 'Little Friends' (PBI) in early winter.

*   *   *   *

For over a month the Guards remained near Nijmegen, resting and refitting. The 'Eye' Club was opened at the Hotel d'Anspach in Brussels, and on 12 October King George VI visited his troops. Most of November was spent in Sittard. During the Battle of the Bulge in mid-December to mid-January the Guards were in reserve north of Namur, before taking part in Operation Veritable with actions at Gennep, Hommersum and Hassum. Once over the Rhine the Guards advanced steadily through Germany, liberating POW camps, capturing a secret naval experimental station at Hesedorp, capturing Stade on the Elbe, and, at Cuxhaven, they accepted the surrender of their old foe, 7th Parachute Regiment.

A fitting epilogue, in the words of Major General Adair:

> I was very conscious of the price we had to pay for victory – the Guards Armoured Division [in the Second World War] had 956 killed, 545 missing and 3,946 wounded. I have since visited their graves: in battle, it was a particularly sad sight to see a burnt out tank and four crosses beside it. I loved them all.

Detail from picture on p. 196. (*Imperial War Museum B-6646*)

CHAPTER 17

'Von Thoma's' 43rd Wessex Wyverns Division

The 43rd (Wessex) Division obviously had its roots in the west of England, with regiments from Somerset (4th and 7th Light Infantry), Wiltshire (4th and 5th Battalions), Dorset (4th and 5th Battalions), Hampshire (7th Battalion), Worcestershire (1st Battalion), and Cornwall (5th Battalion Duke of Cornwall's Light Infantry). The Reconnaissance Regiment was the 5th Gloucesters.

Their distinctive divisional sign was a golden Wyvern with the ferocity of a dragon, the speed of an eagle and the cunning of a serpent. The Germans in Normandy had a variety of names for them, such as (translated) the 'Yellow Devils', or the 'British SS'. Divisional comics, of course, knew better – to them the savage, heraldic golden beast was a 'pregnant prawn'.

The Division was backed by the usual five artillery regiments (99th, 112th and 179th Field, 59th Anti-tank, and 110th Light AA). The Middlesex 8th Battalion was equipped with heavy mortars and medium machine-guns.

On 2 March 1942 Major General Ivo Thomas joined the Division as its GOC. He had served for three years on the front line in the First World War as a gunner officer and was twice wounded, winning the MC and bar, and the DSO. In every photograph of Thomas in the Second World War, he looked as though he was still fighting the battle of the Somme. He wore high oiled boots, light-coloured riding breeches and a battle dress blouse covered in medal ribbons. His field service cap carried a faded red Major General's cap band. In mid-winter he wore a long leather coat. He was, of course, a good horseman, and polo and hunting were his favourite pastimes.

Thomas attracted nicknames. His methods both in training and in battle were described as German in their thoroughness and efficiency, so 'Von Thoma' (after a distinguished German general of that name who fought in North Africa) was one soubriquet, probably originated by Montgomery. He was also christened 'The Butcher' due to being a ruthless, driving soldier, apparently unmoved by heavy losses to his men. He had much in common with General Bernard Montgomery on the battlefield, especially in their mutual preference of a well-planned attack with a preceding heavy artillery barrage, and he impressed his personality and theories of warfare upon his officers and men. So, inevitable training exercises took place – Shudder, Blackcock, Great Binge, Tiger, Harlequin and Porpoise.

On 3 June 1944 General Montgomery briefed the Wyverns about Operation Overlord at Lt General N.M. Ritchie's 12th Corps HQ, and nine days later they sailed from Newhaven. The Division arrived off Ouistreham, at Courseulles-sur-Mer and Mulberry harbour on 24 June, having been delayed by severe storms.

In Operation Epsom the Wyverns followed up behind 15th Scottish and by 26 June were in Cheux, La Gaule, St Mauvieu and Marcelet. It was their first encounter with the Hitler Jugend, young fanatical Nazi youths aged 18 or 19 who fought brilliantly from well-defended positions. Mouen was a successful operation by the Worcesters, and the Wiltshires and Somersets had a hard time in the river Odon's 'Death Valley'.

In early July Operation Jupiter was a classic set-piece attack to secure the high ground between the rivers Odon and Orne. The important objective was Hill 112, which dominated the battlegrounds. It was a ten-acre plateau, sloping on three sides, with no cover on top apart from a copse surrounded by some hedges. Standing cornfields gave some cover to friend and foe. After the immense bombardment by the Allied artillery barrages the Germans called Hill 112 the 'wood of half trees', and the British named it the 'crown of thorns'. The mighty 10th SS Frundsberg Division was well dug in with deep emplacements for its minnenwerfer mortars and SP guns. The 277th Wehrmacht Infantry Division was on the west side around Evrecy, and a Hitler Jugend battle group was holding the north side. In reserve in the village of St Martin was the newly arrived 102nd SS Heavy Tank Battalion of 11th SS Panzer Corps, equipped with 56-ton Tiger tanks.

It looked like being a nightmare. General Thomas was responsible for Operation Jupiter and used classic First World War tactics. A violent prolonged

Le Bon Repos crossroads, 1944.

artillery programme was the prelude to an appalling two-day battle, which is rarely mentioned in the history books. It was a massacre. On 10 July the Division nearly bled to death. The well-trained but raw infantry division from the West Country suffered 2,000 casualties in 36 hours. This was the division entrusted by Lt General Horrocks to be the *lead* infantry division in Market Garden two months ahead.

Operation Express, a two-battalion attack by 4th and 5th Wiltshires to retake the village of Maltot behind Hill 112, started on 22 July. Captain John McMath, signals officer of the Wiltshires, recounted:

> Maltot proved to be a dreadful spectacle, the streets and fields still strewn with the dead Dorsets and Hampshires who had fallen on 10 July. They lay in heaps around slit trenches with hardly more than the turf removed. The houses were shattered, roads cratered and full of debris: everywhere the sickly smell of death and destruction hung heavily upon the ruins. Tiger tanks overlooking the village were still dropping shells with deadly accuracy on our positions.

Oh – and Operation Express is not in the history books either!

There was no let up. Operation Bluecoat followed with 8th Armoured Brigade (Red Fox) in partnership with the Wyverns, to advance through La Suisse Normande of genuine *bocage* country from Caumont to Mont Pinçon. It was only 15 miles and the 'Mount' was only 365 metres high, but it took ten

Moving south from Caumont with the 43rd Wessex Wyvern Division, 31 July 1944. (*Birkin Haward*)

days and many casualties before the Somersets joined 13/18th Hussar tanks on the top of Mont Pinçon.

The relentless demands continued: actions in Le Plessis Grimault; Operation Blackwater to form a bridgehead over the river Noireau; and then, a dubious honour, Operation Neptune to force a crossing of the river Seine at Vernon. The Seine was over 200 yards wide with a strong current, and Thomas was ordered to get across by 25 August. Four days later, after a four-day and night operation in which the Wyverns suffered another 550 casualties, the Seine bridgehead was established and Horrocks' armoured legions poured across on their way north. Soon infantrymen from the 59th Pithead Division, which went into Normandy and never came out, joined the Wyverns. At three investitures for medals and decorations won in the Normandy campaign, only 28 out of 55 officers and men had survived to appear on parade; the rest were dead or wounded. Elements of the Division were dispatched as mobile reserves and garrison units for part of Brussels. On 9 September they arrived at the St Jean hospital, a German barracks in the city. Their duties were escorting prisoners to the rear, guarding amenities such as food, wine and petrol, as well as coal dumps, and map depots, and clearing the Bois de la Cambre and Fôret de Soynes of German stragglers.

There was one story current, that Monty had offered General Thomas the opportunity for the Wessex Wyverns to be *the* garrison of the city of Brussels. To which Von Thoma had answered: 'Not bloody likely, we're a fighting division', or words to that effect!

Brigadier Peter Essame recalled the move to rejoin 30th Corps east of Diest by last light on 15 September: 'The long column filed past the red, yellow and black frontier posts of Belgium. A densely populated country of small houses flush with the streets, estaminets (where many trucks and carriers happened to "break down" or "get lost" and require advice and sustenance), slipshod villas, steam trains still running, the coal mines were working. The Belgians were free but they were hungry. Bottles of brandy and Burgundy appeared. Bearded priests and nuns came out to cheer. Crowds of children swarmed around the cooks' lorries, clamoured for cigarettes and sweets.' The fine weather now broke and heavy rain fell on the Wyverns as they learned of the dramatic – and ambitious – plans for Operation Market Garden. A 60-mile thrust through Eindhoven, Veghel and Uden on 'Club Route', to follow Guards Armoured Division *with the utmost speed*, and pass through after the capture of Arnhem. Then, having reached the Apeldoorn area, they were expected to block the escape routes of General von Zangen's 15th Army and other German forces in Holland. Bridgeheads would have to be made by the Wyverns over the river Ijssel at Zutphen and Deventer.

The Wyverns were responsible for bridging the numerous water hazards ahead. General Dempsey had assembled 9,000 sappers, engineers and pioneers with 2,300 vehicles around Bourg-Leopold. The Army Group Bridge column consisted of four bridge company HQs with bridging equipment and rafts. Eventually they were responsible for the evacuation of 1st Airborne across the Lower Rhine.

Horrocks gave careful instructions about traffic movement but the Wyverns infantry division had over 3,300 vehicles, Guards Armoured had 3,400 vehicles, and the grand total was over 20,000. With the best of plans laid, traffic jams were still very frequent, even more so when General Student's battle groups cut the Club Route.

General Thomas's divisional 'O' Group included the commanders of the 8th Armoured Brigade, the 147th Field Regiment RA, the 64th Medium Regiment RA and the Royal Netherlands Brigade Group. The Division was allotted rations for four days and petrol for 250 miles.

On the evening of 19 September Brigadier Essame was writing: 'The situation of 1 Airborne Division at Arnhem was critical: need for speed overrode all other considerations. Owing to bad weather resupply had failed.' And on the morning of the 20th: 'Contact had been made by wireless. Their situation was critical in the extreme. What was left of the division had been compressed into a tight perimeter at Hartestein, where it fought on, weary, hungry and sadly depleted in numbers.'

In these crucial days the divisional artillery was in action most of the time. 94th Field Regiment was at Overpelt, supported the main Guards attack on the 17th, and, after dark, the 12th Corps' attack on the left when their gun position was mortared. The next day they were supporting both flanks of the main attack, and in the evening 30 Luftwaffe bombers hit the gun positions. On the 19th Major Concannon, FOO with the Guards, reported he was well beyond Eindhoven.

It was after two frustrating days, on the morning of the 20th, that the Wyverns started to move along Club Route through Hechtel. The whole morning was spent static, in an immense traffic jam, as the German 107th Brigade's Panther tanks and SP guns had cut the centre line at Son, five miles north of Eindhoven. Passing many knocked-out Guards Armoured Shermans, Brigadier Ben Walton's 130th Brigade reached the Grave bridge by nightfall. The Recce Regiment with 12/60th KRRC were ordered to protect the right flank against a possible counter-attack. Captain R.F. Hall, 4th Dorsets, recalled: 'Whilst assembling at Hechtel we could see V-2s being launched about a mile away in woods from where we were. They were being fired desperately before they were over-run. First straight up then angling off towards their target. I was then 2 i/c C Company, 4 Dorsets under Tony Crocker. When we reached the bridge at Nijmegen we were stuck with tanks in front and the rest of the Brigade behind. We could see the tidy Dutch collecting up German corpses in carts and dumping them in the river.'

Lt General Horrocks and the GOC met at Malden on the road from Hernen to Nijmegen late on the 20th; as a result, 4th Dorsets were sent to protect the

Men of the 5th Wiltshires wait in the streets of Nijmegen before crossing the bridge
and continuing the advance towards Arnhem. (*Imperial War Museum B-10274*)

Grave bridge and a company was sent to Neerbosch, while 7th Hampshires and 5th Dorsets were sent to help clear Nijmegen. The two bridges, road and rail, were intact. One theory was the Germans planned to counter-attack from Arnhem due south and retake Nijmegen. Major G.R. Hartwell of 5th Dorsets wrote: 'This was quite the most fantastic operation: far from finding any Germans lurking in the town, it was with the greatest difficulty that any progress could be made through the excited occupants who festooned the troops with flowers, filled their pockets with apples.'

On the night of the 20th 214th Brigade had only reached Eindhoven because of the slow-moving traffic on Club Route. Later, on the 21st, Colonel George Taylor met General Horrocks who told him, Brigadier Essame and the other two COs that the enemy was stubbornly holding a line north of the bridge and preventing the Guards from breaking through to reach Arnhem. General Model's first priority was to block off the approach of the Guards. Taylor recalled the meeting: 'Horrocks said, "What would you do, George?" I said, "Do a left hook and use the DUKWs to cross behind the enemy holding Oosterhout". I did not believe they had much depth behind that village. This proved to be so.' The area between the Waal and the Lower Rhine was called the Island. In his memoirs Horrocks wrote:

> With its dykes, high embankments carrying the roads and deep ditches on either side it was most unsuitable for armoured warfare. It was perfect defensive country in which the anti-tank gun hidden in the orchard was always master of the tank silhouetted against the skyline. I pinned my hopes on the 43rd Infantry Div. which had been ordered up from the rear. Their move had been much delayed by congestion, along our one and only road, caused to a large extent by the increasing enemy pressure which was coming in from the flanks. On arrival they would push through the Guards in the morning [of 22nd]. I hoped this fresh infantry division would succeed in joining up with the Polish Parachute Brigade who had dropped on the 21st near the village of Driel. Together they would be able to bring succour to the hard-pressed 1st Airborne.

The German 9th and 10th Panzer Divisions were now putting intense pressure on the narrow corridor – 1,000 yards wide at most – from the west, and furious counter-attacks were coming in from the Reichswald Forest to the east on General Jim Gavin's 82nd Airborne. Brigadier Essame pointed out: 'The country ahead [north of Nijmegen] was a maze of orchards. No viewpoint [for gunner observation posts] could be found. The enemy held firmly the grid-iron of roads south and south-west of Elst in considerable strength. His west flank clearly rested on the maze of houses, orchards and trees around Oosterhout. This the two Brigadiers [Essame and Norman Gwatkin of the Guards Armoured] must take with all speed to enable the advance to be continued.' Unfortunately, 7th Somerset Light Infantry had been delayed getting through Nijmegen. Private D. O'Connell wrote:

> How clean and wholesome were the Dutch houses, red-tiled, red-bricked, clear shiny windows, close-cropped neat lawns. When the Dutch discovered we were British, the barriers went down, hugging and kissing all round, every vehicle in the column had a Dutch Fan Club. Woodbines, Gold Flake and Senior Service fags were brought out by us. We held those Dutch people in high esteem. My Sergeant said if the women could have been better looking he might even fall in love with them. [Later] A muck-up in a Dixie occurred. The column in front got separated from the rest … I became the front carrier in a dash across the road bridge. At one part of the town were love, kisses, fruit and flowers, on the other there was a barrage of bullets. A motley group tailed behind us, light AA guns, some anti-tank guns, some Pioneers, another tank or SP gun and a few more ragtag and bobtail.

Eventually Lt Colonel Hugh Borradaile, CO of 7th SLI, the fifth commanding officer since D-Day, gathered his scattered battalion together and crossed the railway bridge, which could bear the Shermans of 4/7th Dragoon Guards. They then advanced two miles to set up an attack on the village of Oosterhout. The GOC ordered his third brigade, 129th, still some way behind on Club Route, to advance over the road bridge on the right, and then both 214th and 129th would set off for Arnhem. Weather conditions were awful, rain and thick mist,

Sappers working at night on a Bailey Bridge over the Maas.

so RAF support was nil. Ammunition for the divisional artillery was rationed because of the acute supply problems on the centre line. In any case, FOOs could not easily identify targets. 130th Brigade in Nijmegen was to be relieved by 69th Brigade of 50th Division, with the defence of Grave bridge handed over to the Royal Netherlands Brigade. The only concrete road on the Island was the main road from Nijmegen to Arnhem running through Elst, and the Guards simply could not get past the tanks and anti-tank defences, hence General Thomas's left-flanking attack and that of Colonel George Taylor. For the set-piece attack on Oosterhout, the Somersets had much support. The Somersets then tried to turn the right flank and failed, so Brigadier Essame ordered a set-piece attack with H-Hour at 1520hrs.

The Somersets attacked again under a barrage of four field regiments, a medium regiment, heavy 4.2-inch and 3-inch mortars – the lot. By 1700hrs 'A' and 'B' Companies reported that the village was clear. 139 SS prisoners were taken for the loss of 22 casualties, including three killed. Five small AA guns, an 88mm gun and three tanks were captured or destroyed, but General Urquhart was dismissive: 'wasted most of a day, held up by a tank and some infantry'. The Corps artillery was now down to three rounds per gun, and Horrocks sent the Somersets a personal message of congratulation.

The Recce Regiment probed the north-west sector of the Island, scouting into De Hulk, Andelst, Zetten and Randwijk. 'C' Squadron patrolled towards Hien. The enemy they encountered were elderly gentlemen of the Luftwaffe, dressed in smart new uniforms, who had been manning searchlight or AA Flak sites in occupied Holland. They were on their way to Utrecht and were not amused to be put in the bag. Regimental HQ was set up in Slijk Ewijk.

Now it was the Cornwalls' turn. In the dusk, on the road north-east of Oosterhout, Colonel George Taylor quickly formed up an armoured column with ammo and medical stores intended for the airborne survivors, followed, at the rear, by Major Parker's 'A' Company with carriers and mortar platoon. The rest of the battalion, under Major St George Martin, was to follow on foot. The objectives were to reach Driel on the banks of the Lower Rhine, link up with the Polish parachute troops, and make contact with the airborne. After the spirited defence of Oosterhout by the Germans it appeared a tall order. Off they set at full tilt, roaring ahead on the bund (riverside track) until they reached Slijk Ewijk. As Colonel Taylor wrote: 'tracks clanking, motors roaring, dashing headlong ignoring the danger of ambush and mines, we were soon in the streets of Valburg. The Dutch inhabitants, astonished at the eruption of armour and men, went wild with joy, shouting and cheering. The light was fading rapidly as the head of the column reached Driel. The journey of about 10 miles had been completed in under 30 minutes. We felt that even General Patton would not grumble at this.' An equally exciting drama was happening in the rear of the column, as CSM Philp, DCM, recounted: 'Major Parker was leading 'A' Company's group in his jeep travelling much faster than my carrier. Halfway to

43rd Division Wessex Wyverns on the march. (*Stan Procter*)

Driel I was 600 yards behind. In the distance I saw Major Parker passing a tank on the fork roads between Elst and Driel. Within 100 yards I saw they were a column of tanks marked with the black cross. We could not stop but charged on hoping to get through.' CSM Philp shot the leading tank commander and baled out with his carrier crew into a muddy ditch; he lived to tell the tale.

Lt General Horrocks wrote in his memoirs:

> Up to this point [22nd] in the battle no troops could have done more or advanced more rapidly than had 30 Corps, but from now on our rate of progress slowed down and this has been the subject of criticism from several sources, notably by Chester Wilmot in his *Struggle for Europe*. He has suggested that 43rd Division was both slow and sticky. If the leading troops of the Guards Armoured Division were now only six to seven miles short of Arnhem bridge, why then did a first-class infantry division take so long to get up to the lower Rhine? – particularly as their casualties were comparatively small. That is the general tone of the adverse comments.
>
> I have always strongly deprecated this criticism because I spent the morning of the 22nd with Brigadier Essame, the commander of the 214th Infantry Brigade, which was in the lead, and nobody could have done more. He had tried to launch an attack with his leading battalion on the previous afternoon, but the whole brigade had been delayed by the confusion in Nijmegen and some of his troops were misdirected towards the road bridge,

while the remainder crossed to the north bank by the railway bridge. The Welsh Guards were attacking on the sector immediately north of the river, the bridges were being shelled, and movement was difficult along the narrow, twisty roads which ran on the banks with deep dykes on either side. In my opinion only an experienced brigadier like Essame could have succeeded under these circumstances in concentrating his brigade at all on the night of the 21st, and launching an attack with the leading battalion, the 7th Somerset Light Infantry, early next day.

His orders had been to advance with all speed but, and this is most important, he was told that artillery ammunition must be used with the utmost economy. Owing to enemy pressure on our lines of communication we were forced to economise as much as possible.

The large village of Elst, half way between Arnhem and Nijmegen had been completely overlooked by the vast array of military and RAF planners. The original concept was that the Polish Airborne Brigade would drop around Elden on 19 September and either block the main road or put pressure on the Germans attacking the Arnhem bridge from the south. They would then link up with Colonel John Frost's men, or possibly just occupy the key village of Elst, just south-west of Elden, denying it to the Germans. Indeed they could have jumped into position on D-Day in the 37 planes that Lt General Browning's *folie de grandeur* required. To compound the errors, during the fighting in Arnhem Major General Urquhart was given the opportunity to redirect the Polish drop. Elden meant possible success for Operation Garden and the Guards could have linked up with Frost. Driel was chosen because it was nearer to the beleaguered 1st Airborne holding out in Oosterbeek. Browning made the first mistake; Urquhart compounded it.

While the Somersets and Cornwalls were successfully beating their way forward on the western flank, 129th Brigade with 4th Wiltshires leading, supported by 13/18th Hussar tanks on the eastern flank, headed due north towards Elst. Major Hans-Peter Knaust, the German CO at Elst, was handling his battle group with skill.

Tank and mortar fire rained down on the Wiltshires, and Major A.D. Parsons wrote: 'desperate section battles took place, stalking Spandaus up ditches, waist deep in mud and water trying to rush them. All the head-on attacks failed. 'B' Company tried to move through to clear the crossroads but two Mk IV tanks held them up, causing heavy casualties. Two Shermans of 13/18th Hussars were soon knocked out and at last light four more were lost in one minute. The mortars had to be manhandled into place and often had targets only 100 yards ahead. Captain Bedford and Lieutenant Hardiman were killed and the Wiltshires took 37 casualties on that black day. Not for want of trying, Elst was not reached, we achieved next to nothing! Night fell with both sides dug in 50 yards apart.'

For 25 hours Club Route had been cut by a German force of 30 tanks and 200 vehicles from Erp on the right flank astride the centre line north-east of Veghel. 32nd Guards Brigade had to be sent back to re-open the road. General Dempsey and Lt General Horrocks, who had met at Veghel, saw at first hand the very determined German attacks. At this stage they must have realised that there was no likelihood of getting the whole of 43rd Division across the Lower Rhine to reinforce the battered airborne troops. The GOC now ordered 130th Brigade to advance at first light on the 23rd along the bund to Slijk Ewijk, via Valburg, to link up with the Cornwalls in Driel, while 214th Brigade was to capture Elst from Valburg, to the west. Led by 5th Dorsets, 7th Hampshires and 4th Dorsets, in sleet and driving rain, the column set off at 0600hrs, supported by 13/18th Hussars, in another mad dash for Driel. Despite the column being cut in two by enemy tanks firing from Elst, 5th Dorsets reached Driel by 1130hrs and contact was made with the Cornwalls and the Poles.

By 1645hrs 4th Dorsets had reached Homoet, with 7th Hampshires on their left near Heteren. General Urquhart in Oosterbeek received a message: 'leading infantry 43 Div. have arrived south bank. Hope they will be able to cross under mist.' He also wrote in his memoirs: 'General Thomas ordered a comparatively junior brigadier [Ben Walton] of 130th Brigade to take the Polish Brigade under command and attempt a crossing into the perimeter at night. The plan was not going to produce a crossing of sufficient strength to be of any real use.'

Meanwhile, the Cornwalls had laid on a fire plan from the south bank from tanks, machine-guns and 3-inch mortars to distract the German troops surrounding the airborne perimeter. The Wyverns received a considerable amount of 88mm shell, airburst and mortars in return. Colonel George Taylor asked Brigade for a supply of assault boats so that if necessary his Cornwalls could cross the river. A few boats were brought up and given to the Polish Brigade.

It was mid-afternoon before the follow-up 214th Brigade managed to deploy across the Valburg crossroads under constant 88mm and machine-gun fire. Their Battalion HQ was in the local pub near the crossroads. As General Thomas arrived for an 'O' group with Brigadier Essame, a fierce 88mm stonk greeted his arrival, smashed the pub windows and killed several men outside. When there was a second salvo 'Von Thoma' vented his wrath, not on the Germans, but on the person responsible for positioning Brigade HQ in an obvious target site! Eventually, just before dusk, the attack started on Elst, held by Waffen SS, under a divisional barrage. On the right (southern) flank, 7th Somersets had to move cross country with their tracked vehicles and supporting tanks separated on the main road.

The Worcesters had a more difficult time. Private William Gould recalled that:

...a Panther tank had ditched itself and its fire was directed at an angle above
the Worcesters. Four young Hitler Youth soldiers surrendered in the RAP.
The Provo Sergeant G. Ridler and five other ranks were killed by shelling at
Valburg crossroads. The village of Elst was only partly taken by the night
of the 23rd and it was not until the morning of the following day that it
was properly taken. Every house contained Boche with machine-guns and
grenades and the Worcesters took many casualties. Panthers caused havoc
and Major Souper, OC 'D' Company, and Major Gibbons, OC 'A' Company,
were killed by 88mm and mortar shells.

Back at the river's edge near Driel the stout-hearted Poles were ferried across
the fierce current in 16 assault boats by 204th Field Company RE and the 5th
Dorsets. Although supported by every weapon 130th Brigade could bring to
bear, they were unfamiliar with this type of operation and suffered heavy losses.
They left the assault boats on the far bank where they were shot to pieces during
the day. Major General Urquhart noted: 'By early hours of Sunday 24th a total
of 200 Poles had managed to cross. Some were killed before they could be put
into position by Hackett.' The general made no comment about the reckless
bravery of the Poles trying to go to the rescue of the 1st Airborne. Pat Spencer
Moore, Thomas's ADC, 'attended a caravan HQ meeting with Polish Brigadier,
GIT [the GOC] and General Horrocks. On our way up to the meeting we
passed the Polish [survivors] coming back. They looked exhausted and done in.
GIT told me later that Horrocks had told the Pole to get his brigade remnants
back out to rest. Pole, standing very erect and fierce, "I will continue in battle,
General". Horrocks, "You will do as I bloody well tell you". Pole, "General
Horrocks, I will do as you bloody well tell me".'

Colonel George Taylor recounted: 'There was great activity this day [24th].
The attempts to drop supplies were tragic, but a wonderful spectacle of
courage and devotion by the air crews, both American and British. Halifaxes
and Dakotas flying in compact groups against angry black bursts of flak shells.
Only a small percentage of the parachute containers fell in the target area.
Our air losses were heavy.' Horrocks, Thomas and Colonel Taylor climbed the
church tower in Driel and made a thorough reconnaissance of the ground, the
position of the enemy and their own troops. The area occupied by the airborne
troops had no military value. The enemy held the high ground overlooking
the river and its approaches. Bridging to put a brigade across was obviously
impossible. Horrocks ordered Thomas to prepare an urgent evacuation called
Operation Berlin. Cornelius Ryan's book *A Bridge Too Far* mentioned that
Brigadier Ben Walton's orders to Lt Colonel Tilley were 'to broaden the base of
the perimeter' and then 'hang on until reinforced' with food and ammunition
for three or four days. Shortly after 1800hrs Walton told Tilley there had been
a change of plan: 'the whole operation – the large-scale crossing – was off.'
Tilley was to take 'only enough men to do the job', approximately 400 men

and 20 officers. At the St Oedenrode conference with Horrocks and Browning, the plans were made to withdraw the Airborne Division. Major James Grafton, the Dorsets' 2 i/c, was told: 'I'm afraid we're being chucked away.'

Brigadier Essame wrote: 'To get a firmer grip on the river bank on the far side 130th Brigade were ordered to pass over 4th Dorset on the left with a further party of Poles – on the night of the 24th/25th. The crossing site was the ferry [non-working] at the western end of the perimeter, but overlooked in daylight by mortar and machine-guns. A factory about 600 yards inland was selected as the battalion's objective.' The current was likely to increase rapidly after midnight so zero hour was provisionally fixed for 2200hrs. A huge defensive fire plan was planned by the divisional artillery, plus all of 8th Middlesex medium machine-guns and mortars, 13/18th Sherman tanks, and from the Hampshires on the left and 5th Dorsets on the right. But the actual assault boats intended for the crossing had not arrived, although 20 had been promised. It is an unfortunate story. In the darkness two lorry loads of boats took the wrong turning at Valburg and drove into the part of Elst still held by the enemy. Two more lorries slithered off the muddy road into a dyke and could not be rescued. The fifth lorry reached the Poles but they had no paddles.

At 1930hrs 4th Dorsets moved off under murderous fire and arrived at Driel at 2130hrs. Major Grafton, 'A' Company, and Major Whittle, 'B' Company, were to lead the first flight of assault boats; 'C' Company, under Major Crocker, and 'D' Company, with Major Roper, were to follow; 'S' Company, with supplies, was to cross last. Major Whittle wrote: 'We spent three unpleasant hours waiting for the boats to arrive, [which came] due mainly to the energy of Captain Dawes of 5th Dorsets.'

Major Mike Whittle recalled:

Two of the ten boats in my company group were holed badly before reaching the bank. A strong current swept my two leading boats rapidly westwards where the factory 400 yards downstream was ablaze. We were beautifully silhouetted. By using spades as well as inadequate paddles we eventually landed 100 yards east of the factory and got ashore without much trouble. Moved forward to edge of trees 50 yards from river bank but only two further boatloads joined us. Three had been holed before launching, one was swept downstream and landed below the burning factory, four crossed with us, the other two sunk during the crossing. On the spot strength of 'B' Company were two officers [Whittle and Lieutenant Macdermott] and less than 30 other ranks. Where the trees started was a steep bank about 100 foot high and the enemy were well dug in on the top of it. We started an assault and met very heavy opposition. The Jerries rolled grenades down on us. We gained the top with 50 per cent of our strength. We occupied the trenches at the top with about 15 men. We were joined by the CO [Lt Colonel Tilley], Major Roper

and about 20 men of 'C' Company. They set out to the right to try to contact
'A' Company and ran into opposition immediately. The CO's party advanced
up wooded slopes, were soon surrounded and forced to surrender.

The German kampfgruppen confronting the Dorsets were a naval battalion
Schiffsturmabteilung 10, a battalion of Security Regiment 6, the Security
Regiment Knocke and two Luftwaffe field companies.

315 out of the 350 Dorsets launched got across the river – 13 had been
killed and about 200 captured.

Operation Berlin, the withdrawal from Arnhem and Oosterbeek, was
finally approved by Monty at 0930hrs on Monday 25 September. Club Route
was cut again north of St Oedenrode and was closed to 30th Corps for nearly
36 hours. Three enemy divisions had been identified east of the axis and two
more west across the Scheide. It was obvious that the Island was soon to
become a salient. Levels of ammunition were running down, the RAF no
longer had air supremacy and the weather was deteriorating rapidly. Elst,
where two Tiger and six Panther tanks were accounted for, had finally been
captured.

General Thomas was ordered to protect the west flank, and the east flank
from Elst to the south bank of the Lower Rhine, and to keep a brigade group
in reserve to supervise the dangerous return journey of the Airborne and
remnants of the Dorsets. From 2200hrs on the 25th, 130th Brigade was to be
responsible for the river withdrawal and the CRE, Lt Colonel W.C.A. Henniker,
was in charge of the actual ferrying operations. There were to be two crossing
sites: 260th Field Company RE and 23rd Canadian Field Company opposite
the Airborne perimeter, and 553rd Field Company RE and 20th Canadian
Field Company a mile downstream, where 4th Dorsets had crossed. At each
site would be 21 storm boats and 16 assault boats. A divisional barrage would
be fired to cover the withdrawal, and tracer would be fired on fixed lines to
guide the boat crossings.

On the south bank 5th Dorsets were responsible, appropriately, for Operation
Berlin. Special cooking centres were set up and ambulances marshalled for the
wounded. A large barn in Driel, lit by jeep headlights, was a main reception
centre, where tea and hot stew, rum and blankets were readied. The AQMG,
Lt Colonel McCance, had 40 jeeps equipped with stretchers, as on the narrow
slippery roads jeeps were the only vehicles likely to get through.

At 2100hrs the divisional covering barrage opened up and in heavy
rain and pitch darkness the sapper crews carried their boats over the dyke
walls and down to the water's edge. Lieutenant Bevan taped the route from
the assembly area to the embarkation point. Major G.R. Hartwell's 'D'
Company was in and around the reception centre, and Major H.C. Allen's
'A' Company was on the right at the junction of the road and the railway
embankment. No lights could be used, but the enemy harassed the area with

shell and mortar fire. The boat crews suffered many casualties and Sergeant
Rigler's Pioneer Platoon was called in to help and made several crossings. 'D'
Company was kept very busy regulating the flow of traffic. At one stage 150
exhausted casualties were lying in the company area. In the space of half an
hour 200 mortar bombs fell there. Private H.K. Cuffs remembered: 'We had
some Paras coming through who had swum the river; some were dressed
in ladies' clothes which they had found [in Arnhem].' The strong current
carried some boats downstream but the first flight of boats brought back
100 men. Flames from the burning factory were fanned by the strong wind.
Back and forth the brave sappers went, and by first light 2,000 Airborne and
a few 4th Dorsets had been rescued. But at dawn the enemy could see what
was happening and rained down 88mm shells and mortar bombs, and set up
machine guns in the reeds on the far bank. Despite gunner smoke screens,
the CRE called a halt to the ferrying operation after Major W.A. Vinycomb
of 260th Field Company made one last trip in a storm boat, loaded it with
men, and came back under heavy fire.

Lt General Brian Horrocks had the most difficult role to play in Market
Garden. Besides 30th Corps, he had responsibility on the ground for 101st US
Airborne Division. In his memoirs he wrote:

On arrival at my headquarters at 10 a.m. next morning, the 25th, I found a
gloomy gathering awaiting me. The 4th Dorsets had crossed the night before,
but all communication with them had now ceased; few assault boats were
left, and ammunition was running short. In fact one artillery regiment was
down to five rounds per gun.

General Browning and I came to the conclusion that there was nothing
for it but to withdraw the 1st British Airborne Division over the river. That
night, under a cover of a Corps artillery programme, 2,323 gallant airborne
troops reached our lines. It was a tragic scene. As the exhausted paratroopers
swam or were ferried across the river in torrential rain, it seemed that even
the gods were weeping at this grievous end to a gallant enterprise.

And so ended the battle of Arnhem. Now for the post-mortem. General
Urquhart, the commander of the 1st Airborne Division, has complained
that we were very slow in advancing to the relief of his division. In fact
his criticisms are perfectly reasonable when viewed from the airborne point
of view. If I had been in his position, surrounded by the Germans, fighting
desperately for eight days and always waiting for the 2nd Army which never
arrived, I doubt whether I would have been half so reasonable. But if we
were slow then the fault was mine because I was the commander.

The sense of desperate urgency was there all right. It was not for want of
trying that we failed to arrive in time. I don't believe that any other troops in
the world could possibly have fought better than the Guards and the 82nd
US Airborne Division when they captured the bridges at Nijmegen. But, after

all we were cut off three times, and it is difficult to fight with one hand tied behind you.

... The failure at Arnhem was primarily due to the astonishing recovery made by the German armed forces after their crippling defeat in Normandy. Even if the 2nd German SS Panzer Corps had not been in a position to intervene so rapidly, and if we had succeeded in getting right through to the Zuider Zee, could we have kept our long lines of communication open? I very much doubt it. In which case, instead of 30 Corps fighting to relieve the 1st British Airborne Division, it would then have been a case of the remainder of the 2nd Army struggling desperately to relieve 30 Corps cut off by the Germans north of Arnhem. Maybe in the long run we were lucky.

Out of 8,905 Airborne and 1,100 glider pilots who had landed at Arnhem, 2,163 were rescued, together with 160 Poles and 75 Dorsets. Another 200 were making their escape plans north of the river.

For the next ten days the Wyverns stayed on the Island, fending off many severe counter-attacks from elements of 2nd, 9th, 116th Panzer Division, part of 1st SS Panzers, and 108th Panzer Brigade. General Model's intention was to recapture Nijmegen and force 30th Corps out of the Island. General Horrocks sent the Wyverns a message: 'We have burst through the enemy's defences and secured a passage over two of these rivers ... very soon I hope we shall be advancing into Germany and carrying on the war on German soil.' From 7 October to 10 November the Division was in static defence east of Nijmegen. Operation Clipper, the successful attack on Geilenkirchen with 84th US (Railsplitters) Division, followed.

Back with 30th Corps the Wyverns took part in Operation Veritable, the slogging match in deep mud and under constant rain, to clear the Reichswald, with actions at Materborn, Cleve and Goch. In ten days in February 1945 the Wyverns had taken 2,500 prisoners and advanced 10,000 yards down the Siegfried Line. In early March Xanten and Luttingen, on the west bank of the Rhine, were captured. In Operation Plunder, the massive Monty-inspired crossing of the Rhine, the Division crossed in Buffaloes and the advance continued.

The last word must go to the intrepid, brutal and demanding CO, General Ivo Thomas. A day or so after the end of the war was broadcast, he said to his ADC, Pat Spencer Moore: 'We could cut through those Russians like a knife through butter.' And he would have done.

The Wyvern 'Butcher's' bill was appalling: casualties in the north-west Europe campaign were 12,484, with 2,843 killed, 8,300 wounded and the rest taken prisoner.

Dorsets, Cornwalls, Somersets, Wiltshires, Hampshires and Gloucesters – the superb fighting infantry division from the west of England.

CHAPTER 18

Last Battle of 50th Tyne-Tees Division

The 50th (Tyne-Tees) Northumbrian Division had a long and distinguished history. In the First World War of 1914–1918 it suffered 34,000 casualties in the appalling battles of the Somme, the Scarpe, Passchendaele, Lys and Aisne.

In 1940 the Division fought with the British Expeditionary Force (BEF) under Major General Martel in the battle of Arras, which gave the then unknown General Erwin Rommel a terrible shock. Its 150th and 151st Brigades acted with the 5th Division as rearguards for the BEF retreat to Dunkirk. The 50th had the doubtful honour of being the last division to be evacuated, with its strength reduced to only 2,500.

In April 1941 150th Brigade sailed from Liverpool in the liners *Empress of Asia* and *Empress of Russia* via Freetown, Cape Town, Durban and finally, to Port Tewfik near Suez. Winston Churchill was anxious for a *British* infantry division to join the Australian, New Zealand, Indian and South African divisions in General Auchinleck's army. Two other brigades were dispatched in July 1941 to garrison Cyprus, but after three months they were reunited with 150th Brigade. The Tyne-Tees was sent to Palestine and concentrated around Haifa, then it moved across the Transjordan desert via Baghdad to Kirkuk in Iraq. The object was to deter or defeat an opportunistic German move into the Orient. Churchill promised Stalin that the 50th and 18th Divisions would move into northern Persia to block Hitler's Plan Orient. In January 1942, the crisis over, the Division assembled for the first time in the Western Desert – 69th Brigade from Syria, 151st from Iraq and 150th from Palestine. It was an extraordinary year of travel and no fighting. By April 1943, the 50th Division had taken a major role in the Gazala battles and, in five weeks of attritional fighting, had suffered 9,000 casualties.

Then came Operations Manhood, Lightfoot, Supercharge (Alamein), Pugilist (disaster at Mareth) and Wadi Akarit. Private A.H. Wakenshaw, 9th Durham Light Infantry, Lt Colonel D.A. Seagrim, 7th Green Howards, and Private Eric Anderson, 5th East Yorkshires, each won Victoria Crosses. The Division's losses were well over 10,000 but Montgomery, who trusted the 50th completely, wanted it for Operation Husky, the capture of Sicily. In the thick of the fighting, as ever, the Division's casualties were 462 killed in action, 1,132 wounded and 545 missing, probably taken prisoner. Hundreds of Northumbrians lie buried in the cemeteries of Syracuse and Catania.

Jig Green Sector Assault RE support 50th Tyne-Tees Division clearing Le Hamel and Asnelles. (*Birkin Haward*)

On 5 November 1943 their convoy arrived back in the UK for home leave, only to receive the unfortunate news that Monty wanted the Tyne-Tees to land in Normandy on D-Day as part of Operation Overlord, to liberate France and the rest of Europe. CSM George Warters, 7th Green Howards, recalled:

> We were in the south of England on manoeuvres when Monty gathered us all together and gave us a nice speech about how we were going to have the great honour of being among the first troops ashore on D-Day. We didn't take to it very kindly, after three years of fighting we reckoned we'd done our fair whack. We thought we were coming back to be given a break, but Monty's way was to keep you going and going and going ...

At this point half the Division were newcomers with no fighting experience, but the new GOC, Major General D.A.H. Graham, and all his battalion commanding officers were highly experienced.

The 69th Brigade was composed of the 5th Battalion The East Yorkshires, and the 6th and 7th Battalions The Green Howards. 151st Brigade comprised the 6th, 8th and 9th Battalions of the Durham Light Infantry, and 231st Brigade were all southerners – 2nd Devons, 1st Hampshires and 1st Dorsets. The artillery echelon was made up of 74th, 90th and 124th Field Regiments with towed 25 pdrs, 102nd Anti-tank Regiment and 25th Light Ack-Ack Regiment, plus 2nd Battalion Cheshires with medium machine-guns and mortars.

Gold Beach D-Day, 6 June 1944. 50 Tyne-Tees Division come ashore from landing craft. (*Imperial War Museum B-5262*)

Monty's thorough exercises followed: Duck 1, 2 and 3, Fabius, Tiger and many others.

The 50th Division landed on D-Day in Gold sector on King beach with the hamlets of La Rivière on the left, Le Hamel and Arromanches on the right. The 69th Brigade assault was led by the 6th Battalion Green Howards and 5th Battalion East Yorkshires; both suffered heavy casualties but took all their objectives. CSM Stanley Hollis won the fourth Victoria Cross for the Division – the only one awarded for the D-Day landings. Almost single handedly, with Bren gun, then Sten gun and grenades, he destroyed the large garrison inside the powerful Mont Fleury battery. Not content with that, now armed with a PIAT anti-tank weapon and a Sten, he went storming on throwing deadly grenades in a series of amazingly brave actions.

The Division fought in all the *bocage* battles around Verrières, Lingèvres, Hottot, Tilly, Cristot and Andrieu. Then, in August, Saint-Pierre and Condé were taken in Operation Bluecoat, and the Falaise-Argentan Gap was finally closed.

In Flers and Argentan some 100,000 German troops were trapped. Adolf Hitler said, 'August 15th was the worst day of my life'; of the five German Corps commanders still in the pocket, four got away to safety, while 12 out of 15 divisional commanders managed to escape as well! They left 50,000 prisoners of war and another 10,000 dead. Nearly all their tanks and assault guns – about 500 – were captured or destroyed. 50th Division had done well. They had created a salient 12–15 miles in depth and 1–2 miles wide.

Lt General Brian Horrocks sent a message to the GOC: 'I cannot give you higher praise than by saying that the most experienced battle-fighting Division in the British Army has once more lived up to its high reputation. Well done 50 Div.'

Major I.R. English, in his history of 8th DLI, wrote:

> The route of the Durham brigade took them through the area of the Falaise-Argentan pocket and each man was able to see for himself the havoc that the Allies had inflicted on the fleeing enemy. Both sides and often the middle of the road were jammed with wrecked lorries, guns, horses and tanks. Here and there a truck or gun limber set on fire and smouldering. Abandoned staff cars and many vehicles were packed with loot, field glasses, typewriters, pistols and small arms by the hundred, cases of wine and boxes of ladies' clothing. It was a sight few who saw it will ever forget.

It was a battlefield that decided the fate of France.

After Normandy the GOC issued new tactics. Each battalion would travel behind an armoured force that would keep moving ahead: moving by bounds, waiting until the tanks had a lead of 10 or 12 miles, then travelling that distance in one spell, then harbouring up. The tactical duty was to mop up everything the armour left behind or bypassed, and form a firm base behind them. The infantry battalions had about 130 vehicles, which, spaced 40 yards

Durham Light Infantry anti-tank gunners inspect knocked-out Tiger tank at Bretteville crossroads, Normandy. (*Imperial War Museum B-6045*)

apart, took up three miles of road. The riflemen were bundled into 3-ton TCVs, lorries, Bren gun carriers, jeeps: every possible vehicle. The section of Bren gun carriers led, then the vanguard rifle company, Battalion HQ, then the three other rifle companies. The supporting arms were divided among the rifle companies and placed under their command. There were strict orders to travel at 12 mph. 50th Division's route was L'Aigle, Verneuil, St André and Pacy-sur-Eure. On 29 August it crossed the river Seine through the Wessex Wyvern bridgehead at Vernon, and on the 30th it progressed via Crèvecoeur-le-Grand to Amiens. 9th DLI had two brisk mopping up tasks at Beauvais and 8th DLI in Picquigny.

Isolated pockets of enemy sometimes fought, but often surrendered, sometimes hundreds at a time. Occasionally a bridge would have to be fought for, or a wood cleared which might cost casualties. Major Mellor, 'B' Company 2nd Cheshires, with Corporal Evans and Private Cotterill, found themselves in their jeep in Fouilloy, near Beauvais. With the aid of three FFI (Free French Forces of the Interior) they carried out a small war and ended up with 500 prisoners. Major Martin, 'A' Company, took 53 prisoners near Doullens. The Cheshires were offered plums in Tournai, beer in Renaix, matches in Ninove, and in other places tomatoes, cakes, nuts, flowers and fruit. The girls demanded kisses from 'Tommy'. At Le Bas, Sergeant Lamb discovered the Cheshire side drums, which had been hidden there in the 1940 retreat to Dunkirk. 61st Recce Regiment sent its carrier troop under a sergeant to guard a bridge at Oudenarde on 4 September. An enemy column of 250 infantry, a Mark IV Special Tank and three half-tracks approached the bridge. At 70 yards' range the carrier troop's anti-tank gun opened up and, with four rounds, destroyed all four enemy AFVs. The action went on for seven hours and 60 wounded enemy were collected.

Lieutenant Geoffrey Picot recalled the atmosphere in Arras:

> Old men wept for joy. Old men who had fought *their* war and won it a quarter of a century before and had lived through the shame and horror that had come to them. Outside one house a bearded man in shabby clothes stood rigidly to attention and at the salute as we passed by – as a military duty. On all faces were such expressions of thankfulness, joy as I had not seen *anywhere* before. I was confident that they would remember Britain with gratitude for the rest of their lives. For us also it was unforgettable. All the troops were deeply moved.

On 2 September 231st Brigade followed Guards Armoured to Brussels, via Arras and Douai. Lieutenant Picot 'didn't like the cobbled roads in Belgium, [it made] the carrier drivers and motorcycles skid'. He noted: 'the French sang the Marseillaise, the Belgians, Tipperary. The French shouted "we are free" and the Belgians "welcome to our liberators".' They harboured at Enghien, via Ath. On the way two enemy tanks knocked out carriers and lorries and took petrol but left the food rations. 'In the evening in the plain ahead of us, I saw a large city of white gleaming buildings – Brussels.' On 4–6 September 231st Brigade took part in the ceremonial liberation forces' parades. It was led by Major General Adair, GOC Guards Armoured Division, with the Household Cavalry armoured cars, Lt General Horrocks' HQ staff, the 1st Belgian Brigade, units of Guards Armoured, and a company of 1st Hampshires. Their mortar section was in the suburb of Duilbeck, some of them in a brewery. Hundreds of troops were teaching the Belgians to dance the Hokey-Cokey. They thought *Tipperary* was the British National Anthem. The champagne the liberators drank was marked *pour le Wehrmacht*. Rumours abounded. The war was over. Hitler's gone to Spain. Most of the Hampshires believed the war was over. 'It's on the wireless isn't it?' The *Daily Mirror* and the *News Chronicle* implied the end of the war was imminent. Meanwhile 11th Armoured fought a smart little two-day battle to capture Antwerp and 231st Brigade was sent there to garrison the city whilst 151st Durham Brigade garrisoned Brussels. Casualties for the month of August in 50th Division were 64 officers and 1,162 other ranks, mostly incurred in Operation Bluecoat and the advance towards Condé-sur-Noireau.

50th Division was now ordered to force crossings over the Albert canal, the last important water barrier before the Dutch frontier. The Germans had mustered about ten battalions to defend the crossings over the Albert canal between Antwerp and Hasselt. Some of these were Luftwaffe Flak units, Flieger Ersatz regiments, various Grenadier regiments, and a considerable number of determined and experienced paratroops. The Guards Armoured Division's bridgehead at Beeringen was heavily counter-attacked by German paratroops. 11th Armoured was also switched to the Beeringen bridgehead. On the morning of 8 September 69th Brigade crossed the canal between Steelen and Herenthals, south-west of Gheel. The road bridge, of course, was blown. The canal was about 30 yards wide with a very high, steep nearside bank. Lt Colonel Exham's 6th Green Howards would cross first, with 7th Green Howards following. H-Hour was fixed for 0130hrs on 8 September. There were only two assault boats and 12 reconnaissance boats. Heavy rain fell (which was good), but the moon came out at midnight (which was bad).

Rather surprisingly the dawn found both battalions safely across until the sleepy defenders in Het Punt hamlet woke up and opened fire with mortars and machine-guns. By dawn on the 9th the 5th East Yorkshires arrived and were across the canal unopposed that evening. The enemy in Het Punt were now rudely assaulted by PIAT, 2-inch mortar, Bren and rifle fire. Lieutenant Smith, with ten men, captured two officers and 20 other ranks, and rescued some Green Howards who had been taken prisoner. Brigadier Knox's 69th Brigade had performed a difficult task; now Brigadier Gordon's 151st DLI

Brigade was tasked with enlarging the bridgehead and capturing Gheel. Near Steelen, 8th DLI crossed the canal late on the 8th; its 'A' company suffered heavily and its OC, Major Beattie, was mortally wounded. The 2nd Cheshires deployed their medium machine-guns and 3-inch mortars to great effect. 8th DLI, once across, was counter-attacked and lost 29 casualties. During the night sappers built a new Class 9 folding bridge (suitable for carrying light vehicles), which allowed some of the 61st Recce Regiment armoured cars to get across. Sapper Ron Sheather helped build the folding boat bridge over the Albert canal:

> We made a recce to see where to build this bridge about 100 yards to the left of the blown road bridge. There was a high flood bank to peep over to see the other side and estimate the width for the amount of materials needed. Next afternoon the bridge arrived. We began to unload it. The DLIs arrived with their assault boats for the crossing. The machine guns and mortars were ready to move. When it was dark we started to build it when the shelling started. But lucky for us they concentrated where the old bridge had been blown. We finished the bridge and got the Recce cars and ambulances across before a shell hit the bridge. We got the damaged part out and rowed another raft out to replace it. Soon the ambulances were coming back [full] and a lot of prisoners walking back under escort.

As 7th DLI prepared to cross, shellfire destroyed the bridge. By 1100hrs it had been repaired and 6th DLI carriers and anti-tank guns crossed and helped take the village of Doornboom, 1,500 yards north of the Albert canal. Lt Colonel Green was now ordered to attack Gheel itself, about two miles ahead, behind a barrage and helped by tank support. 'A' company was partly over-run but was reorganised by Major George Wood; 'B' Company was infiltrated and mortared before Major Atkinson got things under control. Major Ken Wood with 'D' Company and their 'big friends' pressed on behind the barrage and reached Gheel.

Captain Winston Field, 6th DLI, was ordered to collect as many men as possible from 'A' Echelon and take them urgently to Gheel to reinforce 'C' Company, which was in danger of being over-run. Afterwards he wrote:

> If we were thankful to reach Gheel, Major Ken Wood of 'D' Company was even more glad to see us. His men had been fighting against heavy odds in the fields in front of the town, across dykes, into the town and then from house to house inside the town and now they were being heavily counter-attacked by the enemy who were numerous enough to cut off odd parties and sections in the street fighting. We loaded the wounded into three carriers and sent 40 prisoners off with them right away – just in time – and that left one platoon, Company HQ and my extra men.

Many enemy dead littered the battlefield and 6th DLI took 165 prisoners plus much equipment – at a cost! The CO was wounded and Major George Wood took command. 9th DLI arrived in Stelen and took Winkelom, a village a mile south-east of Gheel. 8th DLI moved beyond Doornboom towards Gheel to support 9th DLI. 'A' Company was nearly over-run by enemy tanks. Their OC, Captain Ridealgh, was killed, and Sergeant Self took command. 8th DLI reached Stokt by nightfall, helped by Sherwood Ranger Shermans.

The regiments of young Luftwaffe ground troops and elements of 2nd Parachute Division, who had just arrived in lorries from Germany, were determined to retake Gheel and destroy the 50th Division bridgehead. Captain Ewart Clay wrote:

During the period 8–12 September 151st DLI Brigade made and held a bridgehead on the right flank of the original one [which included Gheel, Winkelom, Stokt, Doornboom and Willaars, a triangle with each side of about 3,000 yards]. They did so in the face of the most determined

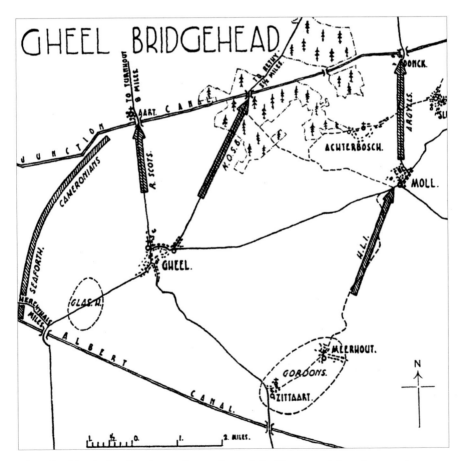

The Gheel bridgehead and assault crossings of the Escaut and Junction canals.

opposition and at the cost of bitter fighting, which led to severe casualties for the Germans. The two German Air Force regiments always had a reputation for good fighting qualities and at Gheel they maintained their traditions until the Durham Light Infantry wore them down and finally disposed of them as fighting units.

Then the Germans brought up the 2nd Parachute Division to try to contain the bridgehead. (This was a repeat of the savage battle at the Primosole bridge in Sicily – same opponents, same results). Early on the evening of 10 September the first enemy tanks appeared against 8th and 9th DLI. One counter-attack came at dusk against 8th DLI with 200 men and 10 tanks determined to reach and smash the Sappers' bridge at Stelen. David Rissik, the DLI historian, wrote: 'The night was one of confusion. The attack was a full-scale one on the Brigade positions. Each battalion stood to all night and there was a good deal of mortaring and shelling. But neither side was willing to move while it was still dark. So the position remained confused and uncertain throughout the Brigade area for the rest of the night.' Besides the divisional gunners who were kept busy firing defensive fire tasks most of the time, the Sherwood Rangers (who lost many tanks to Panthers), the 2nd Cheshires' medium machine-guns and mortars, and the anti-tank battery of Northumberland Hussars all played their part in the four-day battle. At one stage, 6th DLI in Gheel was completely cut off. It was probably the most awful battle the DLI had been involved in since D-Day in June.

On the evening of the 12th the DLI Brigade withdrew over the canal to Pael, three miles west of the Beeringen bridgehead, and 15th Scottish took over responsibility for the Gheel bridgehead. During September 50th Division incurred 918 casualties, mostly in the Gheel bridgehead, and took 2,300 prisoners. Shortly afterwards the shattered German forces pulled back from Gheel and retired over the Escaut canal.

The next major operation was Market Garden; 50th Division would act as reserve to 30th Corps behind the Guards Armoured Division and 43rd Wessex Wyverns. Its eventual task was to secure the high ground of Arnhem. Lt General Horrocks, GOC 30th Corps, gave all the senior officers an upbeat, optimistic speech about the forthcoming operation, to start on 17 September.

The Division's field artillery and mortars of the Cheshire regiment joined in the opening barrage. The ground attack started at 1435hrs and despite 'Division Walther' of five battalions defending the white concrete road to Eindhoven, the Irish Guards' Shermans reached Valkenswaard, five miles south of Eindhoven, by dusk. The 1st Dorsets and 2nd Devons were now called up to clear woods on the left of the Guards advance. 'We went over the Escaut bridge to relieve the Irish Guards,' wrote Lieutenant Picot, 1st Hampshires:

The only operational maps were German with much more detail. We came across a German patrol of 12 men with bazookas stalking Sherman tanks. There was a lot of 'guns over the Rhine' optimism. But it was 65 miles from the Canal to Arnhem. It was a huge barrage in a semi-circle ahead of the advancing tanks. We saw men on parachutes dropping and Typhoon aircraft firing their rockets, and the Guards armour going over the main bridge 700 yards to our right, three vehicles abreast.

Early on the 18th the Dorsets took over Valkenswaard. Their CO became town governor and established liaison with PAN, the Dutch resistance. 9th DLI had to repel a counter-attack on the Escaut bridgehead. On the 19th the Guards advanced north through the bridgeheads at Son, Veghel and Grave and into Nijmegen. There it took two days of severe fighting before the town and its great bridge was cleared. On the 22nd 69 Brigade was in trouble when two battalions of Hermann Göring Parachute training troops and a regiment of tanks cut the main Corps centre-line near Uden, eight miles south of the bridge at Grave. The East Yorkshires in the north were separated from the Green Howards. Fortunately, the divisional artillery and the 101st US Airborne troops fended off the German attackers, who next day repeated their incursion into Veghel. This time the artillery and Guards Armoured stood firm. Sergeant Max Hearst, 5 East Yorkshires wrote:

> We crossed the bridge and took over from the Yanks, our forward platoons were engaging Jerry. When we approached the bridge there was a lot of dead American Paras laid out [in Nijmegen]. Here we met the German storm-troopers, the death or glory boys, they were firing at our lads. One or two of our boys – good marksmen – were picking off these Germans. We dug in both sides and held the position for a number of days. Frogmen came up the river to blow the bridge but they were spotted in time and shot in the water.

Rations were short because of the road congestion. 69th Brigade was thus forced to eat captured German rations. There was an uproar – the jam tasted like rubber, the margarine was rancid and the regimental medical officers confirmed that the meat was bad! 151st DLI and 231st Brigades were ordered to move north and east of Eindhoven to guard the right flank; Eindhoven had been badly damaged by Allied bombers and also by the Luftwaffe. The two brigades moved through Lieshout, Stiphout and Veghel to Boekel. On the Sunday 20 % of the troops could attend their padres' religious services – occasionally under fire. On the 26th the villages of Mill, St Hubert and St Agatha near the German border were occupied. On the same day a determined counter-attack by German forces, again at Veghel, was thrown back after two days' confused fighting. It was no wonder that the attempts to relieve the brave, beleaguered British Airborne in Arnhem were eventually doomed.

The exhausted survivors of 1st Airborne Division were arriving in Nijmegen on the afternoon of 26 September. It became even more important to retain the area on the north side of the river Waal as German infantry and tanks engaged at Arnhem were now freed for action against the Nijmegen bridgehead. The recapture of the bridge was the enemy's immediate objective. The whole of 50th Division was now tasked with guarding the bridge and bridgehead. The battleground between the rivers Maas, Waal and Lower Rhine became known as the Island, an area of flat, rich pastures, mingled with orchards of apple and pear and criss-crossed by numerous canals and ditches. It was also overlooked by the high ground beyond Arnhem. The low-lying ground meant that it was difficult to dig a trench deeper than two feet without striking water. From 25 September battles raged for more than a week for possession of the little villages of Bemmel, Baal and Haalderen, and the woods between them. First of all 5th East Yorkshires captured Bemmel on the 25th, and on the 26th and 27th the two Green Howards' battalions tried to take Haalderen, a village with factories whose tall chimneys made excellent observation points for the enemy. Panzer tanks and 88mm anti-tank guns dominated all the approaches. On the 28th the Luftwaffe, in a series of aggressive attacks, tore a 40-foot gap in the Nijmegen railway bridge, and frogmen damaged the main road bridge. The first serious German counter-attack came on 30 September on the East Yorkshires, with 70 tanks and the equivalent of an infantry division. The rest of 69th Brigade and 5th Guards Brigade were holding the line, and

AT THE OP A VISITING BRASS HAT SAW A WALKING GERMAN SOLDIER & ASKED IF WE COULD KILL HIM — CALCULATIONS WERE MADE — BOMBS FIRED — & 60 SECONDS RUNNING COMMENTARY OF THE SCENE & HIS MOVEMENTS WAS RELAID OVER THE RADIO — THE FIRST 2 ROUNDS MORTAR FIRE HIT HIM — THE SECOND KILLED HIM.

A SECTION SHOOT FROM A FARM YARD NORTH OF BEMMEL (AN INFANTRY BN HQ.) WE – 15 PI. — WERE NOT WELCOME GUESTS BUT IT WAS THE ONLY LAND OUT OF WATER NEAR ENOUGH.

CAPT DICK THORNHILL WHO WAS AT THE O.P.

MICHAEL BAYLEY 2 KENSINGTONS

2 Kensingtons fire their 3-inch mortars in the Peel countryside. (*Michael Bayley*)

another attack was put in on the Wessex Wyverns across the Lower Rhine. The intensity of attack and defence can be judged by 124th Field Regiment, RA, who fired a total of 12,500 25-pound shells during the action, and 'B' Company of 2nd Cheshires, who fired 95,000 rounds of medium machine-gun fire. Twelve enemy tanks infiltrated the 7th Green Howards' position, which with great difficulty they held from 0700hrs to 1100hrs, when the East Yorks relieved them. Squadrons of 13/18th Hussar tanks supported 69th Brigade most effectively. The GOC ordered 151st Durham Brigade and 231st Brigade up to relieve 69th Brigade.

On 4 October 8th DLI attacked towards Haalderen and 9th DLI towards Baal, with the familiar barrage and close support from rocket-firing Typhoons. 8th DLI succeeded and took 60 prisoners, but 9th DLI encountered heavy Spandau fire; 'A' Company lost all its officers except Captain Thomson. By 1600hrs 100 prisoners had been captured as well as many anti-tank guns, mortars and bazookas. 6th DLI moved forward to tackle a factory near Bemmel and for several days carried out fighting patrols. On 7 October the brigade moved back into Nijmegen for a few days rest. Lt Colonel Hammer, CO of 6th DLI, commanded a bridge defence force of AA, anti-tank gunners, searchlights, DUKWs for river patrols, a field security section, a Dutch Civil Police section and four explosives experts. 231st Brigade was also tasked with straightening the line of Haalderen and Baal, and clearing woods. During 4–5 October Lieutenant Picot, 1st Hampshires, wrote: 'It was the first set-piece attack since St Pierre-La-Vieille in Normandy with shelling, mortaring heavy on both sides. Although the attack was successful the Hampshires had 22 men killed in action.'

Early in November Field Marshal Montgomery made a speech to the Division's officers in a cinema in Bourg-Leopold. The gallant Tyne-Tees would return to England as a training division for reinforcements. 9th Durham Light Infantry would join the Desert Rats infantry brigade. There were two schemes: LILOP (leave in lieu of Python) would ensure generous leave, whilst Python meant that veterans who had served for three and a half years or more would be repatriated to England. A substantial minority of the Division, mainly the replacements (358 officers and 8,019 other ranks) for earlier casualties, were posted to other formations. Since D-Day 50th Division had suffered total casualties of 488 officers and 6,932 other ranks. Winston Churchill was furious that this famous division would, in effect, be disbanded, but not even he could cancel War Office policy.

CHAPTER 19

Polish Brigade Tragedy

In September 1939 Britain and France went to war with Germany when Adolf Hitler unleashed his storm troopers, the Wehrmacht, and the deadly Luftwaffe Stukas on Poland. Hitler had signed a ten-year non-aggression pact with the Poles in 1934 – one of the many treaties not worth the paper on which it was printed. Poor Poland was sandwiched between the two monsters: Stalin's communist hordes to the north, and the aggressive Nazi regime to the south. These jackals then divided the spoils as Poland was ravaged. The Polish Buro Szufrow, the secret Cipher Bureau, had managed to break the unbreakable Enigma coding machine used by all the German services including the Reichbahn railway system. Colonel Gwido Langer, the able head of the Bureau, secretly produced Enigma machines at the Ava factory in Warsaw and on 25 July 1939 handed over an Enigma machine from his stock of 15 to his opposite numbers in the British and French secret services. The rest is history.

During 1940 many hundreds of brave young Poles made their way with difficulty to Britain. Some joined the RAF, and many others were trained to operate and fight with tanks. Thus the fine Polish Armoured Division was formed and fought in Normandy, and a Polish Corps fought in the Italian campaign. They all had one thing in common – an almost reckless bravery.

The First Polish Independent Parachute Brigade was established in October 1941 under the command of Colonel Stanislaw Sosabowski, a veteran of the First World War, and of the Polish-Soviet war of 1919–20. He also commanded a brigade in the battles in Warsaw in September 1939. He had no airborne experience, but had more experience of fighting the Germans than most Allied officers. A proud man, he was sometimes indelicate in pointing out the flaws in the plans of his superiors, the traditional duty of a commander, thus creating difficult dealings with his Polish senior officers. He was nicknamed 'stary' (an affectionate form of 'old') or 'Old Sosab', and was immensely popular with his men. Major General Roy Urquhart, GOC 1st Airborne Division, wrote:

A very highly trained soldier, Sosabowski was also a character with a vengeance. Like most of the Poles, he had a natural courtesy which contrasted violently with the sudden outbursts in speech and temper that positively withered any erring individual of whose behaviour or methods he did not approve. Nevertheless, when during the months of training I visited

Major General Stanislas Sosabowski.

his brigade several times, I soon found that he not only had the affection of his men, but was tremendously well respected by all those who served with him – two attributes to a commander which in my experience have not always gone hand-in-hand together.

He was a small, tough, wiry man, but brave in spades! Sosab had served with the reconstituted Polish Army in France in 1940 and had escaped via Dunkirk to England. When the parachute unit was conceived jointly by Sosab and the Polish General Staff in London, the rationale was that an airborne operation might eventually get liberating troops back into Poland. The Brigade's motto translated as: 'By the shortest way'. It remained under direct control of the Polish government-in-exile until June 1944. The Poles established a sophisticated parachute training centre at Leven, near Fife in Scotland. General Sikorski, the Polish commander-in-chief, had negotiated with the British CIGS, Alan Brooke, the complete independence of the Polish Brigade and the principle that it would be used *only* for the liberation of Poland.

However, Major General Frederick 'Boy' Browning, the so-called 'Father of the British Airborne Forces', was intent on expanding his empire from his first arrival on the scene on 21 November 1941. When General Sikorski died in an air crash on 4 July 1943, Browning persuaded Alan Brooke and General Montgomery to employ Sosab's brigade on the European mainland, subject to conditions. No one in those days put conditions to Monty, and on D-Day 1944 the Polish cabinet-in-exile gave way and Browning got his 'evil' way. On 10 August the Brigade came under command of 1st Airborne Division.

The Polish Brigade was now on call from Browning for the various planned drops, which were duly aborted. Operation Comet, scheduled for 8 September, tasked 4th Parachute Brigade with seizing the crossing over the river Maas near Grave. Sosabowski claimed that the Poles were to support Brigadier Hackett's drop at Grave. At the briefing at RAF Cottesmore on 6 September, the Pole repeatedly shouted out 'What about the Germans?' indicating that no information was available about the enemy dispositions. Sosab and Urquhart flew to HQ where Browning waffled away and eventually asked Sosab for his solution to Comet. 'Simple' was the answer, three airborne *divisions* were needed, not brigades! Comet was cancelled on 10 September.

The orders for Market, the airborne army part of Market Garden, took place at Moor Park on 12 September, with D-Day set for the 17th. The Polish Brigade was scheduled for the third lift. The parachute element was to land on dropping zone 'K', just south-east of the Arnhem bridge at a village called Elden, which was ideal for capturing the southern end of the Arnhem bridge. It was polder country and deemed unsuitable for a glider drop. It could also lead the Poles to capture Elst on the road to Arnhem. The Poles' heavy equipment, artillery, transport, ammunition, and Brigade troops would land by 46 gliders on landing zone 'L'. The Poles' main artillery, 12 75mm guns, was actually deleted from the drop and would arrive separately via Normandy. The implicit message was that the Poles were second-class soldiers to be used as extra ground troops. Urquhart then told Sosab that if the bridge was not taken when the Poles arrived, they were expected to capture it!

The third parachute lift was 48 hours late due to poor weather over the airfields in England – two *whole* days in mid-September? So 114 US C-47 Dakotas took off with the 1,689 Poles on board early in the afternoon of Thursday 21 September. Forty-one planes were recalled shortly afterwards when the weather closed in again. The Germans were now four days into Market. They were highly organised with a Flak Brigade of 88mm, 37mm and 20mm anti-aircraft guns that had been sent from the Ruhr to the Arnhem area and had arrived on the 19th. Despite a ferocious barrage, only five C-47s were lost, and they all managed to dispatch their 'sticks' of paratroopers.

Corporal David Salik, a young Polish medical orderly, remembered that on the flight 'we were just eager to jump out. We were young Poles and the Germans were a real enemy – they were murderers, and we all, Jew and non-Jews felt very strongly that we should fight them. And we were all ready to fight. The Germans were shooting at us like ducks.'

Almost at the last moment, on the 20th, Major General Urquhart, unaware of the situation outside his Oosterbeek HQ, had managed to radio a message back to England asking for the Polish drop to be altered to a new dropping zone (DZ) to the west of Driel village, just a mile south of the Lower Rhine. In effect he wanted some more foot soldiers to join him in what was known as the 'Cauldron', thus deliberately reducing the chances of the 30th Corps armour and infantry drive from Nijmegen northwards to Elst getting through to Arnhem. The 1,000 skilled, tough, brave Polish paratroops, even at the late stage of the 21st, might have made all the difference. Lt General Brian

Horrocks was not on top form and seemed bewildered by having to deal with his Major Generals Adair, Thomas, Browning, and then possibly Sosabowski. The distance from Elden, the original planned drop site, to Driel was four miles, but it might as well have been 40 miles. Kampfgruppe (Kapitan Peter) Knaust, reinforced by eight Panther tanks and assault guns, had crossed the Arnhem bridge shortly after mid-day on the 21st and by 1600hrs had reached Elst. It was now strong enough to stop any armoured attack that Horrocks and Adair could muster. Probably Operation Market was doomed from that moment.

SS Colonel Heinz Harmel, commander of the Frundsberg 10th SS Panzer Division, wondered later: 'Why did they [Allied armour] not drive on to Elst instead of staying in Lent [a suburb north of Nijmegen]? At this instant there were no German armoured forces available to block Elst.' He wrote in *Die Frundsberg in Nijmegen* published by Schneider in 1956: 'It gave us time to get Knaust down there. It was ironic really, at the same time we lost the Nijmegen bridge, we were just about over the Arnhem bridge. The Allied infantry were too late supporting their tanks.' In fact Sosab in the lead plane had passed over Eindhoven, turned north, and seen hundreds of chaotic traffic jams below on 'Hell's Highway', with trucks blazing and shells landing. Over Driel he could see panzers on the road from Arnhem. But 1,003 men did land at 1700hrs; in their drop the Poles had five men killed and 25 wounded. Sosab, on arrival, discovered that over a third of his men had failed to arrive due to the weather recall, nor could he get through to Urquhart's HQ by radio. He sent one battalion north to the Lower Rhine for the Heveadorp ferry, and the other battalion to make for the river bank opposite Oosterbeek church. Major W. Ploszewski commanded the 2nd Battalion and Captain Sozocinske the 3rd Battalion.

Lt Colonel George Stevens was British liaison officer to the Polish Brigade and reported from 1st Allied Airborne Army HQ at 0700hrs on 21 September that the Heveadorp cable ferry was *definitely* still in British hands.

General Urquhart had signalled Browning: '[we] still maintain control ferry point at Heveadorp'. This was, unfortunately, totally untrue. Two small patrols had been to look at the cable ferry. The second patrol found no sign of the ferry and found the cable broken, possibly by a shell or mortar bomb. Cornelius Ryan tells the story well about Pieter Hensen's ferry (pp 442–5).

In his memoirs Sosab recalled that after all these misfortunes his brigade 'was being sacrificed in a complete British disaster'. Unable to raise the 1st Airborne by radio, the Polish liaison officer, Captain L. Zwolanski, swam across the 400 yards of the Rhine river, found Sosab and told him that Urquhart wanted the Poles to cross that night and would have rafts to ferry them across. Lt Colonel Myers had promised rafts that never came. Sosab later commented: 'At 3 am I knew the scheme had failed. I pulled my men back into a defensive perimeter.'

There was little, if any, military justification for dropping the Poles around Driel. Even if the Heveadorp cable ferry had been working, the arrival of the lightly armed Poles would not have made any difference to the outcome of the Oosterbeek battle. On Friday 22 September, D+5, the Wessex Wyvern Division arrived in strength at Driel, and that night the Kampfgruppe Brinkmann attacked the Polish perimeter. Hampered by the polder soggy ground, ditches and dykes, the German half-tracks and armoured cars made little progress. Nevertheless, Sosab's men were ferried over the river in a little string of small rubber boats. There were only four boats: two two-man, two one-man. Several wooden rafts carried basic stores. 'A slow laborious process,' Sosab noted. Soon Spandau fire was raking the river crossing and by 0300hrs the operation was cancelled. Only 50 Poles got over safely, with many killed or wounded in the river or on the banks. The ordeal continued on the next night, D+6. Under a heavy barrage 16 boats carried more Poles into the 'Cauldron'; 250 made it to the northern bank, and 200 reached the Airborne perimeter.

On the morning of 24 September Sosabowski went to Valburg for a conference with the three generals: Horrocks, Browning and 'Butcher' Thomas, GOC 43rd Wessex Wyverns Division. Thomas declared that the river would be crossed that night by a battalion of 4th Dorsets, followed by a battalion of Poles, with their second battalion crossing the river further east. Sosab pointed out that feeding more troops in small amounts into the Oosterbeek perimeter was achieving very little; what was needed was a major assault across the river further downstream by the entire division, a plan that had occurred already to Horrocks. Horrocks now took umbrage and told Sosab that if he did not like the plan he would be relieved of his command. It looked already as though Browning, Horrocks, and even Field Marshal Montgomery, had decided that the Poles were to be the scapegoats for any failures at Oosterbeek.

Predictably, on the night of the 24th five lorry loads of assault boats were sent up to Driel. Disaster struck the whole crossing. Four lorry loads never arrived, and the one that did lacked paddles! There were therefore no boats available for 130th Brigade and 4th Dorsets, so the Poles were duly sacrificed. Only 300 Dorsets got across that night; the rest were swept down river by the current and landed in a German position where they were killed, wounded or captured.

Fifty Poles were killed at Oosterbeek or drowned in the final evacuation. Another 42 died in combat south of the river, and a further 111 were missing or were made prisoner.

Finally, Sosab marched the survivors 14 miles to Nijmegen, with their heavy equipment. Browning sent them to help guard the Nijmegen road bridge and the Maas–Waal canal crossings to deter sabotage by German frogmen. On 7 October the Brigade came out of the line and was back in England by air or sea before the 12th.

Vitriol from Browning to Horrocks and Montgomery, and then to the CIGS Alan Brooke, did its work. Sosabowski was relieved of his command on 9 December 1944.

CHAPTER 20

Black Bull: 11th Armoured right flank protection

11th Armoured Division, with its provocative insignia of a violent black bull with scarlet hoofs, horns and face on a strong yellow background, was a formidable, but untried formation when it landed in Normandy in mid-June 1944. It had never been in action before but had been very well trained on the Yorkshire moors by Major General Percy Hobart, whose family coat of arms included a fighting bull. The Division consisted of 29th Armoured Brigade (3rd Royal Tank Regiment, 23rd Hussars and 2nd Fife and Forfar Yeomanry) and 159th Infantry Brigade (1st Herefords, 3rd Monmouthshires and 4th King's Shropshire Light Infantry), and was backed by the 2nd Northants Yeomanry Reconnaissance Regiment (replaced after Normandy by 15/19th Hussars) and the 8th Battalion Rifle Brigade. The four artillery regiments were 13th RHA (Honourable Artillery Company), 151st Field Regiment (Ayrshire Yeomanry) TA, 75th Anti-tank Regiment and 5th Light Anti-aircraft Regiment. An armoured division was composed of approximately 15,000 men, including 724 officers, and an astonishing total of 3,410 vehicles. There were 246 Sherman tanks, one in four of which were Fireflies, with the invaluable 17-pdr gun installed. There were 44 light tanks (Cromwells) and 100 Scout cars, plus 261 Bren gun carriers and half-tracks, which had ring-mounted 0.5mm machine guns.

The GOC was the desert veteran, Major General 'Pip' Roberts, who had earned a DSO and two MCs in North Africa, and at 37 was the youngest major general in the British Army. All the senior officers were also desert veterans, including Brigadier Roscoe Harvey and Brigadier John Churcher. The author's regiment was commanded by Lt Colonel Robert Daniell, who had earned a DSO in the desert, but the only regular battle-trained unit was 3rd RTR.

Soon blooded in Operations Epsom, Goodwood and Bluecoat, the Black Bull distinguished itself time and again. It reached the top of Hill 112 in mid-June before ULTRA warned Montgomery that two SS Panzer divisions were advancing from the south to cut off, isolate and destroy the Black Bull. In Goodwood the Division lost 195 tanks and 735 casualties to massed 88mm dual-purpose AA/Anti-tanks guns on Bourguebus Ridge. In Bluecoat, Montgomery's only genuine victory in Normandy, it smashed its way 14 miles from Caumont to the Vire-Vassy highway, and fought 9th SS and 10th SS Panzer divisions to a standstill.

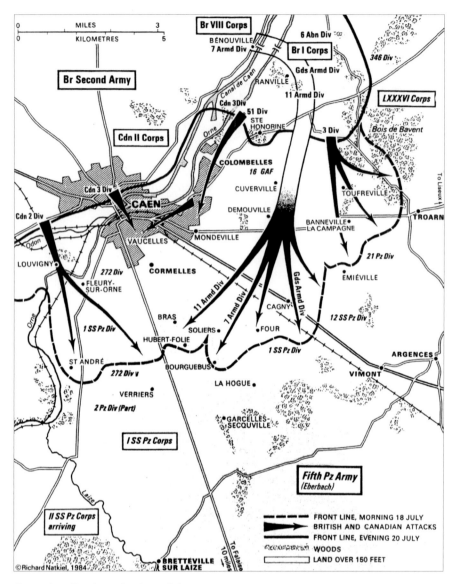

Operation Goodwood, 18–20 July 1944.

The 'Great Swan' was unique in British military history. Montgomery's four armoured divisions and two independent armoured brigades swarmed northwards under Lt General Brian Horrocks. It was exhilarating stuff – Guards on the right heading for Brussels, 11th in the centre for Antwerp, the 7th Desert Rats and the Polish Armoured on the left flank heading for Lille and Ghent. On 2 September the advance was halted for an airborne drop around Tournai, but the drop was cancelled. Numerous V-bomb launch sites were over-run and destroyed and many First World War battlefields were passed on the way through northern France into Belgium, and a date with General von Stolberg-zu-Stolberg.

Operation Goodwood, 18 July. A Red Cross half track and 11th Armoured Sherman tanks are in the background. In the foreground is a Crab Flail. (*Imperial War Museum B-7521*)

So, the advance resumed against hardening opposition. On 8 September 29th Armoured Brigade moved off eastwards, 3rd RTR and 15/19th Hussars came under 159th Brigade and 1st Herefords under 29th Armoured.

8th RB and 3rd RTR went off on a 'peacetime' march through liberated territory – Malines, Aarschot to Diest – where they harboured alongside the Americans who had more or less run out of petrol. Roland Jefferson's route followed the Guards Armoured centre line to Diest, where his RB company met the Princess Irene's Netherlands Regiment. The Inns of Court patrolled the Albert canal as far east as Herenthals; the 15/19th Hussars silenced some enemy guns at Burght on the west bank of the river Scheldt; and 23rd Hussars were diverted to Beeringen where the Guards had already bridged the Albert canal. Everyone was sad to leave the fleshpots of Antwerp behind, except the 4th KSLI who had survived 40 hours of continuous close-quarter fighting across the Albert canal. Its fighting strength was now 211 below the war establishment of 809. On the 9th the Division crossed the Albert canal on a Bailey bridge immediately next to the Guards bridge. By 0600hrs Lieutenant Steel Brownlie and the Fifes were 'having a café breakfast party with the owner and his daughters who played the piano, eating fried eggs, drinking coffee and cognac. Never miss a chance.' 8th RB and 3rd RTR occupied Beeringen and combed the immense surrounding woodlands; a slow and tiring operation helped by Princess Irene's Dutch infantry.

On the following day, 10 September, 8th RB and 23rd Hussars led on the right, and immediately ran into tough opposition a mile north-east at Koersel. Noel Bell's 'G' Company and 'A' Squadron 23rd Hussars looped round to the north and caught the enemy looking the wrong way, but, as they moved on, 8th RB ran into a considerable number of German paratroopers. They were part of General Kurt Student's hastily assembled First Paratroop Army: 'very lightly armed, very badly organised but who fought fanatically, preferring to shoot themselves rather than be taken prisoner. They suffered enormous casualties and the carnage over the whole area was the greatest we had yet witnessed. Darkness fell and we spent the night in a field with the tanks expecting to be attacked.' The grounded Luftwaffe crews, young men of high morale, fanatical and desperate, suffered 500 casualties. Each paratrooper was armed with a bazooka but few tanks or carriers were hit. 8th RB had 11 killed and 2nd Hussars three – a real classic victory by a determined, well-planned attack

Meanwhile, the Herefords and 2nd Fife and Forfarshires pushed north towards Hechtel early on the 10th, and reached Wijcmael against determined resistance, taking 400 prisoners. The heather was burning, and smoke obscured the view. The Herefords then arrived and cleared the enemy with their bayonets. Four hundred German so-called paratroopers were disarmed and herded up by the railway line. Steel Brownie noted 'They had been dug in, in a piece of ground not much larger than a rugby pitch, over which I had been charging for about half an hour.' A marvellous effort. The battle group then headed for Peer, bypassing Hechtel, where practically every Fife tank was bogged down in low-lying marshland. 'We sat there till night fell.' The Herefords had many men killed in the fighting around Hechtel and Helchteren. 4th KSLI and 15/19th Hussars moved south-east and four miles north of Hasselt. Lieutenant Ted Deeming, 15/19th Hussars, wrote:

> It was close country with lots of marsh and short fields of view; treacherous going for tanks and the fighting was severe and confused. The opposition was A/Tk guns of all calibres, at least 2 SP guns and probably a Panther tank, all located east of the road, 3½ miles north of the Albert canal. The regiment inflicted many casualties on the enemy, destroyed two SP guns, four A/Tk guns and three tanks but lost 21 casualties themselves. Squadron Leader Lord Rathdonnell found himself 60 yards away from a Jagd-Panzer IV. His gun jammed, the SP fired and missed and a bazookaman hit the Cromwell, but no real damage!

The following day, the 11th, 8th RB and 23rd Hussars advanced to Peer and met some resistance. It was a beautiful, clear autumn morning and strangely peaceful after the battles the day before. The enemy had vanished as in a dream, leaving many dead behind. But bazookas soon claimed several Hussar tanks, Lieutenant Evans was captured but fortunately recaptured a few hours later. Captain Norman Young, 'I' Battery 13th RHA, had a narrow squeak. Fired at by an 88mm gun, he replied with his 75mm and hit it with his first shot, even though his sights were 400 yards out of true! The battle group advanced to Petit Brogel, Linove and Grand Brogel, where the villagers gave 8th RB a warm welcome.

During the day the Inns of Court had investigated all possible canal crossings between Peer and Neerpelt – all bridges were blown and covered by enemy fire from the far bank, as 23rd Hussars had discovered.

159th Infantry Brigade had a relatively peaceful day. 3rd Mons/3rd RTR cleared up Laak and concentrated round Helchteren. 4th KSLI and 15/19th Hussars took over and approached Bree from the south-west; after some skirmishes they found the bridge, which was then, not surprisingly, blown up in their faces.

On 12 September the Inns of Court kept up their canal patrols and found Bree on the west bank to be free of the enemy. 13th RHA and Ayrshire Yeomanry fired heavy stonks on the defenders between 0815hrs and 0845hrs in support of the 1st and 2nd Welsh Guards, who finally turfed the spirited German resistance out of Hechtel. Many Guards tanks were knocked out in the morning attack amid savage fighting. 3rd Mons/3rd RTR then moved in to occupy Hechtel, or what was left of it. Trooper Ernie Hamilton, 15/19th Hussars, wrote:

We arrived at a small bridgehead [on 13 September] over the Meuse-Escaut Canal to protect the road on the left of the regiment, some 200 yards from the Dutch border. Next morning brought 2nd troop 'C' squadron's first tank battle; to our front appeared four Mark IV tanks. It was here the troop made regimental history; this battle brought us an MC, two MMs and a mention-in-dispatches. We had knocked out the German tanks but not without our own casualties, two tanks hit. My own hit twice, my guns were damaged unable to fire and our 19 set filled with shrapnel like myself. My operator Percie Downing was killed, his first moments in action, he was eighteen years old.

The Division spent another five days around Hechtel, Peer and Petit Brogel, until 16 September when they rested and reorganised in their first real break since L'Aigle. 8th RB and the infantry sent out patrols to the line of the Escaut canal. Roland Jefferson recorded: 'German patrols were active and there was many a skirmish. On night patrols it was an uncomfortable feeling to go out in the dead of night, face blackened.' He carried a 38 radio set, of short range but with a throat microphone. Words were whispered, translated into pulses through the throat mikes, and thus transmitted back. Lieutenant Steel Brownlie and Geoff Hales 'explored Peer's cafés, scrounged for eggs in a liberated Volkswagen, drank much Cointreau (ex-Wehrmacht), had a hot shower in a pit-head baths, had a letter from Maria in Antwerp, were shelled occasionally, played piano in cafés, put clocks back one hour. What next?' During their stay at Petit and Grand Brogel, 23rd Hussars, 8th RB and the rest of the Division enjoyed the vast collection of wines, liqueurs and cigars, 'liquid booty', acquired in Antwerp. On the 13th a deception force, consisting of a company of Herefords and a squadron of Fifes, engaged the enemy around Bree to persuade them that a big attack was coming. FOOs of 13th RHA and Ayrshire Yeomanry occupied observation points in Bree church tower and every other high building on the west bank of the canal, to harass the enemy with minor fire targets.

General Roberts described the new German opposition: 'The Germans now consisted of a number of "battle groups" bearing the name of their commanders [Hermann, Haregg, Hubner and Grassmehl]: their divisions had broken up but the groups still had a very high morale, particularly those of SS or Paratroops: they would often fight on without any officers.' The killing grounds were going to be different too: 'The country was heavily "canalised" and with natural obstacles little work is required to convert them into a strong line of defence very quickly.' To deal with this situation the Division was once again organised into mixed brigade groups with the Inns of Court armoured cars, like busy little fox terriers, aggressively reconnoitring ahead and on the flanks. The general also wrote:

> In Normandy there was always real anxiety: if one made wrong decisions, if the front were penetrated by the Germans, if our line of communication was cut, the result could be catastrophic. Now mistakes or failures could only delay the end. Unless morale was high we would not achieve our objectives; heavy casualties in a fruitless battle will not help morale. We must try to win our battles without heavy casualties; not very easy.

On the start line of Market Garden on 17 September, north of Neerpelt, 13th RHA and Ayrshire Yeomanry joined the immense artillery barrage. Two specific targets were engaged just after midday, and between H-hour at 1435hr and 1450hrs there were three more heavy concentrations. Rocket-firing Typhoons were also in action. On the 18th vigorous enemy patrols crossed the canal in the factory area of Neerpelt and bombarded Ayrshire Yeomanry rather intensely. But there were no casualties and the enemy were pushed back. *Taurus Pursuant* mentions that two small mercenary forces now appeared to protect the canal towns of Bree and Bocholt. They were a mixed bag of Russians and French dressed in various uniforms with German arms and equipment. The Germans were amazed, the Belgians perplexed, the Division amused, and the FFI miffed. On the 18th 4th KSLI replaced Breeforce and Tineforce and also occupied Bocholt. 3rd Mons was holding the line at Wijcmael.

Monumental traffic jam near Eindhoven. The author's Sexton SP 25-pdr regiment (13 RHA) about to go into action. His troop was 200 yards away. (*Imperial War Museum B-10244*)

On 19 September the Black Bull moved across the Escaut canal at Lille-St-Hubert through 3rd British Division's bridgehead. 2nd Fife and Forfarshires, 1st Herefords and a squadron of Inns of Court led, but were held up by a blown bridge at Schaft, then headed north towards Volkenswaard.

Lieutenant Steel Brownlie remembered: 'Around the Escaut canal there was much wreckage; at last we reached the outskirts of Volkenswaard, clean, tidy, very Dutch and undamaged. Just outside there were nine Guards tanks nose to tail, all burned out and graves by the roadside. We harboured a mile beyond the town and saw and heard an air raid on Eindhoven.' The following day the advance continued east-north-east with two centre lines. On the left 8th RB and 23rd Hussars reached Heeze, which they cleared without difficulty. The 2nd Fife and Forfarshires and the Herefords passed through Heeze via Leende. Steel Brownlie's route was 'via a maze of sandy tracks among fir trees, inadequate maps but help from Dutch patriots. Small bridges kept collapsing. We finally harboured, shell and mortar fire all night, near the blown bridge between Zomeren and Asten. No sleep, refuelling risky.' On the right flank 3rd Mons and 3rd RTR had cleared Budel and Soerendonk and were nearing Maarheeze. 13th RHA passed into Holland via Heeze, Zomeren and then Geldrop. It was awkward country for guns, with marshy open ground and coppices giving good cover for snipers. The Ayrshire Yeomanry supported 3rd Mons with crash action targets fired on Toom, north-east of Hamont, and on

2nd Troop 'A' Squadron 15/19th Hussars in Geldrop, 19 September 1944.

15/19th Hussars in Geldrop, 19 September 1944.

Budel, reached by 4th KSLI. The night of the 20th the advance battle groups were altered. 3rd RTR/3rd Mons with 23rd Hussars/8th RB were under command of 29th Brigade, and 2nd Fife and Forfarshires, 1st Herefords with 4th KSLI/15/19th Hussars (on their return to the fold) were under command of 159th Brigade. 29th Brigade was directed north, and 159th Brigade to Zomeren on the Willems canal, via Asten, and then to Deurne, with a view to eventually taking Helmond from the rear. On the 21st 8th RB found Geldrop a 'very friendly place'. Noel Bell's riflemen had time to dive into a local barber's and have a haircut and shampoo, but ran into determined resistance at Gerwen, where 23rd Hussar tanks and a carrier were brewed up.

At the hamlet of Stiphout, radio codename 'striptease' (as in Jane of the *Daily Mirror*), 'C' squadron ambushed a force of five Panthers on their way to reinforce Gerwen. Three were destroyed at about 1630hrs, and two Shermans were brewed up. Despite artillery and mortar stonks on Gerwen, 107th Panzer Brigade defended stoutly, but evaporated during the night.

Maarheeze had been cleared in the morning of the 21st by 3rd Mons and 3rd RTR who then followed 23rd Hussars and 8th RB north via Nunen towards Geldrop. Later 3rd RTR pushed on to Hout, south of Helmond. Meanwhile in the Zomeren area due east of Eindhoven, 1st Herefords, 2nd Fife and Forfarshires and 4th KSLI found the town bridges over the Bois le Duc canal blown and covered by enemy fire. Steel Brownlie's squadron spread along the Willems canal looking for a crossing: 'We worked south in thick country with a high bank on our side of the canal, making it difficult to see the far bank. We harboured near the Zomeren/Asten bridge with rain, shells and mortars coming down. We were shocked.' A daring plan had been hatched for the morrow: 'A and D Companies of the Herefords in assault boats had

'A' Squadron Cromwell tanks of the 15th /19th Hussars carrying American paratroops through Eindhoven, 21 September 1944.

got across to make a bridgehead while the sappers were starting to build a Bailey bridge. This was the cause of all the noise as dusk fell, for the enemy were obviously sensitive and were bombarding the area. The opposing force of Assault Engineers were reputed to be good fighters.'

General Roberts related:

> By 2100hrs two companies of Herefords had crossed. Our engineers began to construct a bridge and a searchlight battery had been brought up to give them a better light. At 0200hrs the enemy pressed home a fierce attack on the bridgehead; work had to be stopped. The Herefords rallied, restored the situation. By morning the bridge was ready.

Major Ned Thornburn, 4th KSLI, recalled: 'The bridgehead had been 250 yards deep but the German counter-attack pushed it in to 30 yards when we were due to cross. Jimmy Bratland with the leading platoon, crossed over and with tank support and hand grenade actions extended the bridgehead to allow my other two platoons across.' And later, after Asten was captured: 'That day we took hundreds of prisoners with great help from the tanks.' The KSLI dug in north-east and south of the village to guard the roads and fended off counter-attacks with their 3-inch mortars. The Asten church was used as a first aid station and was full of wounded from both sides. Lance Corporal George, DR with the KSLI, recalled: 'The air was full of the smell of death and destruction. The streets were full of the dead.' Ned Thornburn and Jimmy Bratland both won MCs at the Zomeren/Asten battles. General Roberts wrote: 'Despite a lot of small arms fire, the foremost tanks were moving on towards Ommel by 0900hrs. I was near the bridgehead at the time and was delighted to see this very dashing action.'

8th RB and 23rd Hussars took over from the Fifes at Ommel. Noel Bell reported: 'The Germans had been using cavalry in Ommel, so many dead horses littered the area. Hell was then let loose and the village came in for shelling and mortaring, the like of which we had not seen since Normandy. The Germans were using huge rocket mortars.' Among the Rifle Brigade casualties was their padre, Jeff Taylor, who was killed trying to locate some wounded and helpless Dutch children. 'A' squadron 23rd Hussars was shelled and 'minnied' in Ommel all day. At night there was some noisy 'relief'. The tame 'Dr Göbbels wagon', consisting of loudspeakers mounted on a vehicle, appealed to the panzer grenadiers to surrender, promising in return food, rest and all the other attractions of a prisoner-of-war camp. Renderings of 'Lili Marlene' were more melodious, but there appeared to be no wild rush of deserters.

On the same day, 22 September, 29th Brigade continued to clear the area between the canal d'Embranchement and the Zuid Willems-Waal canal. 3rd RTR and 'G' and 'H' Batteries 13th RHA were in the outskirts of Helmond, clearing the western approaches. 3rd Mons/3rd RTR remained in the region of Gerwen and 23rd Hussars and 8th RB moved to a position on the Heeze-Zomeren road and collected 30 prisoners, 'raw and lousy recruits, convalescents and ex-Marines fighting with obstinacy born of despair'.

29th Armoured Brigade encountered considerable resistance across the Wilhelmina canal at Zomeren, but 23rd Hussars and 8th RB led off at dawn towards Deurne via Liesel. At 1000hrs 3rd Mons/3rd RTR, which had moved south from Helmond, crossed the Zomeren bridge and advanced towards Liesel. South of Ommel on the Deurne road Major Mitchell, FOO Ayrshire Yeomanry, was astonished to see a group of mounted men approaching from the village. They were not farmers. They were 1944 'Uhlans', who charged the Fife's Shermans and were destroyed. A small revenge perhaps for the Polish lancers who charged the Nazi panzers in 1939–40.

Vlierden was cleared at mid-day by 23rd Hussars and 3rd RTR converging on the town, having knocked out four anti-tank guns. On the Liesel road one Panther and two 88s were disposed of, and by 1900hrs Liesel itself was reached by 3rd Mons/3rd RTR. After his Asten bridge exploits Steel Brownlie rested in a nunnery, where he was offered fresh bread, basins and hot water for a wash.

Sunday 24 September was another grey, drenching day when 15/19th Hussars took over the defence of Liesel. They encountered and destroyed three 88mm guns in close wooded country to the south-east, giving and taking casualties.

A schoolteacher in the village of Zeilberg near Deurne gave Corporal Alastair Tait, RASC with 3rd Mons, a brooch from her dress and pinned it to his battledress – the first English soldier she had met. His section had taken 20 prisoners and as the village was being mortared they all took shelter in a

3 RTR and 3rd Monmouthshires have lunch in the middle of a battle, September 1944.

windmill owned by the Veltman family. Later the village was re-taken by the Germans. 8th RB was in Deurne and Roland Jefferson remembered: 'The great traffic jam, tanks, carriers, AFVs blocked the street and air-burst shells made life a bit dodgy.' By 1100hrs 3rd RTR had cut the Venlo-Helmond railway, entered Zeilberg and threatened the north-east sector of Deurne. In Vlierden the 'Göbbels wagon' sounded off and prisoners came in. Four regiments had a hand in the capture of Deurne: 23rd Hussars and 3rd RTR, with 8th RB and 3rd Mons clearing up by 1500hrs. The Fifes took the lead and passed through Deurne towards Bakel. At St Anthonis a disaster had taken place: Lt Colonel David Silvertop, CO 3rd RTR, and Lt Colonel H.G. Orr, CO 3rd Mons, were ambushed and killed at an 'O' group, and Brigadier Roscoe Harvey and the brigade major were both wounded. An impressive sunset, which stained a brilliant backcloth of colour to the windmills, church spires and flat-dyked countryside, seemed like a very peaceful Dutch postcard. Beautiful yes, peaceful no.

At 1827hrs on the 25th 'H' Battery 13th RHA, in action along the Milheeze-Oploo road, fired a salvo into Germany – the first of many. 1st Herefords entered Helmond and the Inns of Court put a patrol into Boxmeer on the wide river Maas. General Roberts noted: 'At Cuijk south-east of Nijmegen, we joined up with 30 Corps. The Arnhem operation was over.' During Market Garden the Division had advanced 14 miles as right flank protection, capturing half a dozen villages and small towns despite having its centre lines cut and re-cut by aggressive German defenders. It suffered over 500 casualties, including 115 killed in action.

On the 26th 15/19th Hussars found Boxmeer clear, but there were enemy infantry in Sambeek to the south. The recce troop captured a rare species – a German officer who proved of considerable intelligence value. For the next two days the Hussars pushed and probed towards Overloon and Vortum, often being heavily shelled and mortared, losing tanks, taking casualties, but giving as good as they got, including capturing a rare Tiger tank.

For the time being the Division halted in its tracks: 23rd Hussars in De Rips, the Fifes at Rijkvoorts and Handel, 8th RB at Judiths Hoeve, and the remainder of the Division round St Anthonis, Lamperstraat, Mortel and Gemert. There followed a week of rest, cleaning, tank maintenance, Liberty trucks to Helmond, cinemas, baths, local concert parties, evening church services in converted barns, football, basketball and a brisk barter trade with American troops. But Boxmeer was No Man's Land. Artillery targets were fixed on German pockets around Overloon and Venray.

The Division went on to win two Victoria Crosses and to lead Monty's armies through Germany across five formidable river and canal barriers to Lubeck and the Danish border. In 11 months of fighting the once 'green' and 'virgin' Division suffered 10,000 casualties, including nearly 2,000 killed in action.

CHAPTER 21

Monty's Ironsides: 3rd British Division

A fine regular division, which fought under Wellington, and was known in the First World War as the 'Iron' Division, 3rd British distinguished itself with the British Expeditionary Force in 1939, under command of Major General Bernard Montgomery. When he arrived in October to take over his new command on the Franco-Belgian border, almost the first thing he did was to inspect his troops and write a severe memorandum on 'Discipline'. Six months later he wrote to Lt General A.F. Brooke, later to become Chief of the Imperial General Staff, then commander of 2nd Corps. Montgomery criticised heavily four or five of his own senior staff, noting: 'I consider that in a front line fighting division it is necessary to have commanders who have the character and personality that will inspire confidence in others. They must be mentally robust and be possessed of initiative, energy and "drive". They must possess enthusiasm and be able to impart that enthusiasm to those under them.'

During the 'phoney war' before the German *blitzkrieg* tore through the French, Dutch, Belgian and British armies in May 1940, Montgomery trained his 'Iron Division' rigorously by day and night with emphasis on fighting patrols, siting of weapons, digging in, sniping and weapons training. As a result, 3rd Division fought brilliant defensive actions at Louvain, the Dyle river, the Escaut canal, the counter-attack at Wattrelos, the defence of the Yser canal and finally, at the Dunkirk perimeter. When Brooke was ordered back to England, Montgomery was promoted to Lt General to command 2nd Corps.

For the next four years 3rd British trained and trained in a score of exercises and did not fire a shot in anger.

Major General Tom Rennie became GOC 3rd British in October 1943, having commanded the re-formed 51st Highland Division. His three brigade commanders were Cass (8th), Cunningham (9th) and Smith (185th). The infantry regiments were 1st Suffolks, 2nd East Yorkshires and 1st South Lancashires in 8th Brigade; 2nd Lincolns, 1st Kings Own Scottish Borders and 2nd Royal Ulster Rifles in 9th Brigade; and 2nd Royal Warwickshires (Monty's old regiment), 1st Royal Norfolks and 2nd Kings Shropshire Light Infantry in 185th Brigade.

The Commander Royal Artillery (CRA) had under him 7th, 33rd and 76th Field Regiments RA, all with towed 25-pdr guns, and 20th Anti-tank Regiment, 92nd Light Anti-aircraft Regiment and 2nd Battalion The Middlesex Regiment, with its medium machine-guns and mortars.

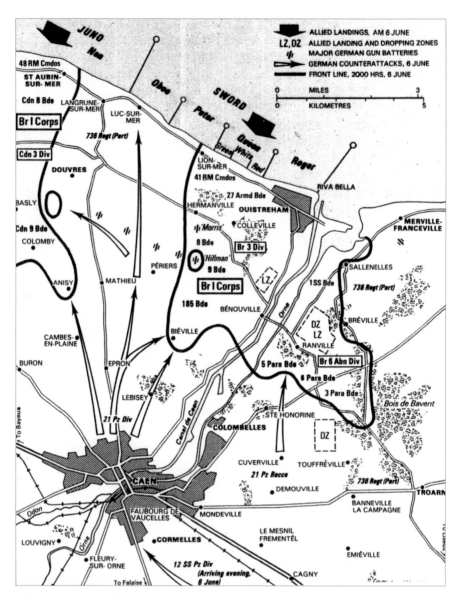

Allied landings north of Caen, 6 June 1944.

Predictably, Monty chose his old division to land in Normandy on D-Day, 6 June 1944. On Sword Queen Red beach it encountered the German 736th Regiment defending the two small resorts of Riva-Bella and La Breche.

The D-Day landing was brilliantly planned and executed; minesweeping flail tanks, Crocodile flame-throwers and 34 (out of 40) Dual Duplex amphibious Sherman tanks destroyed the main defences in front of the 1st South Lancashires and 2nd East Yorkshires, who had the terrible honour of leading the assault troops respectively towards Hermanville and Ouistreham.

Troops and carriers clearing their way off Queen Beach. (*Imperial War Museum B-5104*)

1st Battalion South Lancashires move past 'Big Friends' between Vire and Tinchebray.

Unfortunately, General Montgomery had set an unrealistic objective for D-Day: that of capturing the large town of Caen. After subduing the strong points inland of 'Morris' and 'Hillman', the advance guards of 21st Panzer Division stopped the Division in its tracks three miles south of Caen. But it was, nevertheless, a magnificent day.

It was vital to expand the Normandy bridgehead with battles for Cambes and Lebisey, then the terrible Operation Mitten against 192 Panzer Grenadiers holding the salient of Le Landel, La Londe and La Bijude in late June.

King's Own Scottish Borderers in Caen. (*Imperial War Museum B-6683*)

Carriers of 2nd Battalion Royal Warwicks along a battle–scarred lane near Lebisey. (*Imperial War Museum B-6646*)

Operation Charnwood followed in early July against 12th SS Panzer Division, holding the southern suburbs of Caen.

Major General Rennie was wounded on 13 June and succeeded by Major General L.G. 'Bolo' Whistler. Eventually, on 10 July, the Division along with others succeeded in capturing Caen after the RAF had blown it to pieces.

Operation Goodwood was another Monty spectacular with his three armoured divisions tasked with a massive breakthrough from north-east of Caen south towards Falaise – a distance of 25 miles! During the three days,

18–20 July, Panzer Group West and the 88mm screen on Bourguebus ridge destroyed the British armour thrust. 3rd British Division fought as left flank protection around Toufreville and Banneville on the way to Troarn, plagued by mortar fire and mosquitoes. In Operation Bluecoat in early August it advanced eastwards from Caumont towards Vire. Corporal Sidney Bates was awarded a posthumous Victoria Cross at Pavé. The 11th Armoured Division shared trenches and positions between their 3rd Battalion Monmouthshires and 1st Norfolks, hence the 'Nor-Mons' battle group. This was protected by the Shermans of 2nd Fife and Forfars and the 25-pdr Sextons of the author's 13th RHA. Operations Walter and Wallop followed in southern Normandy before 3rd Division was taken out of the line. For nearly a month the Division was out of action, absorbing reinforcements and having useful training in house clearance, counter-mortar and infantry–tank co-operation.

From the Flers area the Division moved north-east to Villers-en-Vexin, St Clair and Etrepagny, just north of the river Seine. It was an almost blissful time with rural picnics, dances, dinner parties and football and basketball matches against the locals. Pipe majors with attendant pipers enchanted everyone. There was short leave to Paris, which had just been liberated by the French (with the Americans doing most of the fighting). The CO of 2nd Royal Ulster Rifles met a charming young lady who later became his wife.

One reason for this limbo time in Eden was that all petrol, oil and lubricant were required to keep the armoured thrust north to Belgium moving briskly. So 8th Corps was grounded, inactive and not at war. On 5 September, after the capture of Brussels and Antwerp, the highly experienced Major General Whistler wrote in his diary: 'Reports from the battlefield are staggering in showing the size of victory. I believe the war against Germany is over.'

As part of 8th Corps with 11th Armoured Division, 3rd British Division was to protect the right flank of the daring drive to link up with the three Airborne Division drops from Eindhoven to Arnhem. On their way through northern France, Sergeant Fred Hartle, 1st KOSB, wrote: 'East of Louvain was the area where the Bn had met the invading Germans in 1940 and had to retire with our backs to the sea at Dunkirk – but that's another story!'

On 18 September the flank advance started with an assault crossing of the Meuse-Escaut canal to seize the main road and railway on the north side. From Lille St Hubert 9th Brigade led with a midnight attack. The canal, 40 yards wide and with 10-foot high banks, would be spanned later by a Class 9 and a Class 40 bridge. 2nd RUR was on the left of the original blown bridge, 2nd Lincolns on the right and 1st KOSB in reserve provided the storm-boat carrying parties. From 0300hrs 474th Searchlight Company provided the new night-time tactic of 'artificial moonlight' and at 2345hrs the divisional artillery programme started.

The RUR had an uneventful crossing, but, while boats were being launched, they lost casualties to mortar fire and later to counter-attacks on the far side. Captain Laving and 2nd Lieutenant Morgan were killed, but the enemy lost nearly 100 men killed, wounded and captured, plus a large quantity of guns: bazookas, mortars and machine-guns. Major de Longueuil's 'C' Company distinguished itself, Sergeant Peel threw 36 grenades shrewdly, and Rifleman Greene, 'B' Company, earned the MM. An accolade must also go to Captains Gaffikin and Baudains of 'B' Company who, heavily disguised in 'civvies', had carried out a daylight recce before the attack. So the village of Broek was taken and a bridgehead was established. Ken Bradshaw wrote: 'bridging and rafting went ahead with great gusto, anti-tank guns and jeeps were shipped across. The sappers' Class 9 bridge was built and by 1000hrs the RUR were firm, secure and prepared for any eventuality.'

The bridge at Lille St Hubert allowed the 11th Armoured Division to cross over the canal. However, for the Lincolns it was rather different, as Major Glyn Gilbert, OC 'C' Company, recalled:

> Up the bank we scrambled lugging our boats and easing them down the steep slope into the water. The enemy response was immediate and fierce. Very heavy mortar fire opened up directed at the canal and village and several MG and a 20mm were firing on fixed lines down the canal. We immediately suffered heavy casualties crossing the bank. The boat on my right received a direct mortar bomb hit. We left two sunken boats and over 70 NCOs and men killed and wounded in the canal and on the banks. George Bennett had most of his jaw shot off. Peter London and Denis Querky, two platoon commanders, were dead. The Germans had fought a good action at little loss to themselves.

By 0215hrs all the rifle companies were across and digging while Battalion HQ consolidated in Broek. Fred Hartle, 1st KOSB wrote: '9 Platoon had a new officer, Lieutenant Taylor. Sergeant Goode had been acting platoon commander and I was acting platoon sergeant. We crossed the canal in little canvas boats. A farm on the other side was on fire, lit up the whole area. At dawn, heavy mist and in poor visibility Lieutenant Taylor told me to take a point section up in front. [Later] I could hear the platoon coming up behind us. Their rifle butts were catching against their shovels. I could also hear them talking a mile away.' Fred spoke sharply to them! Subsequently Lieutenant Taylor was killed in his first action, along with three or four of Fred's platoon.

The pioneers, under Lieutenant Pogson, built two Class 5 rafts and ferried all the battalion transport across. 246th Company RE built their 160-foot Class 9 bridge in record time between 0100hrs and 0700hrs, and 17th Field Company RE built their Class 40 bridge, which was finished by 1700hrs the next day, the 19th. Now the GOC ordered 8th Brigade to cross the canal on the right of Lille St Hubert and two Canloan officers in the South Lancs, Alfred Cope and Eric Fryer, were killed during the crossing. The East Yorks linked up with 'A' Company of the Lincolns to battle with young SS officer cadets in a wood, and 32 of them surrendered the next morning.

Next, 185th Brigade came up and Captain R.R. Rylands, 2nd KSLI, remembers: 'I went forward to see the South Lancs Coy attempt a crossing. It was rather noisily done and their first platoon fell into a trap, some being ambushed behind the high bank where they had got over, others being caught in the boats. We helped to extricate some of the latter and offered fire support, but this was refused ... 'W' Coy moved up and took over from the remaining South Lancs who withdrew. Some cross-canal sniping ensued.' At 1945hrs on 20 September 'X' and 'W' Companies crossed in assault boats one mile north of the blown bridge on the main road from Caulille to Weert, established their bridgehead and advanced south down the canal against heavy opposition. By the night of the 21st they had suffered over 30 casualties. Meanwhile, 1st Suffolks took 60 prisoners in Hamont for the single loss of Private Hollis, killed in action. He was given a slap-up funeral with full civic honours, as huge crowds formed a cortège to his grave.

Major Robert Moberley, 2nd Middlesex, wrote: 'several million German rations were captured in Hamont, the pork and beans and cheese were quite good. But we all hated the ersatz coffee, biscuits, "knackebrot" and the cigars were quite amusing.' On the other hand the gunners of 33rd Field Regiment RA reported: 'The honey biscuits and frozen vegetables were approved but the meat was not popular.' Cheese in 'toothpaste' tubes was an edible novelty. Ray Paine, 2nd Lincolns, had strong feelings too: 'We lived off German frankfurters (a small smoked sausage) – very spicy – Ugh!' Oss was another huge German supply depot which supplied 30th and 8th Corps with Wehrmacht rations for two weeks until the Normandy bridgehead supplies caught up.

Unbeknown to most, the airborne troops fought and died in Arnhem, 50 miles due north.

The GOC's diary of 20 September reported: 'The Div. is now concentrated – or rather it has curled its tail up and thrust its head over the Escaut. Damn fine Div! To do the crossing 9 Bde were the clever boys – and my staff! Anyway the job got done quite brilliantly. It was about a 250-mile move up to begin with and we were very short of equipment, ammo and also food. This Army under Monty and Dempsey is a pretty remarkable show. Their plans and conceptions are quite staggering.' 'The Div. Club', Norman Scarfe commented, 'made a determined effort to establish itself in luxury in Brussels, but was prevailed to move to the village of Peer.'

On the evening of the 19th a company runner, Private Charles Ramage from Townhead, Glasgow, got lost. He saw a village, made a canny recce and was spotted by the villagers who flocked excitedly out of their houses to hail the bewildered liberator – the village was Achel, just inside the Belgian border! But the battalion suffered many casualties from small arms fire as the Borderers moved into the village. Iain Wilson, the KOSB padre, wrote: 'The villagers were rapturous, wept on our shoulders, drew us to their hearts and kissed us, pressed fruit and flowers upon us.'

Sergeant Fred Hartle's 9th Platoon KOSB was now commanded by Canloan Lieutenant Rose. Fred was ordered to take a Bren carrier with crew to check and clear a village ahead: 'some shots were fired at us from a wood, and a salvo of shells whistled over our heads and landed in the village behind where the remainder of the platoon was positioned. Lieutenant Rose was wounded in the eye, taken away to hospital, so another officer was lost in such a short time.'

On the morning of 20 September 8th Brigade moved due east and 1st KOSB advanced towards Achel, north-west of Lille St Hubert, after crossing spongy fields and boggy countryside. Captain J.B. Cranston reported: 'A determined German machine-gunner, he was a deadly shot, held us up for more than an hour.' The opposition was partly SS of 12th Panzer Division – old Normandy foes – part airborne and Luftwaffe.

On the morning of 21 September 8th Brigade crossed over the Dutch frontier and occupied Weert with 1st Suffolks leading, followed by East Yorks and 76th Field Regiment RA. Major Claxton led 'D' Company across the Dutch border at 1230hrs; it was a desolate area of sand, scrub and fir plantations and they were met by heavy Spandau fire as they approached the railway from the dune. Shielded by smoke from their own 3-inch mortars they pressed on, but at 2200hrs heard explosions east and south-east as the canal bridges and ammo dumps were blown. Lt Colonel Craddock kept 1st Suffolks going across the sandy wastes of Boshover Heide, and by 0315hrs on the 22nd they had reached the Weert canal.

In Weert itself the streets were soon decked with orange flags and beribboned portraits of Queen Wilhelmina, Princess Juliana and Prince Bernhard. They sang a shrill nursery song rather like 'Aye, aye, ippy, ippy aye'. The Dutch newspapers rebuked the kids for asking 'Tommy' for cigarettes and chocolates: 'Remember your manners, Dutch children don't scrounge,' and schoolmasters taught children how to sing a well-rehearsed 'God Save the King'. Windmills received new coats of paint in honour of the liberation, with red, white and blue sails and a strong splash of orange on the base of the mill. Little girls wore orange frocks or pinafores, and little boys wore orange shirts. Even the monks and nuns wore orange 'favours' to show loyalty to the royal family. The embarrassed Jocks danced on the village green.

The Belgian and Dutch resistance movements were invaluable. Besides beating up and arresting suspected collaborators, they telephoned around the countryside, finding out and reporting back the local German troop dispositions. And they rounded up German stragglers. Their courage over the last few years was indisputable; the underground movement had sheltered Allied airmen shot down over their country and had devised intricate escape systems. Lt Colonel Bill Renison, CO East Yorks, noted in his journal:

We made ourselves very comfortable and very popular in Gemeert – the battalion home station during the long winter campaign. Battle dress was pressed up again with female assistance. The troops wore soft hats off duty and could walk freely round the town. We played Retreat on the 27th in front of the town monastery. We billeted the troops in garages and barns. The Boche always turned people out of their own homes. A great temptation to the troops was the price of one cigarette, a Dutch guilder!

Near Weert, Lieutenant Eddy Jones, South Lancs, recalled:

At dawn we passed in an industrial estate, a large scale battery hen farm. As the companies went past men took off their helmets and filled them with eggs. I said to my batman 'Cook a dozen or so of those for our breakfast'. We liberated two million eggs – a month's quota for delivery to the Wehrmacht. The divisional gunners soon found that the great church belfry tower made an excellent OP until an unfriendly German 88mm gunner thought otherwise!

Marcus Cunliffe, 2nd Royal Warwicks, described the countryside which had effectively destroyed any chances that Guards Armoured and 43rd Wessex Wyverns had of relieving the beleaguered Airborne in Arnhem: 'Desolate sandy heaths, belts of pine trees, meagre little farms, the roads were mere tracks, mines were difficult to detect, vehicles were constantly bogged, the fields were water-logged and the causeways stood nakedly above the fields.' It was very difficult for armour and infantry to progress against a determined enemy.

For a week in cold wet weather 8th and 185th Brigades plus 3rd Recce Regiment, patrolled the eastern axis of 8th Corps from Weert, 20 miles north to Asten, Liesel, Deurne and Helmond. 1st KOSB moved from Achel to Budel in Holland, where the troops quickly disposed of the watery beer left in the cafés and then, on 24 September, moved to Liesel. Here patrols went out to Meijel and the line of the Deurne canal. The Scotsmen (and others) were given the freedom of Helmond with its clubs, cinemas and theatres. During the last three days of September the battalion was guarding the important crossroads at Milheeze, five miles north of Deurne. The Middlesex sent 6th Platoon carriers into Helmond, where they were mobbed and soon had 20 Dutch citizens on each carrier. The drivers wore orange jockey caps, orange ribbon and orange tricolour favours. The local liberation committee organised dances in the railway buffet room. Frank Neuerberg, a Dutch nephew of Lieutenant Clarke, South Lancs, joined the battalion as interpreter and served until the end of the war. Lieutenant Eddie Jones met a unit of 82nd US Airborne, whose HQ was in a charming villa. The rather overweight American general, without a jacket and in his braces, was smoking a large cigar. Eddie duly saluted the rather surprised general, who called all his staff by their first names, as they did him. 'Lesson of democracy in action!'

2nd KSLI moved up to Zomeren and relieved the Herefords of 11th Armoured near Asten. Guy Radcliffe wrote: 'Most depressing place, the weather was vile, pouring rain, the country low and waterlogged, the roads and tracks covered with mud and the ditches full of the decaying bodies of the enemy dead.' On 29

September the battalion moved back to Zomeren, then to Asten to allow US 7th Armoured's attack through Overloon and Venray to Venlo.

The long cold winter was spent in the Peel country, followed by Operation Veritable to break the Siegfried Line and Operations Ventilate, Heather and Plunder to cross the Rhine and advance on through Germany to capture Bremen.

During the whole 11 months of the north-west Europe campaign, the 3rd Division had over 11,000 casualties, including 2,586 killed in action. In the Normandy campaign their casualties from D-Day until the end of August were 8,000 – a terrible blood bath.

Blasted, ruined Bremen, 26 April 1945. (*Birkin Haward*)

AVREs on the road to Bremervorde, 1 May 1945. (*Birkin Haward*)

CHAPTER 22

The Netherlands' unique Tank Battle

For obvious reasons the attractive but mildly waterlogged Netherlands had never suffered an armoured tank battle – not tanks doing their nasty work against enemy infantry or machine-gun nests and other targets, but tank against tank. A substantial part of the country is polderland and another substantial part is the Peel country, so there are limited opportunities for such combat. In any case, well-developed German armoured tactics were devoted to *blitzkrieg*, fast armoured assaults with Luftwaffe Stukas overhead and good going under the tracks, such as autobahns. Northern France was ideal and, to some extent, so was North Africa. The German armoured strategy, which worked so well, was to entice the British tank squadrons to charge headlong, in the fashion of the Light Brigade cavalry in the Crimea and various battles under the Duke of Wellington, straight into a well-set trap of powerful dual-purpose 88mm AA/Anti-tank guns. As recently as July 1944 the British armoured divisions had had 200 assorted Sherman and Cromwell tanks knocked out in 36 hours by the powerful 88mm screen on the Bourguebus ridge that dominated the cornfields south of Caen.

There was, however, one quite important tank battle, which took place in the Netherlands in September 1944 and continued into October. It was a whole series of actions, often on a daily basis, between the best British armoured division and a first-class German armoured battle group.

The two Allied battle tanks, the American Sherman and the British Cromwell, were mechanically reliable, easy to manoeuvre and fast, but they were thin-skinned and under-gunned, except for the one 17-pdr gun on a Sherman Firefly. The German Panzer Mark IV was their equivalent, but a Panther was undoubtedly a superior beast and was acknowledged as such. The relatively rare Tiger tanks were almost impossible to defeat, unless possibly by a 'sabot' shell fired at close quarters. On the other hand the huge weight of the Tiger mitigated its movements on the Dutch battlefields.

Between 16 and 18 September the German 107th Panzer Brigade Group, 3,000 strong, unloaded their armour at Venlo station beside the river Maas, 12 miles north of Roermond, 12 miles south-west of Overloon.

The 107th Panzer Brigade, commanded by Major Freiherr von Maltzahn, was part of Army Group B and had been re-routed by train from Tilburg from its original task of confronting the 1st US Army at Aachen. After detraining, it

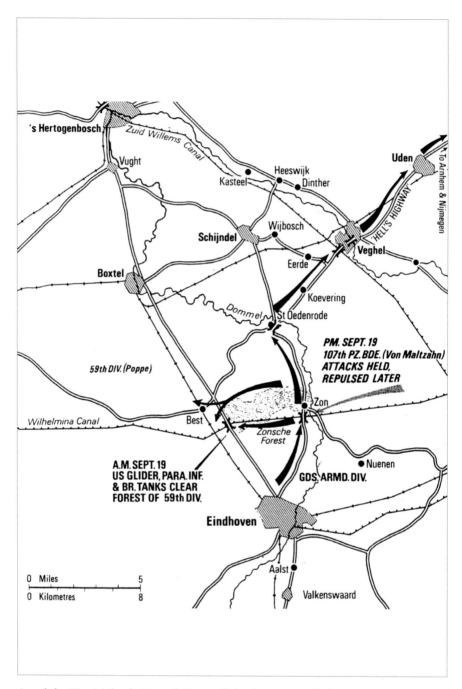

Attack by Von Maltzahn's 107th Panzer Brigade on 101st Airborne Division, 19 September 1944.

The Sherman tank.

The Panzer MK V Panther.

moved in clattering, exhaust-shrouded columns towards Helmond. It had been totally re-equipped with a battalion of 36 formidable Mark V Panther tanks with 75mm guns, plus Panzergrenadier Infantry Regiment 1034 mounted in armoured half-tracks, supplemented by a self-propelled assault gun company, an engineering company in half-tracks, and transport and supply detachments. It had a Flak/anti-aircraft 'umbrella' of 37mm guns mounted on tracks to deter the Allied 'Jabos' (Typhoons and Tempests). The Panzer Brigade could and did fire 250 Flak machine-guns at aircraft, knocking quite a few down. The Brigade moved by night to avoid air attack. It was a tough, very well–equipped battle group, determined and full of fight.

Its first task was to attack across Son, capture St Oedenrode, both north-west of Eindhoven, and slice off the head of the British 30th Corps' advance to Grave, which was a key 82nd US Airborne objective. The ground, of course, was flat, sandy and not too boggy, but nevertheless the 45-ton Panthers had to be very careful where they prowled.

However, at a secondary bridge at Son, American troops with bazookas and a 57mm anti-tank gun prevented the tanks from crossing the canal. The Brigade lost two Panthers there so the formation moved back to Molenheide.

Von Maltzahn's first encounter with 11th Armoured Division was with the 15/19th Hussars, equipped with Cromwell and occasional Challenger tanks. The Hussars were tasked to link up with 101st US Airborne Division at Son and Eindhoven and to protect the long lines of communication. On the 17th,

Winter warfare: Infantry boarding RTR Shermans.

the start day for Market Garden, 'B' and 'C' Squadrons fought in support of the Dorsets and Devons of 50th Northumbrian Division, losing three tanks to mines. Via Valkenswaard they passed through Eindhoven in brilliant sunshine with Dutch Orange-Nassau flags flying everywhere. 'A' Squadron went under command of 506th US Parachute Regiment and the others stayed around Son and protected a supply-dropping zone on a large heath north of the canal. In the afternoon of the 19th joint operations around Best produced 50 prisoners. 'C' Squadron, however, 'lost' a 17-pdr Challenger, which the Germans took to Best, but it was retrieved five months later. Trooper Crump of 'A' Squadron destroyed two Panthers with seven hits out of eight shots! On the 20th Captain Christopher Weatherby led a patrol of one troop of Cromwells from 'A' Squadron, with two scout cars from the Royals and a platoon of infantry. He met a detachment of 107th Panzer and destroyed three Panthers and several half-tracks at Nederwetten, three miles from Son. The next day at Neunen, a few miles south, the Shermans of 23rd Hussars engaged seven Panthers and a Tiger tank, destroyed two, and the rest were heavily shelled by 13th RHA. However, 107th Panzer Brigade fought back and the Hussars had a score of casualties. Another 11th Armoured tank unit, 3rd RTR, fought around Ommeel and Geldrop with almost daily actions against 107th Brigade, knocking out five anti-tank guns and a Panther.

For four days, 22–26 September, von Maltzahn's battle group came under command of the much larger Kampfgruppe Walther, whose initial responsibility had been defending the Neerpelt bridgehead against 15th Scottish and 50th Northumbrian Divisions. Their next role was to be an attack on Veghel to split the Airborne corridor.

88mm dual-purpose gun.

Crocodile flamethrower north of Schilberg, Operation Blackcock. (*Imperial War Museum B-13942*)

3rd RTR was in action continuously around Vlierden and Liesel, knocking out the occasional Panther and several 88mm guns. On the 25th 2nd Fife and Forfar Yeomanry destroyed two Panthers on the Bakel road and a few days later, another three in the wooded country southwards around Overloon and Venray.

The supply of Shermans and Cromwells was never-ending but once a German tank was knocked out, unless it could be repaired quickly under cover of darkness, it would never fight again.

The running tank battle against von Maltzahn's armoured battle group went on almost daily for nearly three weeks. By October the unique battle on Dutch soil was over.

CHAPTER 23

Desert Rats: 7th Armoured Division left flank

The 7th Armoured Division became known as the Desert Rats because it earned its initial fame fighting in North Africa at the beginning of the Second World War. It tore the poor, wretched and effete Italians apart in 1939 and 1940, suffered setbacks against Rommel's panzers, and took part in Monty's famous battles from El Alamein to Tunis. In one dramatic week the Division won three Victoria Crosses – Ward Gunn, John Beeley and Jock Campbell – in the battles for Sidi Rezegh.

Briefly, in the Italian campaign, the Division fought in Operation Avalanche, in the Salerno bridgehead, and then in the advance to the Volturno and Naples before returning to England in January 1944.

The Desert Rats Division derived its nickname and insignia from the jerboa rodent, an unlovely tough little beast that soon became famous. The author wore the smart, sophisticated version as the commander of Java Troop in 3rd Regiment RHA in 1945–47. When they arrived back in the UK, the Desert Rats were a race apart with brown, sun-tanned faces, arms and legs, and they appeared to many people to be rude, cocky and arrogant – a law unto themselves. They spoke a foreign language with words like *shufti*, *shai*, *maleesh*, *imshi*, *sayeda* and *buckshee*, and of course, *ackers* and *bints*! They sang peculiar songs such as the haunting Wehrmacht marching song 'Lili Marlene', albeit with unusual vulgar words. Their army costume was bizarre: gaudy silk coloured scarves, brilliantly coloured pullovers and an eccentric array of headgear. Their officers wore scuffed 'brothel-creeper' suede shoes and highly coloured corduroy trousers, and some of them sported luxuriant moustaches and carried fly whisks.

Some of the Desert Rats had been away for five or six years and felt, quite rightly, that the 'green', untried divisions which had been training in England for three or four years should lead the way in Europe. Not a bit of it. Monty was an infantry general but usually wore a Royal Tank Regiment silver badge on a black beret. So he sent his favourite armoured division, the Desert Rats, into Normandy to land on 9 June. 7th Armoured was also Winston Churchill's favourite division and in his memoirs and records there are more mentions of it than any other formation. He even sent Stalin a message shortly after D-Day saying that now that the Division had landed some exciting things would happen. They did. In a battle in and around Villers-Bocage the Division was

Sketch by a Desert Rat of an armoured assault in Normandy.

ambushed by a Tiger panzer group and smashed up. It fought in the great armoured battle of Operation Goodwood and by the end of June had suffered 1,000 casualties. Operation Spring followed in July and Bluecoat in early August and another 1,000 casualties were sustained.

For most of the campaigns the 11th Hussars, the famous Cherry Pickers, led. The tank regiments of 8th Royal Irish Hussars, 1st and 5th Royal Tanks were equipped with fast, reliable, under-gunned Cromwell tanks. They were backed by the motorised infantry of 1st Rifle Brigade and the 3rd and 5th Royal Horse Artillery 25-pdr gunners. The infantry brigade that had suffered the bulk of the casualties was 1/5th Queens (from Guildford), 1/6th Queens (from Bermondsey) and 1/7th Queens (from Southwark).

Practically everybody who fought in the incredible 'Great Swan' did what Monty asked of them: 'get cracking around'. The Desert Rats' objective was Ghent via Gournay, Poix, Picquigny, Doullens, St Pol, Béthune and Seclin. They enjoyed the dozens of exuberant 'liberations', as Trooper Hewison, 1st RTR, noted in his diary:

> Everyone is out to watch us rumble past – babes in arms to centenarians, smiling, waving, laughing, shouting, clapping, throwing kisses, weeping, chucking dahlias and rhododendrons and all sorts of flowers on to the tanks, passing up fruit, cider, milk and lord-knows-what when we stopped for a few minutes.

The northern advance was through an enormous industrial maze of canals, dykes, railway embankments (all easy to defend), factories, coal mines, shafts and slag heaps, *pavé* roads and many little villages.

The recce squadron of 5th Inniskilling Guards (the Skins) went through northern France where the Queen's Brigade had fought with the BEF in 1940. It was, as recounted by Corporal John Pilborough: 'a victory parade where the people thronged the streets, cheering every vehicle that went by … at nightfall we crossed the Belgian frontier at Toufflers. If our reception in Northern France had been enthusiastic, here it became ecstatic. The red, white and blue French flag gave place to the red, yellow and black colours of Belgium. There was hardly a house without one and most cafés had several. There was dancing and music in every café. Tipperary was sung, the blackout was forgotten. It was a riot.'

Some small towns and villages were defended. If really seriously defended they were bypassed for the follow-up infantry divisions to deal with in their 3-ton trucks.

The Maquis or FFI (Free Forces of the Interior) were helpful: pointing out targets and giving interesting but mostly unreliable information about *les sales boches*. They guarded prisoners, and often their unsavoury habits of dealing with *collaborateurs* offended the British tankies, but of course they had not lived through four years of unpleasant enemy occupation.

Some of General von Zangen's 15th Army, travelling in parallel to the west, crossed paths and swords with rough little actions. In Oudenarde the Desert

Sketch of machine-gunners by a Desert Rat.

Rats filled the barracks with 2,000 German prisoners, and in the capture of Ghent, partly shared with the Polish Armoured Division, another 10,000 prisoners were handed over to the Belgian 'White Brigade' for fairly safe keeping. The prisoners were mostly from Lt General Wilhelm Daser's 70th Infantry Division.

The Panzer Grenadier regiments of Lt General Poppe's 59th Infantry Division were in occupation of a line south and north roughly from Auxi le Chateau through St Pol and Bours, west of St Pol-Lillers, and garrisoned the more important towns with about 200 men supported by anti-tank guns as happened in Auxi and St Pol. At Lillers it was often touch and go and the Maquis were invaluable in the street fighting. It was difficult owing to the absence of maps and the many blown bridges. Indeed some patrols were cut off. A large patrol of the 5th Dragoon Guards, the Skins, holding the bridges at Wingles and Béthune, was surrounded by the enemy for three days and nights and unable to evacuate the wounded or a substantial number of prisoners. The 11th Hussars (Cherry Pickers) were indomitable, pushing and prodding their armoured cars up minor roads and through small towns, constantly on the radio to HQ.

After the liberation of Ghent the Division spend ten days resting and maintaining the Cromwells, half-tracks and carriers which had covered nearly 300 miles. Fuel was short and many units were living off captured German rations: tinned stew, tinned Limburg cheese and curious black bread. The Queens Brigade was first back into action as part of the left flank protection in Operation Garden, near Herenthals on the Canal de Jonction, 20 miles east of Antwerp. There were frequent patrol clashes, shelling and mortaring. One battle group of 8th Hussars, 1st Rifle Brigade and 5th Royal Tank Regiment was loaned to 15th Scottish Division near the Dutch frontier town of Hoogiend, situated in a flat open wasteland of dreary sand dunes and sparse fir trees, scarred by deep black dykes. That was on 18–20 September and was followed by another loan, this time to 53rd Welsh Division south of the Meuse/Escaut canal for three days. Then they joined 51st Highland Division west of Eindhoven to capture Middlebeers. Fighting against SS troops armed with bazookas and mortars, it became a house-to-house battle which lasted for two days.

8th Hussars moved north from the battlefield of Gheel on 23 September. Captain Bill Bellamy recalled: 'The heavens opened. We trundled our way through the bleak flat afforested heathlands near to Mol and Lommel, reached Eindhoven in the late morning. If the drive had been miserable, the ensuing wait was worse. We harboured at Heeze just inside Holland, the rain drenched us and we sat in silent dripping misery. Not a happy day.'

The next day the Desert Rats moved south of Eindhoven to protect the left flank and centre lines of the extended 43rd Wessex Division, both straining every nerve to link up with the Airborne Division dropping zones. They had

Sketch by Desert Rat of an armoured car, probably lost.

to retake and reopen the 20-mile centre line between Eindhoven and the Zuis
Willemsvaart bridge at Veghel. It was a difficult road, narrow and embanked
most of the way, running through flat, sandy fields, interspersed with stretches
of birch and pine forests. They, and the inevitable dykes, gave cover to the
bazooka teams.

Sergeant Jim Boardman of the Skins (5th Dragoon Guards) reported on the
24th: 'the regiment was now under command of the Queens 131st Brigade.
The road was packed with vehicles nose to tail unable to move forward or
back, but the Military Police once again played a wonderful role in sorting it
all out. By 0700hrs (on the 25th) we reached the main square in St Oedenrode
where we met a very angry Corps Commander, Lt General Brian Horrocks,
who was desperately trying to get forward to join his own TAC HQ.' The
Skins encountered the US 506th Paratroop Battalion who 'were feeling kinda
lonesome having been dropped into the blue'. Even worse no American K
rations had been supplied so the kindly Skins dished out 'meat & veg' for their
breakfast.

Rex Wingfield with 1/6th Queens reported on the action to keep the centre
line open between Eindhoven and Veghel:

One regiment of tanks and an Infantry Battalion was left to hold our gains.
The rest of us mounted on Cromwells turned back to clear the roads. We
soon found the targets of last night's firing – ten gutted RASC lorries, one
blasted to fragments. That had been the ammo truck. Two hundred yards
further down the road was a roadblock of logs. By it lay another burnt lorry
and four blackened bodies. A clatter of tracer bounced and sang off the tank

as a Spandau opened fire from the roadblock. Cordite fumes blasted from our tank gun into our faces. A six-pounder shell hit right in the middle of the logs. The beams sailed upwards. A field grey rag doll jerked high into the air. We burst through, firing our Stens and heaving grenades into the back of the smoking roadblock. The performance was repeated three times in four miles and then we pulled into the relief column. Each morning we had to clear the roads in front and behind before we could move on. Guards Armoured tried to smash through beyond Nijmegen to Arnhem to reach the poor devils. Only one road could be used as the surrounding land was either too soft or under water. One road they had. That road was zeroed exactly by 88mms. As soon as a tank poked its snout beyond a building, it was hit. We tried to use the ground on the lee side of the embankment road. The tanks bogged down and churned themselves into a hopeless mess.

The salient between St Oedenrode and Veghel was protected by the Queens Brigade. 5th RTR probed west towards Dinther and Heeswijk and 1st RTR and the Skins north towards Nistelrode and Heesch. Trooper William Hewison kept a vivid diary; this is his account:

Sep 28 in Veghel. Jerry is fairly strong on this side of the corridor with Spandau, mortars and heavier artillery including 88s. One B Sqn tank's knocked out by a bazooka, the commander killed. Yankee paratroopers still maintaining patrols in this locality. [Sep 30] Had a nasty day, ran into all sorts of stuff – small arms, sniping, bazooka, Spandaus, 88 and 105s. Lost 3 tanks brewed. Sergeant Smith's, Johnny Wooder was alright, operators Pete Eccles killed, Shep and Sergeant Smith moderately wounded with blast & shrapnel. 2nd tank had to get it, had three killed – turret people. Driver and George Travis brought it back to Echelon. 3rd Tank – Capt. Stephens with two simultaneous 105mm or heavier on front and rear. Micky Perrin killed, Jock Brady and the rest baled out and tank immediately brewed, Jock with burns and blast wounds, others Okay. Bags of MGs firing all day and brassing up with HE. [On 31st] refugees came past this morning very early – pitiful sight with very small children and old folks with a few of their chattels and blankets carried off in all kinds of contrivances.

Since D-Day the Division had suffered 2,901 casualties, many of them magnificent warriors from the early desert days, dying in the polder and Peel country.

Rex Wingfield, 1/6th Queens, met the 4th Dorsets of 43rd Wessex Wyverns returning from the Arnhem pocket: 'A shuffling column of men came down the road. We rushed to greet them. We shook their hands. They were dirty faces, grimy, unshaven. God! Those eyes! Glazed, ever moving, twitching, not seeing, staring south, ever south. We lit cigarettes and passed them around.' Market Garden was over.

For three weeks the Desert Rats held the line from Veghel to the Maas and north of Oss, a front of 14 miles. Patrols on both sides, supported by Brens and Stens or Spandaus and Schmeissers took their daily toll. The Division had 237 casualties from 28 September to 21 October.

In the long, hard, cold winter of 1944–45 the Desert Rats were kept fully stretched. Operation Don took place in Brabant; it was an attack to take Tilburg, over the rivers Dommel and Aa by the 51st Highland Division, and to seize s'Hertogenbosch by the 53rd Welsh Division. In this operation the Skins and 5th RTR were under command. The 131st Queens Brigade was tasked to clear Middelrode, Doornhoeck and Berlicum in Operation Alan. The German defenders were 712th Infantry Division and the kampfgruppe from General Chill's 59th Infantry Division. Eventually both operations were successful and in the New Year Operation Blackcock followed. 12th Corps had to clear a triangle formed by the rivers Roer, Wurm and Maas and destroy or capture 176th and 183rd German Infantry Divisions in the process, which

Sketch by a Desert Rat of an infantry assault on a village in Holland.

A battle scarred road to s'Hertogenbosch.

The harsh winter of 1944-45.

Bren gun carrier on the German border.

they did after 15 days and nights of constant fighting with horrible weather and minefields everywhere.

And so to Operation Plunder, the massive Montgomery-inspired Rhine crossing. The Führer would have been proud of the Hitler Youth Hannover Cadet School, who in early April 1945 gave the Desert Rats and the 11th Armoured Division a bloody nose in the formidable natural hilly defensive line of dense woods, the Teutonburger Wald. This was an escarpment 25 miles long and a mile wide on a south-east vector some ten miles south-west of Osnabruck.

Sergeant Bob Price of the Skins recalled: 'Ibbenburen remains in my mind as the most horrible experience a tank troop leader could undergo while supporting infantry. It was so frustrating for us and so demoralising for the PBI.' The fanatical and skilful resistance with deadly enemy sniping and every defensive weapon produced a frightening Wagnerian battle. The instructors, often elderly men, and their cadets put up such a defence that the Corps commander reckoned it was a stalemate, and the armoured divisions bypassed Ibbenburen on 4 April. It took another two days for the 52nd Lowland Scottish and 53rd Welsh Divisions to subdue the heroic Ibbenburen defenders. Indeed it required heavy artillery regiments with 7.2-inch guns to complete the task.

The advance continued via the relief of Fallingbostel POW camp on 16 April. There were 12,500 prisoners in two camps, about half under command of RSM Lord, Grenadier Guards, who kept up appropriate standards of 'pressed battledress and scrubbed equipment'!

The 9th Durham Light Infantry joined the 7th Armoured Division after the demise of 50th Tyne Tees when Market Garden finished. The indomitable Queens Brigade, with three stalwart London cockney battalions, was now reduced by amalgamation to two battalions. Britain's fighting manpower was being diminished every day. The recruits or replacements from heavy artillery or light anti-aircraft regiments had had little training as infantrymen and perhaps suffered needless casualties.

Stadtlohn, Borken, Vreden, Ottenstein, Nienburg and every river or canal crossing was bitterly contested. The nearer to Bremen, the more intense the resistance. The Cherry Pickers, operating between Bassum and Syke, encountered 14 SP guns and three companies of Panzer Grenadiers supported by two Tiger tanks. The 1st Parachute Army was dying hard in the last few weeks of the war.

On 29 April negotiations started with Major General Wolz, commander of the Hamburg garrison, for the surrender of the city to the Desert Rats. Admiral Doenitz and General Keitel had been consulted. So on 3 May a posse of German generals – Wolz, Kinsel and Admiral von Friedberg – surrendered to Major General L.O. Lyne, GOC 7th Armoured. Appropriately, Lt Colonel Wainmen and the Cherry Pickers led the way into a large city that had been pulverised by the Allied bombing raids. The Desert Rats moved up to the Kiel canal on 7 May and 'Victory in Europe' followed on the 8th.

Soon complicated negotiations took place with the Russians for a notable victory parade in Berlin. 'About the middle of June a rumour spread around the regiment,' wrote Captain Bill Bellamy, 8th Hussars, 'that we were to go to Berlin. About the same time a load of battleship grey paint appeared from German Naval Stores, Lübeck, to enable us to clean up the tanks.' Lieutenant Tom Ritson wrote:

> We drove down the autobahn near Helmstedt ready for the long drive to Berlin. We had spruced up somewhat, guns cleaned, uniforms pressed and brew cans removed from sight. We drove for much of the day in a downpour through the Russian occupied area past Magdeburg and on to the western part of Berlin. From the Grünewald, a large city park full of burned out buses, we drove into the Charlottenburg district, pulling up at the Olympic Stadium.

To Bill Bellamy 'it appeared to be more like a journey into enemy territory than a meeting with friends. Sergeant Alan Howard, a dedicated communist/ socialist whose uncle had fought in the International Brigade during the Spanish War, told us what a joy it would be to meet our Russian allies.' And Trooper Clifford Smith, 11th Hussars wrote: 'Amidst the ruins a feeling of isolation as being on an island surrounded by Russians.' Verdon Besley, Queens, recalled the Olympic Spandau barracks: 'a lovely barracks but in a filthy condition with huge bugs going up the walls and human excrement on the floor. We tried to clean it up until the MO shut it down and fumigated it. We bivouacked down outside.' Tom Ritson wrote:

> Berlin in July 1945 beggars description. It was then two months since the Russians had stormed the city street by street in bitter fighting. No serious attempt had been made to clean it up. At least half of all the buildings had been destroyed. There was no electricity, water or drainage and the weather was hot … the stench of the dead bodies in the ruined buildings and the corpses coming to the surface in the various lakes within the city area. We were continuously warned of the dangers of polluted water, mosquitoes and rats.

Captain Bobby Wolfson, RA, remembered that rats 'the size of a cat would climb up the outside pipes into the sleeping quarters jumping from bed to bed'.

The first parade took place on 6 July. The Union Jack was hoisted in the Grosse Stern at the foot of the Franco Prussian War memorial and Lt General Sir Ronald Weekes inspected the 1st Battalion Grenadier Guards (borrowed for the occasion), 1/5th Queens, 2nd Devons and the Canadian Composite Battalion (also borrowed). 5th RHA arrived on 10 July and moved into Kladow barracks and Divisional HQ on the 18th. Field Marshal Montgomery arrived on the 12th to invest the three Russian commanders, Marshal Zhukov, Rokossovsky and General Sokolovski. They all gave each other colourful and appropriate medals! This time the Grenadiers and 8th and 11th Hussars lined the route as Guard of Honour. Bill Bellamy recalled: 'We travelled the length of the Charlottenburger Chaussée as far as the Brandenberger Tur, the great triumphal gate, marking the divide between British and Russian zones. Then the Tiergarten [zoo] and the Siegessaule. The trees in the parks on both sides of the avenue were stripped of their leaves – the aftermath of a first world war battle. The fighting must have been horrific.' On the 13th the first full-scale divisional parade, a rehearsal for the victory parade, took place. Two days later the delegates for the Potsdam Conference started to arrive, including of course the prime minister, Winston Churchill, and Anthony Eden and Clement Attlee. Then followed another frenetic week of last minute rehearsals, flag poles and stands being erected for the great day – Saturday 21 July. The bands were provided by the Royal Marines, 11th Hussars and 2nd Devons, and the troops on parade were found from 3rd RHA, 5th RHA, 8th Hussars, 11th Hussars, 1st Battalion Grenadier Guards, 1/5th Queens, 2nd Devons and representatives from the Navy, RAF and RAF Regiment.

3rd RHA fired a 19-gun salute in honour of the prime minister and Field Marshals Montgomery, Brooke and Alexander. As Tom Ritson recalled: 'A few days later Mr Churchill was dismissed by the electorate and Mr Attlee returned to Potsdam in his place.' Verdon Besley wrote: 'We were all ready, the Queens right in front of Churchill waiting to start when there was a cascade of motor bikes escorting President Truman, with their sirens sounding, and the parade started.' Bill Bellamy observed:

> The Russians outnumbered the British. They were quite smart in their loosely cut service dress, flat hats, gold or silver epaulettes, and polished jack-boots and they all had so many medals! As we approached the saluting base, being leader of the 8th Hussars column I had a very clear view. Mr Churchill stood slightly to the fore wearing a light coloured Service Dress and a peaked dress hat. He was standing, looking directly up the Chaussée and saluted us in answer to the Colonel's salute. Standing next to him was Mr Attlee in civilian clothes and bareheaded. Then Field Marshals Alan Brooke and Montgomery with the tall bareheaded figure of Mr Anthony Eden to the left. General Lyne was standing to the PM's left, together with a senior naval officer. I also spotted Mr Morrison. Then it was all over and we were past.

The new 'Winston' Club of the 7th Armoured Division for other ranks was later opened formally by Winston Churchill, where he made his famous speech that included *inter alia*:

> Now I have only a word more to say about the Desert Rats. They were the first to begin. The 11th Hussars were in action in the desert in 1940 and ever since you have kept marching steadily forward on the long road to victory. Through so many countries and changing scenes you have fought your way. It is not without emotion that I can express to you what I feel about the Desert Rats.
>
> Dear Desert Rats! May your glory every shine! May your laurels never fade! May the memory of this glorious pilgrimage of war which you have made from Alamein, via the Baltic to Berlin, never die!
>
> It is a march unsurpassed through all the story of war so far as my reading of history leads me to believe. May the fathers long tell the children about this tale. May you all feel that in following your great ancestors you have accomplished something which has done good to the whole world; which has raised the honour of your own country and which every man has a right to be proud of.

CHAPTER 24

Red Crown & Dragon: 53rd Welsh Division

The 53rd (Welsh Division) was the only formation in the British Army to be mainly composed of Welsh soldiers. The Royal Welch Fusiliers (RWF) were the heart of the Division with all three battalions of 158th Brigade (4th, 6th and 7th), the 71st Anti-tank (RWF) Regiment RA and the 116th Light AA (RWF) Regiment. In 160th Brigade were the Welch Regiment (4th and 1/5th Battalions) and the 2nd Battalion the Monmouthshire Regiment. The 71st Brigade, nicknamed 'The International' or 'The Foreign Brigade', were deployed with the 1st Battalion Highland Light Infantry (mainly from Glasgow), 1st Battalion Oxfordshire and Buckinghamshire (Ox and Bucks) and the 1st Battalion East Lancashires. In full support were the 1st Battalion Manchester Regiment with its medium machine-guns and mortars and the three 25-pdr towed guns of 81st, 83rd and 133rd Field. The divisional spearhead in relatively open country was the 53rd Reconnaissance Regiment RAC. The divisional insignia was a bardic red crown on a black background and the RWF sported a red dragon.

The Division had had little battle experience. In 1940 several companies fought briefly in the short Norwegian campaign. For years they garrisoned Northern Ireland, and even Wales, and underwent numerous exercises. But when the popular Major General 'Bobby' Ross led his 15,000 or so troops into Normandy on 23–24 June 1944, although superbly trained, they were a 'green' division, as were seven other divisions.

The shock of arrival in the bridgehead was described by Lieutenant Peter Utley, 'B' Squadron Recce Regiment: 'We moved into the detritus of the assault [D-Day and the push inland]. The smell of putrefaction was all about us, but the worst smell was from the incinerated bodies of tank crews in their burnt-out vehicles. I tried as best I could to keep my troopers away from such sights. In their thin-skinned vehicles [armoured cars] unfortunate comparisons were bound to come to mind.'

Initially the Division concentrated around Soubles, Bény-sur-Mer and St André. The lethal battles followed: first Operation Epsom, then Jupiter and Greenline, in the deadly close countryside of the *bocage*. Le Cahier, Le Bon Repos and particularly Evrecy, will always be remembered. During the final battles to close the Argentan-Falaise Gap in August 1944, the Division captured 5,500 prisoners. By the end of August the 'green' division had suffered 3,819

2 Kensingtons Bren carrier passes knocked-out German tank in Rauray. (*Imperial War Museum B-0137*)

casualties. The young Lieutenant Tasker Watkins of 1/5th Welch Regiment won the Victoria Cross on 16 August near Martigny and Hill 233, leading bayonet charges on enemy machine-gun posts.

Normandy had been a horrifying experience for the Welshmen and their 'foreign' colleagues in arms. Their nine infantry battalions had borne the brunt of each attack and most of their young leaders are buried in the dignified British war cemeteries scattered across Normandy.

However, there was now an unexpected 10–14-day break from attritional fighting as the Division mopped up behind the three armoured divisions going north, hell for leather, through northern France into Belgium and Holland.

Lieutenant Pender, 1st HLI, recalled: 'We crossed the Seine on 30th August, the Somme [Picquigny] on 2nd September, through Givenchy and Menin where we stayed the night and watched the Last Post being sounded at the Menin Gate in memory of the Allied Armies dead of 1914–18, played by the town's fire brigade. All the way to Antwerp was one endless nightmare. There were some compensations, flowers, wine, fruit and pretty girls who all cheered their liberators to the highest. The Jocks showered the children and girls with chocolate and food.'

The 1/5th Welch route to Antwerp was via Muids (Seine crossing), La Mesnil-sur-Vienne, Gournay-en-Bray where the FFI shot a priest, Le Héronde to Surcamps, a night journey of 80 miles, then Lillers via Saint Pol-sur-Ternoise.

Fusilier John Ottewell, 7th RWF, remembered: 'Travelling at night through the Flanders plain was an eerie and poignant experience. In the fading light the trench lines of WWI were vaguely discernible. With closed eyes one could almost visualise their "No Man's Land" screaming and cheering as they waded through the slopping mud to oblivion. Somebody struck up "Roses Are Blooming In Picardy". Within minutes the entire convoy, the Welsh "Treorchy Male Voice" in muted harmony, tenors and baritones were rendering that "tearful" love song.....'

At Fleurbaix in Belgium, the GOC fleetingly established Divisional HQ where he had spent the winter of 1914–15 in trench warfare.

So eventually 53rd Welsh arrived in Antwerp on 8 September to a tremendous welcome, to tidy up after 11th Armoured Division's three-day town battles. Apart from some enemy in Merxem, the northeast suburb, the Division acted for a week as a garrison.

On 13 September Monty visited the Division and talked to many officers and men. Two days later the Welsh went to war again as left flank and base protection for the great Market Garden operation. The Recce Regiment and 158th Brigade, who were to make the assault crossing of the Canal de Jonction north of Lommel, 36 miles east of Antwerp, on 15 September led via Steelen, Vorst, Beeringen (Albert canal crossing) north to Bourg-Leopold and finally to Lommel. A further objective due north was Luyksgester in Holland.

Unfortunately for the Welsh Division, and for 15th Scottish on their left tasked with the capture of the town of Gheel, the commander of the hastily

Celebrations in Antwerp, 4 September 1944. (*R.T. Lancaster*)

assembled German Parachute Army, General Kurt Student, had already sent his battle group Fallschirmjaeger Regiment 6 (parachute regiment) part of 2nd Parachute Korps, to block and hold the line of the Canal de Jonction de la Meuse. The highly experienced and decorated Lt Colonel Friedrich von der Heydte, a veteran of Crete and Normandy, commanded this powerful force which included Kampfgruppe Zedlitz 937th Regiment, the Hermann Göring Training Regiment, four infantry battalions each with about 200 men, plus a heavy mortar company, motorised anti-tank company, various machine-gun companies and recce and engineer companies. Then von der Heydte was joined by the Blocking Force Heinke with two SS Panzer-Grenadier battalions, Segler and Krause, a force of 15 Mark IV tanks with the long-barrelled 77mm gun, and Artillery Regiment 10 from 10th SS Panzer Division. There was also, unfortunately, a rogue Dutch SS unit.

So, from the Neerpelt bridgehead five miles to the east, to Moll and Gheel, 12 miles to the west, a powerful hotch-potch of German Wehrmacht, paratroops, Luftwaffe ground troops, coastguards and Flak troops were quickly shuffled into shape and were preparing to give a brutal shock to the British Army left-flanking on Market Garden.

The assault on a two-battalion front on both sides of a demolished bridge was by 1st East Lancs on the left, 7th RWF on the right. The Canal de Jonction de la Meuse was two-and-a-half miles running east–west. A steep 'bund' runs along its length crowned by a dense strip of young fir trees. The crossing points for the East Lancs were about 200 yards apart. The 50 yards width of the canal would be crossed by 16 class V rafts built by the Pioneers and REs, holding 18 men each. A 'flight' of two boats would thus take a platoon. The 2nd Mons carried out duties of 'obstacle company' with carrying parties, called ferrymen, generally assisting the assaulting companies of 'D' Company on the right and 'C' Company on the left. A substantial fire plan from seven field regiments, two medium regiments, plus the Manchesters' 4.2-inch mortar and medium machine-guns would provide supporting barrages. Opposition was from dedicated German paratroopers who fought with courage and great skill.

At 2330hrs on 16 September the East Lancs boats went down the steep stone-faced bank into the water. It was a dark night, belting with rain, and with visibility only 10–15 yards. Although on the right flank two boats sank with two men drowned, both companies got across relatively unscathed. The move through narrow rides in thick forest at angles to advance meant that all companies became isolated and lost in the dark. Predictably, wireless communications broke down. Lt Colonel Burden tracked down his leading companies, ordered them to halt and advance again at first light. At dawn three out of four companies had 'changed' places, only 'C' was in the right place. Moreover, most enemy forces had been bypassed in the dark. They then opened fire briskly on the rafting operations on the canal. Confused fighting went on all day on the 17th. Major Griffin led 'A' Company in four separate attacks on isolated fortified huts in the woods. By the time 1/5th Welch came through in the evening the East Lancs had 30 casualties.

7th RWF made their first ever assault water crossing, which went according to plan, although 'A' Coy on the right met heavy Spandau fire. 'B' and 'C' were quickly across the canal and cleared the far bank towards 'A'. 'D' Company of 1/5th Welch was borrowed and by 0500hrs on the 18th all five companies were dug in on their objective. Lt Colonel Dickson then pushed 'C' and 'D' at 1100hrs towards the Heider Heide, again with success. The 7th RWF suffered 34 casualties, captured 28 prisoners and did a lot of damage to the enemy paratroopers.

From Steensel 1/5th Welch captured Hoogeloon on the 21st with a bag of 61 prisoners. However, it was Major Goldsmid who led his two troops of recce cars and carriers into the village and was mainly responsible for the enemy's 200 casualties. On the 18th 6th RWF led 160th Brigade across the canal and next day 71st Brigade followed.

For the next two weeks the Division was involved in half a dozen nasty unit battles that are described chronologically. Philip Cowburn, the Recce historian, relates what happened after the regiment had crossed the canal: '[we] fought our way into this country of moorland, wood and marsh, occupied by a resolute battle group of 6th German Parachute Regiment. All squadrons fought with distinction round the villages of Reusel, Bladel, Eersel, Hoogeloon, Casteren, Netersel, Middelbeers and Hilvarenbeek in that corner of north-west Brabant'.

On the 20th 4th RWF attacked and captured Wintelre having passed through 158th Brigade's bridgehead on the 19th. The village, ten miles inland, was strongly held and it took a two-day battle to clear it. 'A' Company was counter-attacked near Bysterveld and suffered badly and 'D' Company was under heavy fire from Hoogeloon. The village church spire was an enemy OP. Eventually, at 1430hrs on the 21st, after a heavy concentration of divisional artillery fire, the enemy started to give up and by the evening the village was taken. The enemy lost 60 killed and many more wounded, and 4th RWF took 168 prisoners, plus 11 enemy guns of various calibres. But the Fusiliers had 80 casualties, 'B' Company alone losing 33. Unfortunately, Brigadier Bloomfield, following 4th RWF into the village, was badly wounded. The Brigade, without firm management, played Musical Chairs for the next few days. 4th RWF was told to stay in Wintelre for a few days and dug in. They were promptly moved on the 22nd to relieve 7th RWF at Westel-Beers. 7th RWF moved to Hoogeloon, then by vehicle to Duizel. 4th RWF settled in again and 7th RWF were ordered back to their recent positions. And 4th RWF? They returned to

Escaut canal.

Wintelre! Not very good staff work for hundreds of exhausted Fusiliers. The moves were *not* explained to the COs, certainly not to the rank and file. Brigadier M. Elrington arrived to command 71st Brigade on 28 September. The rest of 71st Brigade was more fortunate. 1st HLI captured Oostelbeers and Middelbeers, two villages three miles north-west of Wintelre, but only after a three-day battle.

The Ox and Bucks were ordered to infiltrate the enemy lines towards the Wilhelmina canal, 20 miles north and parallel to the Junction canal. So, on 19 September they crossed the Escaut canal by pontoon bridge, ten miles south-west of Valkenswaard, and then, via Meerveldhoven, near Eindhoven, they passed Oerle, Hoogeind and Scherpendhering on their way to the village of De Kruisberg. On the way, at Eijkereind, an entire school of novice priests turned out on the road to sing 'God Save the King'. After many adventures the battalion arrived at the blown bridge at Oirscot on the Wilhelmina canal, west of Best. 'D' Company moved along to clear the south bank of panzer grenadiers of Kampfgruppe Zedlitz, but they were counter-attacked, heavily shelled and lost six men killed and nine wounded. Lt Colonel Hare took over command of 71st Brigade for a week when Brigadier Blomfield was wounded.

After 158th Brigade had made the initial bridgehead north of Lommel, they moved north on the 21st to Eersel, Duizel and Hapert, which had been previously occupied by 71st Brigade.

On the 23rd 6th RWF moved to Postel, south-west of Witrijt. Their late night arrival '…was greeted by monks from the local monastery who turned out in their long white robes and greeted us [Capt. Roberts] with a local barrel organ with such tunes as "It's a long way to Tipperary" and "Pack up

Scene from a bombed-out city.

your troubles". We thanked them for their (noisy) welcome, begged them to be quieter as the enemy was still quite close and might shell the village. Unwillingly they condescended to silence the barrel organ.'

Netersel, a village north of Bladel, was jointly cleared by the Recce Regiment and 1/5th Welch. Lieutenant Boraston, 'B' Squadron Recce, wrote: 'Our task was to hold on to the village of Netersel, prevent the enemy getting back into it. An enemy 88mm just missed Sergeant Mote's car and the next car, but we were more or less pinned down.' 'Bud' Abbot recalls: 'Here we lost "Dusty" Miller and others due to wounds from shell and mortar fire. We manned a slit trench with the Germans dug in just a field away.'

The 7th RWF reverted to 158th Brigade on the 21st and set off early through Veld-Hoven and Knegsel towards Vessem, and spent the day clearing the village of the 937th Infantry Regiment. 'B' and 'D' Companies took 32 prisoners to the delight of the inhabitants. The following day they pushed into Donk to add another 22 prisoners and tried to take Westelbeers. A determined enemy using flame-throwers caused casualties to Major Tomlinson's 'D' Company, but a battalion attack was cancelled as 4th RWF came up to relieve 7th RWF, who moved to the St Oedenroede area.

As the airborne reinforcements passed overhead on Sunday 24th, 133rd Field Regiment supported 2nd Mons in their attack on Voorheide. They had advanced from the De Maat and Postel area from the bridgehead and went into action at 1800hrs. The gallant Pioneers located the mines under fire *in the darkness*, and pulled them out by hand with a cable. At 0300hrs 2nd Mons were counter-attacked by four companies of paratroopers. Savage and confused fighting took place, and bazookas, grenades and Spandaus were deployed against buildings occupied by three Mons companies. All company areas were penetrated at times, and complete platoons and sections were surrounded. Heavy defensive fire by divisional artillery and the Manchesters' 42-inch mortars saved the situation.

Major R.N. Dean, OC 'A' Coy:

The enemy had counter-attacked out of the dark, four companies of paratroops to our three and for a time the village was in complete pandemonium where the only recipes for continued firing were to stay in a slit and shoot Germans off the windy skyline or stay in a room and shoot them off the dim windowsill. In the latter case the cost of bad shooting was a hand grenade thrown into the room, a deafening disruption of domestic rubble and someone badly hurt. The cost of speaking on a wireless set at all was the hand grenade or 'bazooka' from the Germans outside. At one time Voorheide was held by both German and British, one on the outside of the houses and the other inside. Invitations to 'surrender! You are surrounded' were met by streams of good British verbal obscenities and a burst of automatic Sten fire from skylight or cellar peephole.

The 6th German Regiment parachutists left over 60 casualties on the ground. The Mons lost 18 killed, 22 wounded and seven prisoners. General Ross sent a message, 'Well done, 2nd Mons'.

Of the dozen or so battalion battles involved in the operations north of Lommel, perhaps the most savage was that of the assault on Reusel on the west of the 53rd Division salient. The town was one of the road junctions most important to the German defence, and was defended by 600 paratroops of whom only 100 were destined to survive. Every house had been fortified and the divisional artillery of 25-pdrs would do little damage to the German strong points. On the 24th the carrier platoon of 6th RWF came under fire. 'A' Company under Major O.E.H. Hughes advanced under heavy Spandau, anti-tank and artillery fire. It secured the outskirts of the village but could move no further. 'C', under Major Grindley, and 'B', under Major Lord Davies, were sent right flanking but they were observed and pinned down. By late afternoon, after many hours of heavy fighting, the three rifle companies were still hundreds of yards short of the town. Lt Colonel Snead-Cox decided to withdraw at nightfall. At dawn Captain Barnett led a patrol into Reusel unopposed. It was a trap: 'B', 'C' and 'D' Companies were shelled as they were forming up for a dawn attack. 'C' Company, despite heavy casualties, captured some buildings on the south side, but 'B' Company were also in serious difficulties from machine-gun fire from a church converted into a strong point. SS troops including Dutch SS mounted a bold counter-attack that forced 'C' and most of 'D' to withdraw.

For a day and a half 6th RWF had tried their best and failed. Now 4th Welch attacked the following night, approaching Reusel across the front of 6th RWF, but was held up by the church strongpoint.

For three days 4th Welch grimly cleared house to house, street to street. There were many casualties in that time. The paratroopers succeeded not only in holding the attack but also in infiltrating the enemy Spandau groups, some 20 strong between platoons and companies. The fighting became very confused. The least movement drew enemy fire, and mortar bombs seemed to be bursting everywhere. Sections were burnt out of houses by panzerfaust and phosphorus grenades; stores were burnt and reserve ammo exploded. Battalion HQ had great difficulty controlling such a confused battle.

Close quarters fighting continued for three days. When 4th Welch was ordered to withdraw, a half section was cut off in and around the church. They had no wireless. The German/Dutch SS opposition probably spoke English, so Sergeant J.H.W. Williams came up and directed the withdrawal in the *Welsh* language. During the day the half section and the remainder of the battalion were successfully withdrawn under cover of 'Allied' artillery. A flight of Typhoons dived at the church firing their rockets. Anti-tank guns and 17-pdrs of the Anti-Tank Regiment fired at the church and brought the steeple down, but the paratroops fought on. Major A.J. Lewis recalled: 'Many people believed in the protection of God during that withdrawal. We certainly seemed to be protected by some Divine Power.'

The divisional sappers had done a good job building bridges, including a nine-ton bridge at Lommel over the Meuse-Escaut canal and 40-ton bridges over other river crossings. The line of advance of 12th Corps, of which 53rd Division was a part, remained via Oud-Turnhout to Boxtel via Retie, Arendonk and Kasterlee. The Division was to move north to capture Reusel and dominate the Poppel-Esbeek-Diessen area, but 6th RWF found Reusel empty on 3 October.

Captain David Bolland's diary:

Wednesday, 27th September. 83 Field Regt went off with 158 Bde towards Schinder where Jerry is being troublesome trying to cut our lines of communication – again – north of Eindhoven. The BBC announced that the Airborne troops have been withdrawn from Arnhem. This came as a bitter pill to most of us who knew just how much effort had been put into the whole thing. Many lives must have been lost. Friday, 29th. To HQRA, a visit by the Inspector RA and BRA Second Army. How typical the RA was of the Regular Army, slightly patronising towards the wartime soldiers and full of his stories about all his pals. Tuesday, 3rd October. Visited 31 RHU, 30 miles SW of Brussels. Very cold, very wet and very cross. Still crosser when I discovered we were only to get 56 out of our 190 bodies [reinforcements

St Vith in the Ardennes. (*Harrison Standley*)

for the Divisional Artillery Regiments]. On 6th October 160 Bde and 71 Bde moved NE to a defensive position about Elst, a few miles south of Arnhem into a defensive position. 158 Bde had already moved through Eindhoven to St Oedenrode.

Captain Tim Dumas of 4th RWF wrote about morale:

As a Coy CO I must say that one had complete confidence that any battle or engagement would in the end be successful. We had complete air superiority and good weapons. But the German 88 gun was worrying for an infantryman; an incoming shell could normally be heard and allow one to get down, whilst the 88 exploded before you could hear it coming. A quite senior Fusilier Barden, a Cockney from Kent said to me, during another bombardment in Bemmell. 'Them little things can't 'urt yer'. The next moment he was dead. A mortar bomb had landed right by him.

The two weeks of holding and expanding the Lommel bridgehead, and evicting German paratroopers and von der Heydte's many determined kampfgruppen, had taken a massive toll of 53rd Division.

The next three weeks were spent as garrison to what was called the Island between the rivers around Arnhem and Nijmegen. This was the infamous polder area of deep wide ditches, flooded fields, dykes and bunds, occasional fruit tree orchards and tree plantations, which was and now littered with destroyed Shermans, Cromwells and Stuart tanks, mainly from the Guards Armoured Division. Garrisoning this region involved many artillery and mortar duels in a continual programme of patrols and raids.

At the end of October the Welsh warriors took a major part in Operations Pheasant and Alan to capture the important town of 's-Hertogenbosch. They fought later in the Ardennes in the 'Battle of the Bulge'.

By the end of the war in May 1945, 53rd Division had suffered nearly 10,000 casualties.

Detail from picture on p. 12. (*Imperial War Museum BU-509*)

CHAPTER 25

The Red Lion Rampant: 15th Scottish Division

The 15th Scottish Division had fought in many battles in the First World War including Loos, the Somme, Arras, Ypres and on the Marne to Buzancy. A territorial formation, it was reborn at the outbreak of war in September 1939. Its parent was 52nd Lowland Division, which provided all the key commanders. 15th Scottish had an unhappy, chequered existence until April 1943, when it became part of 1st Corps and was upgraded to 'Higher Establishment'.

The 44th (Lowland) Brigade derived mainly from the Lothians and the Border counties, and consisted of the 8th Battalion the Royal Scots, 6th Battalion the Royal Scots Fusiliers and 6th Battalion the Kings Own Scottish Borderers (KOSB). The 46th (Highland Light Infantry) Brigade derived mainly from Glasgow and consisted of 9th Battalion the Cameronians, 2nd Battalion the Glasgow Highlanders and 7th Battalion the Seaforth Highlanders. The original 45th Infantry Brigade was replaced by 227th (Highland) Brigade with 10th Battalion the Highland Light Infantry, 2nd Battalion the Gordon Highlanders and 2nd Battalion the Argyll and Sutherland Highlanders – an all Highland formation.

Major General G.H.A. Macmillan became their GOC when the Division was transferred to 8th Corps as part of the vital 'break-out' corps destined for Operation Overlord in Normandy. Montgomery made sure that all his 'virgin' formations were thoroughly fit and well trained for what lay ahead. Like all infantry divisions it had its own formidable team of 'gunners' – 131st, 181st and 190th Field Regiments RA with towed 25-pdr guns, 97th Anti-tank and 119th Light AA Regiment, plus 1st Battalion the Middlesex Regiment with medium machine-guns and mortars. 15th Reconnaissance Regiment RAC led the Division whenever the battleground was open enough.

On a brilliant morning on 13 June (D+7) the Division landed on the eastern beaches between Gold and Sword and two weeks later was blooded in Operation Epsom, 26 June–1 July. The main objective was the little river Odon and then the formidable Hill 112, which commanded views of the whole of the Allied bridgehead for the German defenders. Cheux, Saint-Mauvieu and Grainville were heavily fortified villages on the way to the river bridges at Gavrus and Tourmauville. What became known as 'The Scottish corridor' was only 2,500 yards wide and open to attacks from three sides.

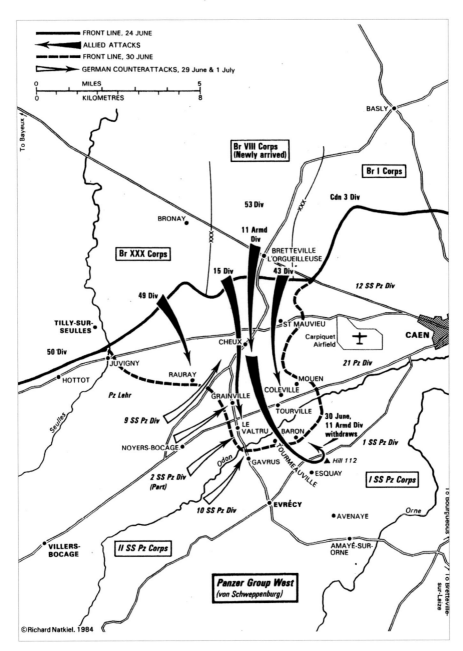

Operation Epsom, 26 June–1 June 1944.

Epsom lasted five days. 15th Scottish Division had been torn apart. 130 officers were killed or wounded, and 257 other ranks were killed and 1,547 wounded. Just as sadly, a further 780 men were missing, either killed or made prisoner. Monty wrote: 'Scotland can well be proud of the 15th Scottish Division and the whole division can be proud of itself.'

Westminster Dragoons clear the way at Hermanville-sur-Mer in front of 15th Scottish Division. (*Imperial War Museum B-5445*)

In July Operations Jupiter and Greenline followed, and during Bluecoat, on 2 August, the GOC, Major General Macmillan, was wounded by a shell splinter. Brigadier C.M. Barber from 44th Brigade was promoted to be the new GOC; he was nicknamed 'Tiny' because he was 6 ft 6 in. tall!

By the end of August the proud Scotsmen had suffered over 5,300 casualties in the 50 days of the Overlord bridgehead, during which they were in action for 37 days. Captain Robert Woollcombe, 6th KOSB wrote: 'with tight-lipped, bitter verve they fought.... Above all we saw the dark face of the Waffen SS. And this we broke, in Normandy.'

Montgomery had fixed ideas about most units in his command. He regarded the two Scottish divisions (15th and 51st) as being by far the best for assault crossings of rivers or canals, as was shown clearly much later in the battle for the Rhine in Operation Torchlight on 23 March 1945.

The hot pursuit by the three armoured divisions towards Brussels, Antwerp and Ghent often left the infantry to follow up and subdue small towns and villages with German garrisons which had been bypassed. This, of course, required different techniques. Lieutenant MacLellan, 2nd Glasgow Highlanders, wrote: 'In clearing buildings, I had trained my men to get to the uppermost floor as fast as possible and clear downwards. I personally raced for the third floor of one building and found a dormitory that had obviously been evacuated in a hurry.' Much of the divisional transport was lent to support the 'Great Swan' north.

The Division set off north and covered 25 miles on 3 September, 15 miles on the 4th and 75 miles on the 5th, through the chalk lands of Picardy and Artois. Lieutenant MacLellan noted: 'We passed through Amiens, Arras, Vimy Ridge, Lens, skirted Lille and entered Belgium on 5 September through the little town of Belleghem where we received a terrific welcome.' The next day they reached Oudenarde. The KOSB crossed the Somme west of Amiens on the way to Saint Pol, then over the Calais-Arras highway, north-east to Béthune, and on to La Bassée towards Lille and the Belgian frontier. They stopped at a First World War cemetery where KOSB soldiers lie buried. In Halluin, on the border, the KOSB received a riotous and happy welcome before continuing into Belgium across the river Lys to Wevelghem. It was a royal procession with banners proclaiming 'Welcome our liberators'. The 15th Scottish Recce Regiment went through Doullens, Houvin, Arras, Lens, Carvin, Seclin and Roubaix. Whenever the armoured cars or carriers halted, girls and children chalked on them the names of their towns, their own names and slogans. There were kisses, flowers and fruit. On the frontier French and Belgian gendarmes cheered side by side. The Recce had come 300 miles through France in 14 days and now drove on beneath the red, yellow and black Belgian flags. On their map boards, blue circles showed that not far ahead the enemy waited, so they now headed for Belleghen, Kirkhove and Avelghem.

In the area west of the line Antwerp–Ghent–Lille–Béthune–Hesdin some 160,000 German troops who had been expecting the main Allied invasion to come in the Calais area were now streaming northwards. Some of them would attempt to break into the area along the line Thielt–Deinze–Courtrai–Menin–Roulers. Each day the brave Recce cars and carriers scuttled briskly ahead, drawing fire and taking casualties and always reporting back by wireless contact. Many small towns and villages changed hands, which made the inhabitants extremely anxious as the Germans always carried out reprisals if they returned. The RSF occupied a village astride one of the escape routes. The 44th Lowland account relates: 'After killing or capturing all the Germans there, the RSF company had an amusing night ambushing enemy convoys which unsuspectingly kept driving into the place.' The Argylls crossed the Belgian frontier on 7 September at Mouscron and had a carnival evening at Bossuyt. The troops were loaded with apples, pears, plums, tomatoes, eggs, wine and coffee. There was an orgy of kissing!

During the 7th the Royal Scots crossed the river Lys canal and then fought their way to Roulers, taking many prisoners. The RSF crossed the Courtrai-Bossuyt canal, took Deerlyck and ambushed enemy columns in buses, returning with 75 prisoners. Captain J.S. Cunis, FOO of 181st Field Regiment, occupied a comfortable observation point in a tall block of flats in Courtrai. He had a hot bath, eggs and bacon, and when the morning mist lifted he got to work. On three roads clearly visible, not more than a mile away, were long columns of slow-moving stolen country carts piled high with loot. These targets of opportunity continued to appear throughout the day, and Cunis kept his 25-pdr gun teams busy. On the 8th the Recce Regiment led the RSF to capture Deinze, the KOSB to Zulte and the Royal Scots to Hansbeke. 227th Brigade moved south of Ghent, mopping up pockets, and stayed in the area until 11 September. Antwerp and Brussels had been captured a week before and some leave parties were sent off to the fleshpots of Brussels. 46th Brigade was echeloned along the Escaut canal for 11 miles north of Oudenarde and remained there till 10 September.

In Deinze, near Mechelen, Major Moreton of the Argylls, acting as Mayor to the town, was entertained to a champagne dinner in the town hall; a dance was held and the pipes and drums beat 'Retreat' in both towns. The pipe major received bouquets from the Belgians which he laid on the local war memorials.

The Glasgow Highlanders were sent off to help the Queen's Infantry Brigade of 7th Armoured Division clear a large factory area across the Canal du Nord. The German force had been resisting the Polish Armoured and the Desert Rats for nearly a week in Ghent. A large, well-defended town, it needed a lot of infantry to clear it and became a platoon commander's battle. "B' company lorries were just in front of us', wrote Lieutenant MacLellan, 'and the second truck ahead of mine got a direct hit killing and wounding several soldiers. Shelling in a built-up area is a frightening experience, even more so than on a reverse slope. You cannot tell where the shells will land with any degree of accuracy and when they explode, besides shrapnel, there are also splinters of glass, wood, concrete, dirt and metal coming at you.'

No.17 Platoon took 200 prisoners out of the total bag of six officers and 233 prisoners. By the morning of the 11th Ghent was free at last, but the Glasgows took 66 casualties in their two days of street fighting and factory clearance. The Division had spent the 10th near Malines (Mechelen). The town burghers celebrated by playing a recital of Scottish tunes on the famous carillon.

As part of the huge complicated plan for Operation Market Garden – the bold thrust for the Rhine crossings – 15th Scottish Division was to relieve 50th Tyne Tees Division in the Gheel bridgehead beyond the Albert canal. It was like a series of chess moves. 50th Tyne Tees, when relieved, would move east into the De Groot bridgehead, which would then enable Guards Armoured to lead the 30th Corps advance north to Arnhem. On 12 September the 44th and 46th Brigades moved embussed from Malines to debus south of the Albert canal and to cross over into the Gheel bridgehead.

The bridgehead was quadrilateral in shape, with the Albert canal, six miles of it, at the southern end. The little towns of Gheel, Aart, Donck, Moll, Meerhout and Zittaart lay north before the Escaut Junction canal is reached between four and eight miles north-west and north-east. The German 16th GAF Division had pushed 50th Division out of Gheel itself. The task of the 15th Scottish was to clear the whole of the countryside between the Albert and the Junction canals.

The battle plan was for 44th Brigade to clear Gheel up to the railway and move north to Junction canal, and for 46th Brigade to extend the bridgehead north-west towards Herenthals. 227th Brigade would then push the bridgehead north-east, capture Moll and seize the bridge at Donck. 15th Recce Regiment had sent patrols deep into the bridgehead north of Gheel, into Moll, where two of their armoured cars were knocked out.

By 0800hrs on 13 September, shortly after 200 GAF troops had moved out, the Royal Scots occupied Gheel. The GOC, Major General Barber, decided to use the tactics so successfully employed at the crossing of the river Seine. He ordered 44th Brigade, with comprehensive sapper support and bridging material, to go headlong for the Junction canal defences. From Gheel the Royal Scots would take the three-mile road north to Aart and the KOSB would take the road north-east towards Retie. On the left flank 46th Brigade, led by the Cameronians and followed by the Seaforths, would advance three miles west of Gheel in a defensive role to protect enemy movement out of Herentals. 227th Brigade would extend the bridgehead on the right-hand flank, HLI leading, through Meerhout towards Moll and Donck, followed up by the Gordons.

All went well to start with. The HLI liberated Moll, empty of opposition, and the Argylls reached Donck. The Gordons were in Meerhout and Zittaart. Both 46th and 44th Brigades closed up on the Junction canal and 15th Scottish

The battle for the Gheel bridgehead, 12–15 September, cost 15th Scottish Division about 540 casualties, including 141 killed in action.

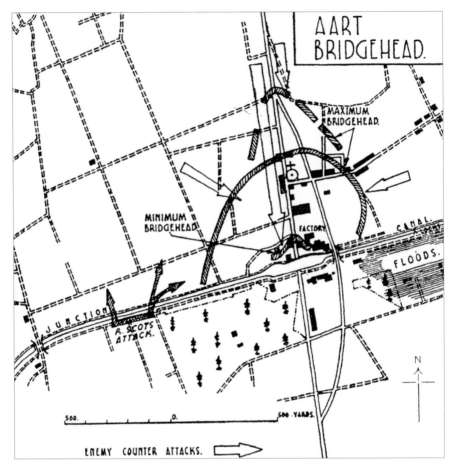

Royal Scots force a bridgehead over the Junction canal.

now held the nine-mile line of the Junction canal with, predictably, all bridges blown ahead of them.

The KOSB incursion during the dark night of 13–14 September was a gallant failure. A platoon crossed over the damaged lock on the road to Retie and was cut off and captured as mortars and 88mm guns swept the canal in enfilade. Major Rollo, who had won the MC in Normandy, was fatally wounded. The German defenders then manipulated the canal locks and flooded the battleground. The CO, Lt Colonel Richardson, ordered his forward companies to withdraw – through three feet of water.

Two miles to the west lies the village of Aart, with its road, bridge, church, crossroads and a large, square factory. Lt Colonel Lane Joynt, CO of the Royal Scots, organised an assault to capture Aart using assault boats provided by 279th Field Company RE. Starting at 0400hrs the whole battalion went over the canal, although 'A' Company suffered heavily from two-barrelled flak guns firing in a ground role. The sappers, under Major P.T. Wood, endeavoured to bridge another nearby lock site but the enemy's flooding destroyed his efforts. On the evening of the 14th he succeeded in rafting 6-pdr anti-tank guns over to the Royal Scots. Confused fighting went on in and around Aart with support for the beleaguered Royal Scots from tank, SP guns and artillery. By nightfall they had captured 100 prisoners from the Luftwaffe regiments attacking them.

General Student now sent in his Hermann Göring Training Regiment who launched a ferocious attack at 2200hrs down the main road from Turnhout. The Luftwaffe troops, led by SS, attacked the Royal Scots from the east under covering fire. An hour later two well-handled SP guns with infantry support came in from the west. Confused fighting, much of it hand to hand, went on all night in the bright light of burning houses and haystacks. 'A' and 'C' Companies were torn apart, 'D' only just held and 'B' was surrounded. On the morning of the 15th the bridgehead had been reduced in size, with a few Royal Scots platoons on both sides of the main street holding out. At about 1000hrs the Germans disengaged to allow a bombardment of the tiny bridgehead. Brigadier Cockburn sent the RSF by assault boats to reinforce the battered Royal Scots, landing on the north bank of the canal to the east of Aart.

They soon expanded the bridgehead by 1430hrs but the Hermann Göring Regiment put in two heavy counter-attacks and compressed the area held by the Scotsmen. Finally, Brigadier Cockburn sent the KOSB across to try to expand the bridgehead north and eastwards. They arrived to find the Scots and RSF in considerable confusion, fighting for their lives.

Major General Barber then ordered 227th Brigade to a concentration area near Donck to make an assault crossing seven miles to the east.

Whilst 44th Brigade was fighting to avoid being overwhelmed, Field Marshal Montgomery arrived at Divisional HQ to present medal ribbons: 'I hope that you will tell your folk at home that I came here today and told you that the 15th Scottish Division had done magnificently.' The Recce Regiment provided the guard of honour and was complimented by the GOC on its smartness and bearing. It was a crazy war. In the basement of a building in Gheel the officers of 2nd Glasgow Highlanders held a mess dinner dressed in kilts, brought up to the front by the Quartermaster. Their CO praised three of the Canloan officers for their deeds in Ghent: Russell Parke, Louis Boudreau and Roger MacLellan (who was awarded the MC for his successful actions in Ghent).

Meanwhile, the three gunner regiments fired DF targets and concentrations around the bridgehead. The Recce Regiment stayed south of the canal, quartered among the hospitable people of Moll and Meerhout, patrolling the factories, straggling suburbs, woods and marshes in the canal area to prevent German infiltrations. At 0400hrs on 16 September the Gordons tried to cross the Junction canal near Donck but were pinned down by intense and accurate machine-gun fire. Brigadier Colville withdrew them after several hours of intensive fighting. Throughout 15 September, despite the KOSB getting across the Rethy bridge to help the RSF and Royal Scots, the enemy held the initiative and mounted several fierce counter-attacks. The heaviest came in at 2000hrs and the RSF was pushed back but held on – just.

Early on the 17th the survivors of the Royal Scots were pulled out of the bridgehead and ferried to relative safety. In their three-day battle they had lost 230 officers and men (31 killed in action, 53 captured) and went back – poor devils – to Gheel to reorganise. In the early afternoon the Scottish Division watched the Dakotas, Stirlings and gliders flying towards Arnhem through puffs of anti-aircraft shells. It was the beginning of the ill-fated Market Garden operation.

After dark the Argylls crossed in assault-boat ferries into the Aart bridgehead to relieve the battered 6th RSF, who were withdrawn at 0730hrs on the 18th. They too went back east of Gheel having suffered 172 casualties in three days (18 killed in action, 50 captured).

General Student obviously was determined to contain the Scottish threat and his battle groups hammered away all day on the 18th at the KOSB and the Argylls. 'We lived like moles,' wrote Captain Woollcombe, 6th KOSB, 'clinging to our slit-trenches in the sandy soil and beat off thirteen counter-attacks, several of which came in battalion strength supported by tanks. Our gunner OPs were shot out of the church spire and shot off the factory roof – or at least they should have been – only they just stayed on. Our perimeter was ringed with defensive fire tasks laid from the gun areas around Gheel town. The Lord's Prayer, the Creed, the General Confession – they were my repertoire. If the shelling still continued, I started over at the beginning.' Shells were rationed for 44th Brigade with ammunition priorities given to Market Garden.

The divisional FOOs from 181st and 131st Field Regiment observers were ensconced in the large square factory in the centre of Aart, and helped greatly to break up the German assault with their dedicated calls for defensive fire. During the night of 18/19th the Gordons were ferried across to relieve the KOSB.

44th Brigade had lost 26 officers and 513 other ranks in the Aart bridgehead. Nine officers and 134 other ranks were killed. The Germans lost 200 prisoners, the Scots 160. But the German cemetery outside Aart is very full, with more than 200 tombstones.

On 19 September, Lt General Neil Ritchie, GOC 12 Corps, wrote to Major General Barber explaining that a high proportion of the enemy's available reserves (General Student's 1st Parachute Army) had been drawn against 15th Scottish in the Gheel bridgehead: 'The Division has had some very tough fighting and has suffered casualties as well. It is small consolation but the initial success of Market Garden operation does owe a lot to what the 15th Scottish Division has achieved.' So the sacrifices made at the Aart bridgehead had not been in vain. 'We were puzzled as to what was being achieved by the severe fighting here and by the vehemence of the enemy's reaction,' wrote Captain Robert Woollcombe. 'The idea had been to force a way of advance into Holland for Second Army. The Brigade fought for three days and four nights, lost over 500 men [actually 900 in the division] and in the meantime the main thrust of the Army developed elsewhere. Finally the bridgehead was abandoned altogether. However we undoubtedly slew many enemy.' 6th KOSB had 166 casualties. It certainly wasn't a victory for the Scotsmen. General Student had contained the Gheel bridgehead despite terrible German losses. 'Sagged about and scattered down the village [Aart] street the lone bodies of German paratroopers slowly rotted, sacrificed and mutilated through hopeless acts of bravado. You stepped over them every time you went back to the command post at the canal.'

Lieutenant Roger MacLellan related:

> Later that day we [Glasgow Highlanders] packed our kilts and left by truck to move toward those voluminous air drops. The roads were full of traffic – tanks, lorries, jeeps, guns, the whole works of an army on the move. The going was painfully slow, we would pull over to allow ambulances to pass to the rear and for ammunition trucks to pass to the front. We'd be stopped until rivers or canals were bridged – some by Baileys, others by floating Kapok – and again move slowly forward. We pulled into hospital grounds south of Eindhoven. But when the town was bombed that night we dug in deeply. The next day [22 September] we moved up to the Wilhelmina Canal for the attack on Best and were allotted a wooded area just south of it.

Lieutenant MacLellan wrote without, of course, realising that in two days time he would be wounded rather badly and flown back to a Canadian hospital in Farnborough.

Market Garden was in its sixth day and although the Airborne Division in Arnhem was still holding out bravely, the long thin corridor via Eindhoven and Nijmegen was also under immense pressure from German battle groups. The 30th Corps centre lines were being cut by General von Runstedt's 1st Parachute Army to the east and the German 15th Army with 50 tanks to the west. The area of the centre line between Eindhoven and St Oedenrode had already been cut, but the axis restored again. The main objective of the Division was to strike north towards s'Hertogenbosch to relieve pressure on the left flank of the Market Garden corridor.

The town of Best, six miles north of Eindhoven, was in the way and heavily defended, as the Seaforths found to their cost. Both road and railway bridges across the canal had been blown. Despite its steep 20-foot banks, men could wade across the sagging structure of the bridge. This was almost the Peel country of Holland: dead flat, desolate heath, many ditches, small streams, occasional woods, orchards and hamlets. The slit trenches were half filled with water and tracked vehicles had to stay on roads, often raised above the countryside. In front of 46th Brigade, on its right, was the large Zonsche Wood. Straight ahead was the so-called main road from Eindhoven to Boxtel via the straggling village of Best. A lateral road went half right for three miles to the town of St Oedenrode. A railway line was parallel to, and half a mile to the west of, the road to Boxtel. Best is dominated by a church and monastery, and near the railway line, south-west of the town centre, were parallel sheds known as the Cement Factory. By dawn on the 22nd the Seaforths were across the Wilhelmina, with jeeps and anti-tanks. Lt Colonel Hunt sent 'D' Company to occupy Best, which it did in a rather casual way. Every house was occupied by the enemy and the Seaforths quickly lost 33 casualties. Brigadier Villiers immediately sent the Glasgow Highlanders across and the sappers completed a Class 9 bridge. But no tanks could get across. Intense mortar fire and Spandau bursts halted Lt Colonel Campbell's Glasgow Highlanders. All the 46th Brigade patrols in the darkness of the day before had failed to bump the enemy defences, which were firmly dug in along the railway or snug in the Cement Factory and the cellars of the houses in Best.

By dusk on the 22nd the Glasgow Highlanders were scattered in and around Best, having taken the church and monastery. The KOSB arrived during the afternoon and veered to the right through Zonsche Wood, which had been cleared by American paratroopers at the start of Market Garden, and occupied Steenweg, a village 600 yards north of Best. The enemy garrison of Best was estimated at two battalions with the same mix that General Student had sent against the Aart bridgehead.

The 44th Lowland Brigade, led by the KOSB, had moved up through Eindhoven, past the huge Philips radio works and across the Bailey bridge. Captain Woollcombe noted the grim evidence of over-run guns, men and equipment lying about in the Zonsche Wood: 'enemy dead packed the ditches. The Yanks had certainly laid about them. We moved through a mass of empty weapon-containers, ration cartons and the big white flutters of discarded parachutes.' In daylight the KOSB relieved the German corpses of their fine (looted) watches and wads of German and Dutch paper money, but unfortunately not valid Allied currency!

On the 23rd Brigadier Villiers put in a three-battalion attack. The KOSB was to link up with the Glasgow Highlanders holding the eastern part of Best, then the Glasgows and the Seaforths would put in a two-battalion attack westwards, with the railway line, station and Cement Factory as their objectives. It took all day for the KOSB to advance 400 yards with house-to-house fighting, so at 1530hrs the second attack from Best started over the Zonsche Steeg (the inter-battalion boundary). Despite a barrage from one medium and two field regiments with Middlesex 4.2-

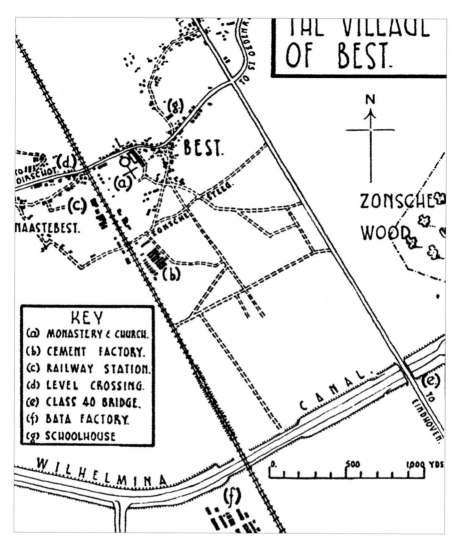

The grim battlefield around Best.

inch mortars and medium machine guns, the joint attack failed to take the Cement Factory, but captured the railway station. A patrol discovered that General Student's forces had abandoned the bitterly contested Aart bridgehead! Near the railway line south of the canal was a large Bata shoe factory, which provided an excellent observation point for the Middlesex and Field Regiments.

On 24 September General Student's forces cut the main Army centre line between St Oedenrode (five miles north-east) and Veghel – hence the necessity for the Scottish Division to keep hammering away at the enemy defences in Best. It was pouring wet and a strong enemy counter-attack more or less overwhelmed the Glasgow Highlanders. 'B' Company under Major Millar was over-run. Lieutenant MacLellan was now acting OC 'A' Company as Major Anderson had been wounded, as had several of MacLellan's Canloan friends. 'My men came under deadly crossfire and I ran over to assist.' A machine gun bullet hit his knee. 'I was shaken and so terribly angry at myself for being so careless as to get myself shot and felt sad that I had let my men down when they needed me most.'

The next day, the 25th, 227th Brigade moved across the Wilhelmina canal with their objective, Naastebest, a mile west of the railway line near Best. Despite RAF Typhoons smashing up the Cement Factory (but not its tough defenders), the Gordons were brought to a standstill with heavy casualties. The Cameronians on their right made little progress towards the railway. At 1630hrs Brigadier Colville called off the attack. However, on the right flank Lt Colonel MacKenzie's RSF, having cleared Vleut and Hoefke, reached Dolendonk.

On the 26th 46th Brigade made a determined attack out of Best to clear the fortress of the Cement Factory. Together with four SP guns the gallant Seaforths did just that, losing in the process four officers and 38 men. On their right the Cameronians, with considerable losses, cleared the western sector of Best up to the railway line. For the next six days Seaforths and Cameronians stayed where they were, exhausted, reduced in numbers but unbeaten. The GOC now decided to bypass the German resistance in Naastebest with a three-battalion drive towards St Oedenrode and the Dommel river, west towards Liempde. With the Argylls in the centre, HLI on the right and RSF on the left with RAF Typhoon support, they moved off initially into thick scrub and then dense woodland south of Liempde. Later the Argylls pulled out and spent a week near Vleut, then to Bakel.

At night the woods were alive with the chatter of small arms and the glow of tracer bullets. Night was the time of foot patrols. On one night Corporal Elliott and two others from 'D' Company Argylls brought in 43 prisoners, two Mongols but also 41 Germans! The HLI and the RSF, in their sweep north on the 26th, took 80 and 73 prisoners respectively, and the KOSB got into the hamlets of Kremsel and Boskant, south-west of St Oedenrode. Early on the 27th the whole of the 227th Brigade was in defensive positions between Donderdonk and the Boxtel road north of Best. Lt Colonel Richardson sent 'C' Company KOSB against Gasthuishoef, under cover of an artillery concentration. 'D' Company was badly mauled and 'C' Company was counter-attacked from Fratershoef. Difficult fighting went on till 2000hrs, when 'A' Company rejoined from the Son bridge patrol and helped restore the situation.

Later that night RSF put in an attack north of Kremsel, lost a number of men but took a small hill near the river Dommel with 45 prisoners. Back at Best the Seaforths sent a patrol to the railway wagons south of the Cement Factory and found it clear. The enemy, however, still held Naastebest. The next day, the 28th, the Royal Scots led out of Gasthuishoef, held by KOSB, to attack

Fratershoef to the north-west, taking 40 prisoners. But a heavy counter-attack came in on the Royal Scots by a Luftwaffe GAF unit who were met with artillery DF targets and withdrew under a smokescreen. The German defenders were scrupulous at allowing Scottish RMOs and stretcher bearers to bring their wounded in, and Lt Colonel Lane Joynt, CO Royal Scots, reciprocated at Fratershoef. On the divisional front on the 29th little of importance occurred except for the usual intermittent mortaring and shelling. On the 30th it was not so: at 1830hrs a strong counter-attack came in on the three battalions of the Lowland Brigade south of the river Dommel, which after an hour's fight was repulsed with heavy losses. Further south the Cameronians got their patrols into Naastebest. But there was a sting in the tail on 1 October. A fighting patrol of the Cameronians was ambushed just outside Best; five were killed and eight wounded.

Now followed Operation Haggis, a peaceful and perhaps unique handover by 15th Scottish Division to 51st Highland Division over 1–4 October. In the 11 days of fighting to clear Best and the north-east to St Oedenrode, the Division lost 925 casualties including 120 killed in action and 279 taken prisoner. The Glasgow Highlanders, KOSB, Seaforths and Gordons came off worst. In the words of Captain Woollcombe:

> The heavy grey days passed. Days of infiltration and counter-attacks, perpetual stand-to and artillery fire churning along drear tree lines. God-forsaken tracks that led nowhere or anywhere. The snarl of the hidden

Major General 'Tiny' Barber, the tallest general in the British Army, receives a bar to his DSO from Field Marshal Montgomery, 16 September 1945.

Spandaus in a fir plantation, RAF Typhoons circling in the sky. And lonely derelict farms, more dull names – Gasthuishof – Fratershof – for these names were now the work of the devil. And thoughts turned with persistence to when relief might come.

During Market Garden 15th Division suffered more casualties – 1,356 – than the three divisions of 30th Corps, which had 1,333 casualties.

Detail from picture on p. 208. (*Imperial War Museum B-13942*)

CHAPTER 26

Monty's Marauders

General Bernard Montgomery was by profession a dedicated infantryman who had learned that the careful use of massed artillery, as in the First World War, and careful use of armoured formations would – and did – win him his campaigns in North Africa and Sicily, and would now do so in North-west Europe. He also relied on all his trusted African veterans to be first into the European breaches. They included the independent armoured brigades who fought as a team but owed no allegiance to any divisions – infantry or armoured. This was, in a way, a problem. The armoured divisions were a self-sufficient composite of all the arms that, usually, worked very well together. The independent armoured brigades would either act on their own to create opportunities, or fill a gap in the advance or retreat, as directed by the army commander – armoured knights on a chess board.

In the maelstrom of the Normandy campaign four brigades went in: 4th (black jerboa rat) and the 8th (red fox's mask), but the 27th and 33rd went in and never came out again due to casualties and the many sad 'mergers' that had to take place. So this story is about the two famous survivors.

4th Armoured Brigade

In January 1940 the Mobile Division in Egypt was renamed 7th Armoured Division and its Heavy Armoured Group became 4th Armoured Brigade in parallel with the Light Armoured Brigade, which became 7th Armoured Brigade. Lt Colonel 'Blood' Caunter led 4th Armoured Brigade in the highly successful campaigns against Mussolini's enthusiastic but inefficient army in Cyrenaica and Libya. It was, however, a different story when the German panzers under General Irwen Rommel appeared. Nevertheless, for three and a half years the Brigade held its own – Alamein, Mareth and west into Tunisia, sometimes independently, sometimes with the parent, now christened the Desert Rats. Next came Sicily, southern Italy and back to the UK in February 1944.

The much-travelled, highly experienced formation landed in Normandy under Brigadier Michael Carver, who was destined to become a Field Marshal. Under his command were three tank regiments equipped with Shermans, plus

12 Firefly 17-pdr tanks for the first time. They were: The Royal Scots Greys, 3rd County of London Yeomanry (known as the Sharpshooters); 44th Royal Tank Regiment backed by 2nd Battalion KRRC; and 4th RHA armed with Sexton SP 25-pdrs.

During the Normandy campaign Carver's brigade supported 15th Scottish Division in Epsom. They then supported a string of divisions, starting with 53rd Welsh, then 43rd Wessex Wyverns, 53rd Welsh again, 3rd British, 53rd for a third time, then Lt General Guy Simonds' 2nd Canadian Corps in the thrust for Falaise, followed by Major General 'Tiny' Barber's 15th Scottish Division for a second time, then 53rd Welsh for a fourth time, 7th Armoured .... The 4th Armoured Brigade's advance north was through St Pol and Lille despite many attacks from General von Zangen's 15th Army retreating northwards from the Pas de Calais. It halted at Oudenarde, scene of Marlborough's famous battle, and engaged the German 71st Division on 5–7 September on the river Escaut–Lys canal front. At first light on the 7th the Scots Greys, 44th RTR and the 3/4th Sharpshooters launched counter-attacks, inflicting heavy casualties and taking many prisoners. The next ten days were spent north of the Scheldt and west of Antwerp around Termonde and St Nicolas.

During Market Garden 44th RTR was assigned to link up with US 101st Airborne Division between Eindhoven and Nijmegen. Brigadier Carver's formation, now in 8th Corps with the task of pushing the Germans back towards the river Maas, was given responsibility for Brigadier Piron's Belgian Brigade. According to Carver, Piron was 'rather a sticky commander who when he seemed reluctant to obey my orders and take some positive action, I threatened to have him removed'. Carver's autobiography *Out of Step* chronicles his clashes with at least three divisional commanders and with Lt General Brian Horrocks, his corps commander. The Brigade, having cleared the Willemsvaart canal around Weert, spent the rest of September sparring with aggressive German parachute troops. During October Carver also was given responsibility for the Royal Netherlands Brigade.

In the New Year the 29th Armoured Brigade (with 11th Armoured Division) had been awarded the first batch of British-made Comet tanks, which were hotted up Cromwells with a better gun. So, in the horrible dreary battle of Operation Veritable, the 4th were borrowed by Major General 'Pip' Roberts and acquitted themselves nobly in cold, wet weather and boggy ground with actions night and day until the end of Veritable on 4 March. They then crossed the Rhine, took part in the attack on Bremen, crossed the river Elbe above Hamburg and, on 2 May, the Brigade led 6th Airborne Division north-east to Wismar and a meeting with the Russians.

Carver, a brilliant, popular tank commander, who crossed swords with practically every senior officer in the British Army, wrote: 'It had been a long trek from Mersa Matruh.'

8th Armoured Brigade

At the outbreak of war in 1939 the 6th Cavalry Brigade was part of the 1st Cavalry Division and was composed of the Warwickshire Yeomanry, Staffordshire Yeomanry and Cheshire Yeomanry. From early 1940 it was based in Palestine carrying out mounted police duties and quelling disturbances between Arabs and Jews. History does repeat itself …. Early in 1941 it took part in the Syria – Persia – Iraq campaign, encountering Russian cavalry in Teheran. In July the old 1st Cavalry Division became the 10th Armoured Division with the unusual red fox's mask insignia. After all, the Yeomanry regiments had spent a lot of peacetime soldiering chasing Reynard! The newly mechanised 6th Cavalry Brigade became the 8th Armoured Brigade but with different fighting formations: The Household Cavalry, the Royal Scots Greys (late of Blenheim, Ramillies, Oudenarde, Malplaquet, Waterloo, Balaklava, Sevastopol, South African War, and First World War, including the pursuit to Mons and Flanders) and the Notts (Sherwood Rangers) and the Staffordshire Yeomanry. When the Division returned to Palestine in 1942 the 8th Armoured Brigade, now an independent formation, was allowed to keep the red fox's mask insignia. Going from horses to General Grant heavy tanks or General Stuart light tanks, known as Honeys, was an ordeal for many dedicated horsemen. In the Western Desert they devised tank tactics similar to nineteenth-century naval warfare, but Rommel's panzers were successful in enticing their cavalry-type charges into deadly screens of 88mm anti-tank guns. In the battle of Alam Halfa on 30 August–1 September, the team of Sherwood Rangers and Staffs Yeomanry, plus the newly arrived 3rd RTR, suffered badly at the hands of the Afrika Korps panzers. But on 2 September when the Germans withdrew, they left 21 burned-out tanks along the brigade front.

For the great battle of El Alamein the Brigade deployed again as part of Major General Alec Gatehouse's 10th Armoured Division, equipped with a mixture of Crusaders, Grants and the brand new American Sherman tanks. The Brigade reached the start line in front of Mitereiya Ridge at midnight on 23 October, in the New Zealand Division's seven-mile wide 'box'. Despite a heavy artillery barrage, the Brigade drove into an avalanche of artillery, anti-tank and Luftwaffe bombing, which, together with extensive minefields, caused huge casualties. On the evening of the 24th Rommel sent in a powerful 100-tank counter-attack out of the setting sun – a favourite German trick – with intense shelling behind a smokescreen and small groups of panzers manoeuvring skilfully from ridge to ridge. It was a tank battle between professionals and amateurs. Nearly 100 Brigade tanks were destroyed or disabled.

Under Montgomery's skilful leadership, and with a lot of help from Bletchley Park's Ultra, which gave away most of Rommel's plans, the advance continued slowly but relentlessly west to the heavily fortified Mareth Line. The Brigade took part in the magnificent left hook around the Matmata Hills and over 80 miles of soft sand and broken ground into the valley of Wadi Merteba. In Operation

Plum the New Zealand Division and 8th Armoured Brigade charged in a 'blitz' attack straight up the Tebaga Gap at midnight on 19 March. 3rd RTR were on the left, Staffs in the centre and the Notts on the right against the German 164th Light Division, 21st and 15th Panzer Divisions, and four Italian divisions. The final dramatic charge was called Supercharge II or The Grand National. The Sherman tanks were in front, the Crusaders behind and the carriers in the third line. They were helped by the RAF, a massed artillery barrage and a providential sandstorm. Eventually, after a spectacular and frightening battle under cover of dust storms, the Germans and Italians gave up, leaving many dead and 700 prisoners. Three Italian divisions were destroyed and the two crack German divisions lost most of their weapons and vehicles.

After a final battle at Enfidavelle, Tunis and Bizerta fell on 7 May. Rommel, a sick man, had left the field of battle after Mareth and returned to Germany, and eventually, on 13 May, Marshal Messe, Commander of 1st Italian Army, surrendered a total of 250,000 troops. In its African campaign the Red Fox's Mask Brigade had suffered almost 1,000 casualties with 214 killed in action. After a week spent in Augusta, Sicily, it returned on the troopships *Tegelburg* and *Neuw Holland* on 9 December 1943 to Gourock in the Clyde estuary.

There were many changes in the next six months before Operation Overlord. 3rd RTR went to 11th Armoured Division as its only regular tank regiment, the Staffordshires went to the 27th Armoured Brigade, and there were two newcomers, 4/7th Royal Dragoon Guards (RDG) and 24th Lancers, backed by 147th Field Regiment RA (Essex Yeomanry) and 12th KRRC as motorised infantry support.

As one of Monty's favourite 'marauders' the 8th Brigade was in the lead on D-Day, 6 June 1944, supporting 50th Northumbrian Division as they attacked Gold Beach. 4/7th RDG backed 69th Brigade, which was directed on La Rivière on King Red Beach. The SRY backed 231st Brigade on Jig Green and Red Beach, directed on Le Hamel and Port-en-Bessin. All went reasonably well but the RDG had 31 casualties and SRY 24, with about 20 tanks knocked out between them.

The Brigade fought in Operation Epsom and bitter battles at Lingèvres, Verrières, Tessel, Rauray and Hottot. 4/7th RDG distinguished themselves at Lingèvres, destroying half a dozen Panthers. The SRY, supporting the 29th Polar Bears Division at Fontenay and Rauray, did invaluable work. The 24th Lancers, who had been in the thick of the *bocage* country fighting, had to be disbanded on 23 July as, since D-Day, they had had 41 killed in action, 98 wounded and 49 tanks knocked out or badly disabled. In turn they had destroyed 11 and knocked out 20 Panther or Mk IV tanks plus 10 SP guns. Over 600 Lancers went to new homes and 13/18th Hussars, a regular regiment, came from the disbanded 27th Armoured Brigade.

The Hussar regiment had a distinguished pedigree. Known as Queen Mary's Own it had won battle honours at Waterloo, Balaclava, Ladysmith and Mons. It also had landed on Queen Beach on D-Day, supporting 3rd British Division.

Brigadier Erroll Prior-Palmer came from 27th Armoured Brigade to lead 8th Armoured. So the war went on. In Operation Bluecoat, starting at La Senaudière south of Bayeux on 30 July, the Brigade supported 50th Northumbrian and 43rd Wessex Wyverns towards Jurques and Ondefontaine, where 10th SS Panzer Division was predictably ferocious. Captain N.N.M. Denny of 'A' squadron 13/18th Hussars won fame when, on the evening of 6 August, after two days fighting in La Varinière, he led two troops of Shermans through German infantry, across an anti-tank ditch and thick scrub, and up a steep escarpment to the top of the famous Mount Pinçon. They held their position on the summit until their 'little friends' of the 4th Somerset Light Infantry arrived to help. Generals Montgomery and Horrocks were delighted. From the top the battlefields could be scrutinised for miles around, and enemy concentrations stonked by the gunners or strafed by the RAF Typhoons.

The Brigade helped the 43rd Wessex Wyverns in Operation Neptune to force a bridgehead over the river Seine and by 29 August set off for Gasny-Fourges-Dangu and Gisors, where the population was delirious with joy, flag waving, handing out apples, flowers, wine and kisses. Near Beauvais a Tiger and three Panthers were knocked out by the SRY and in Doullens they knocked out five guns, captured 100 Wehrmacht and destroyed the flying bomb site. The old battlefields of Arras and Vimy Ridge were passed, then Lens, Seclin and Houplin. Captain John Stirling, 4/7th RDG noted: 'In Seclin the local Maquis who had just looted the German military wine stores distributed champagne, liqueurs and cigars to all comers. We took on a little Veuve Clicquot.' And in Lille: 'An absolute tidal wave of wildly excited humanity swept down on the

SOMEWHERE IN THE FALAISE GAP.

'Somewhere in the Falaise Gap' by Michael Bayley, 2 Kensingtons.

The liberation of Lille.

Infantry with Churchill tanks somewhere in Holland.

tanks and engulfed them. Never before had so many lovely girls been seen whose only aim was to kiss the tank crews, to whom, tired and dirty and dishevelled as they were, it seemed like a glimpse of Paradise.'

On 4 September the Brigade crossed into Belgium and operating with 50th Northumbrian Division formed a flank guard screen between Lille and Ghent, a distance of almost 50 miles. Belgium seemed a more fertile land, the people cleaner and better dressed. Every house flew a Belgian flag and usually a Union Jack or Stars and Stripes as well. Lieutenant Stuart Hills recalled: 'We SRY were doing left flank protection for 30 Corps and passed through Chereng, Baisieux, Tournai and arrived at Renaix covering 25 miles. My troop was to guard a bridge. We were the first British troops in the village and festivities continued throughout the day [4th]. We drank, sang and danced in the village pub and everyone went mad. Bill Cousins and I met a charming young girl who took us home and gave us five eggs *each* for our supper.'

On 7 September the Brigade moved east through Alost, Willebroek and Malines to Aarschot. Some units, including 13/18th Hussars and 12th KRRC, managed to pass through Brussels – absolute bliss – then Louvain, perhaps a trifle slowly, and north to rendezvous at Aarschot. Their destination was Gheel and they had to pass through the village of Oostham, north of Beeringen, where 12th KRRC and 4/7th RDG encountered bazooka teams, infantry and several SP guns. Captain Stirling reported: 'Resistance was stiffening and rearguards of SP guns and tanks found the country criss-crossed with canals and dykes ideal for defence. Each squadron now took it in turn to catch a bang on the nose.' But Brigade HQ and A1 Echelon were caught napping harboured north of the Beeringen bridge; a German paratroop party stalked them through the woods destroying 33 vehicles including fuel lorries and water carts. There were 26 casualties, including 16 Red Fox who were taken prisoner. The following day the German paratroops gave 12th KRRC a hard time, pushing them out of Oostham, where they lost four half-tracks and anti-tank guns and took a number of casualties.

The battle that then ensued for Gheel is partly related in the chapter on 50th Northumbrian Division. Lieutenant Stuart Hills, SRY, recalled: 'The 9th marked the beginning of the worst battle 'C' squadron ever fought in and which took a heavy toll of 'B' as well. The company [of 6th Durham Light Infantry] only had 30 men. After we had gone 100 yards the inevitable Spandau [machine-gun] opened up. The infantry had a rotten time and I could see them falling to my left and right. My troop had two 17-pdrs [Sherman Fireflies], Sergeant Nesling and

The crossing of the Albert canal. Tanks and transport cross the bridge put up by engineers.

Corporal Burnett in support of my own 75mm, so our firepower was limited.'
The 17-pdr is ideal for tank killing roles but is slow at firing its rather poor high
explosive. Hills' squadron had crossed the Albert canal at Beeringen on the 10th
and supported the Durham Light Infantry in the capture of the town of Gheel:

> We then ran over the trenches and the infantry poked the Boche out at the
> point of the bayonet .... Jerry emerged from all sides and gave himself up (I
> got a very nice gold watch). The civilians came out and another town was
> 'liberated'. I had fired between 50 and 60 HE [shells] to get us in and the
> 17-pdrs four apiece, which was all they had. [And a bit later] The enemy
> were at our back door. The troop on our right were all knocked out. Night
> was falling. We were kept busy the whole night with SPs and tanks that Jerry
> kept pushed forward. I 'brewed' one just after dusk … at dawn we heard
> Jerry's tanks milling around and soon after he began shelling in earnest. I
> shall be quite truthful. The infantry left their positions and their anti-tank
> guns. We had to take their striker cases to disable them. And so it continued
> throughout the morning. The tank was covered in bricks, plaster and glass
> with dust everywhere. We were all pretty tired and apprehensive.

151st Brigade of DCLI had over 400 casualties. The SRY had 46 casualties,
11 tanks brewed up and two more damaged. The German counter-attack
recaptured Gheel but eventually withdrew. Hills recalled when the SRY re-
entered the town: 'The place was a shambles and there were hundreds of our

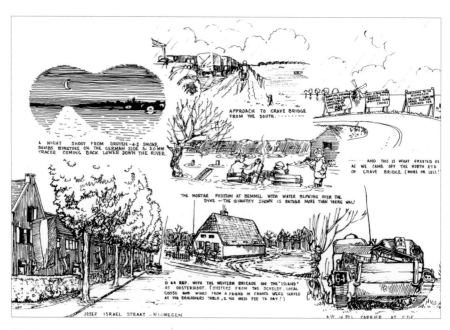

Sketches of the Market Garden battlefields. (*Michael Bayley*)

own and dead Boche lying around.' The German 6th Parachute Division had fought brilliantly and brutally and had given the experienced but exhausted 50th Northumbrian Division, whose ranks were now full of young intakes from disbanded artillery formations, a terrible beating.

SRY then moved 37 miles south through Tessenderloo and east to Beeringen to rejoin 4th Armoured Brigade, which, under command of Guards Armoured Division, was tasked with the capture of Bourg-Leopold, once the Artillery School of Belgium. It was forbidden to shell the town as 300 Belgian political prisoners were held there. 12th KRRC found the town empty of Germans and 13/18th Hussars entered, spraying every building with machine-gun fire and high explosives, just in case. Quite a few well-armed paratroopers were found hiding in cellars. The Belgian Brigade then formally occupied the town.

8th Armoured Brigade next joined 43rd Wessex Division in Market Garden to help protect the long, vulnerable centre line and to link up with the 82nd US Paratroops at the Grave bridge over the Maas. 13/18th Hussars reached Hechtel on the 19th and Zeeland the next day, and 'C' Squadron crossed the Nijmegen bridge at 0900hrs on the 22nd to support 4th Wiltshires advancing towards Elst. The regiment fought and met stiff opposition. It remained around Oosterhout and Homert, the so-called Island, for another month.

4/7th RDG linked up with 7th Somersets: 'We drove over the 600-yard long railway bridge at Nijmegen strewn with dead Germans, swung left along the dyke road running high above the north bank of the river,' recalled Captain John Stirling. 'The road was skyline suicide: to the left the bank was very steep, to the right the woods.' In Oosterhout 'we captured 150 prisoners; two guns, three tanks and an 88mm gun were knocked out. At 5 o'clock the road was free for 'B' Sqn to make their brilliant dash up to Driel with infantry on the back of the tanks to link up with the paratroops.' At dusk a mobile squadron under Major David Richards and 5th DCLI set off to join the Polish Airborne Brigade. On the 23rd 4/7th RDG from Valburg supported 1st Worcesters in

A Sherman tank of the 13/18th Hussars by the Rhine. The Island, October 1944.

A typical jam in a German town east of the Rhine.

an attack on Elst, and fighting against the Panzer SS holding the large village went on for three more days before the Worcesters eventually captured the town. By then it was too late for the beleaguered British 1st Airborne, who were surrounded and almost destroyed.

Meanwhile, the SRY had been asked by their American paratrooper friends to 'clear the Reichswald', a task which in the event required practically every *division* of the British and Canadian Armies to achieve. Nevertheless, ever willing, 'A' Squadron with 'D' Squadron of the Royals (Reconnaissance Regiment) went off in the direction of the Reichswald and became the first British troops to enter the Fatherland, which was announced later on the BBC radio news.

The Brigade thoroughly enjoyed working with the Americans around Nijmegen in actions around Beek, Mook and Wyler.

The Red Fox's Mask Brigade continued to fight in the vanguard of the British Army in Operation Clipper to capture Geilenkirchen; Operation Blackcock to clear the rectangle formed by Sittard, Roermond, Heinsburg and Geilenkirchen; in Operation Veritable in February 1945 to clear a large area in the Rhineland through the Reichswald; in Operation Leek to capture Weeze; Operation Plunder in the river Rhine crossing and bridgehead; and Operation Forrard on towards Bremen and Bremerhaven, where 13/18th Hussars 'assisted' at the surrender of 15th Panzer Grenadier and 480th Divisions.

Both of Monty's Marauders had fought strongly and nobly from the Desert to the Baltic – a formidable record.

CHAPTER 27

Student's Ferocious Counter-Attacks

Field Marshal Walther Model, commander of Army Group B, was fortunate in that he had, by chance, a quorum of first-class experienced battle commanders in his shattered, widespread polder and Peel killing grounds. SS General Wilhelm Bittrich, commander of 2nd SS Panzer Corps, reacted quickly and decisively on 17 September when, to quote Robert Kershaw, the Allied parachute drop appeared to be 'snow in September'. Bittrich organised 17 'alarm groups', which were immediately sent to small towns and villages in the 2nd SS Panzer Corps area around Arnhem. His kampfgruppen of the 9th SS Hohenstauffen and 10th SS Frundsberg Divisions were mainly responsible for the lack of success of Operation Market.

General der Fallschirmtruppe (paratroops), 1st Army Kurt Student, with considerable help from Generalleutnant Kurt Chill, the elderly, irascible GOC of 84th, 85th and 89th Divisions, was responsible for giving much of the British Army a terrible bloody nose along the canal defence lines east of Antwerp. Student was the hero of the German parachute forces. In the 1940 *blitzkrieg*, in Corinth and then in Crete, his paratroops had won notable battles. Student looked like a prosperous, efficient business executive with a dominant forehead, pale face and high-pitched voice. He was greatly admired by the Führer. However, when he had proposed parachute operations on Cyprus, the Suez canal and Malta, they were all rejected by Hitler who said they would cost too many lives.

The sudden capture of Antwerp had really startled Hitler, who immediately ordered the urgent reinforcement of the Scheldt fortresses or *festung*, and measures to halt the Allied advance in the Netherlands. Student was in Berlin on 4 September, commanding an airborne training establishment, while his crack parachute regiments were being used as infantry in various theatres of war. Suddenly he was informed that he had been promoted to command the new 1st Parachute Army, which did not exist, even on paper. Hermann Göring, the Reichsmarschall of the Luftwaffe, had revealed that there were six Luftwaffe parachute regiments under training and two more could be raised from paratroops convalescing in depots. These numbered some 20,000 and would be increased by a further 10,000 Luftwaffe air and ground crew who were redundant because of lack of aircraft fuel. These able-bodied, eager young men were longing for a fight. The bulk of the Luftwaffe training schools were emptied

Model (left) confers with Student, Bittrich and Harmel.

of potential pilots, observers, navigators, signallers and ground staff, who were sent to Holland either in complete units or as kampfgruppen. Student was told that two divisions – 719th under Generalleutnant Karl Sievers, a 'fortress' division of elderly soldiers who had never seen action, and 176th under Oberst Christian Landau, a *kranken* or wounded convalescent formation – would come under his command. In addition there were units from the Navy or Luftwaffe plus 25 tanks. Student was told by General Jodl, Chief of Staff at Hitler's HQ, to fill the gap from Antwerp to Maastricht along the north bank of the Albert canal. Already there was intense activity as the first troops dug in and constructed strongpoints, and engineers placed explosive charges under all the bridges. 719th Coastal Division gave a good account of themselves in the suburbs of Antwerp.

Orders were sent for 3rd, 5th and 6th Fallschirmjäger (paratroop) Regiments to be brought up to strength from the Luftwaffe's 1st Air Force and its Training Division. Also the 346th Division from Von Zangen's 15th Army arrived and were so formidable that they forced the British 50th Division to evacuate a bridgehead over the canal on 6 September. The Hermann Göring Training Regiment, ten battalions of Luftwaffe infantry and flak troops with heavy 88mm dual-purpose guns and close range anti-tank weapons, from the 6th Military District, were all quickly deployed in action.

General Student arrived from Maastricht on the 5th and drove along the canal encouraging the troops and inspecting his miniature Siegfried Line.

He made his HQ at Vught just south of s'Hertogenbosch and sent daily reports to Field Marshal Model. His force consisted of Lt Colonel von der Heydte's Parachute Regiment No. 6, the first battalion of Regiment No. 2 and five more newly raised regiments. Three of these formed No. 7 Parachute Division under General Erdmann. Student had acquired 25 SP assault guns and tank destroyers and 20 mixed flak units. All these details are in Student's book *Arnhem Letzer Deutsche Erfolg*. Model gave Student even more responsibility: the whole area running from the North Sea to Maastricht, a front of 120km (75 miles). He was also given command over 88th Korps under General Hans Reinhardt, which included 719th Regiment, a Dutch SS battalion and some Luftwaffe detachments. Altogether Student's army had a fully stretched front of 36 battalions. They were weak in armour and artillery but had a large number of the powerful dual-purpose 88mm guns.

The German staff work was extremely good but the many disparate groupings of Luftwaffe, SS, Wehrmacht, coastguards, garrison troops, flak and even police into kampfgruppen made orders inevitably more complicated. Lt Colonel Fritz Fullriede, a veteran who had been awarded the Knight's Cross, commanded abteilungen (combat units) of the Hermann Göring Division. He wrote: '8 Sep. The enemy is already over the Albert canal at Beeringen. On order from General Student's Para HQ that *all* airforce troops were to be taken under command I dispatched the 2nd Abteilung on the road before Harderwijk post haste to Eindhoven.' Unfortunately, on 10 September, in a three-day pitched battle in Hechtel, north-east of Beeringen, the 2nd Abteilung was almost destroyed: 'Almost all the tanks, armoured artillery, anti-tank and flak elements were lost. *All due to the mistakes of our joke of a high command.*'

On 13 September Student's forces were lined up east of Antwerp to the junction of the Albert and Meuse-Escaut canals. Opposing the two British bridgeheads were Kampfgruppe Chill and the newly formed Kampfgruppe Walther. All these troops reported to General Reinhardt. Student had direct control over Erdmanns Kampfgruppe (Regiment No. 7) and 176th Division. Colonel Walther, an experienced paratrooper, had the equivalent of ten weak, mainly ex-Luftwaffe infantry battalions, and armour under SS Captain Roestel. His kamfgruppe existed for about a month and was probably Model's most powerful armoured group in Operation Garden.

On 17 September, D-Day for Operation Market, General Student was working at his HQ at Vught. At about mid-day he went on the balcony: 'Wherever I looked I could see aircraft, troop transports and large aircraft towing gliders. They flew both in formation and singly. It was an immense stream which passed quite low over the house.' Student's reactions were, of course, not fear, not danger, but envy: 'I wish that I had ever had such a powerful force at my disposal.'

Further north Model was equally astonished. Robert Kershaw, in his book *It never Snows in September,* had cleverly deduced the answer to the 'missing glider pilot Market Garden plan'. An American Waco glider had crashed near Vught and a *feldwebel* discovered a collection of documents and promptly brought them to 88th Corps HQ staff to translate and decipher. In essence they said: '101 American Airborne Division has been tasked to secure crossing points over the water obstacles at Son, St Oedenrode and Veghel and hold them until the attacking British ground forces – Guards Armoured Division, 50th Infantry and 43rd Infantry Divisions – link up. The latter are assaulting toward Eindhoven.' Student deployed two paratroop battalions from 's-Hertogenbosch: one towards Veghel, the other, Kampfgruppe Ewald, towards St Oedenrode. General Poppe's 59th Division, part of Von Zangen's 15th Army, arrived from Tilburg and, via Best, went into action at Son.

Lt Colonel Friedrich Freiherr von Heydte, whose Paratroop Regiment 6 had given the Americans a hard time on the Utah bridgehead in Normandy, now repeated the process in the Neerpelt salient.

Student was determined to block and halt the inexorable but slow progress northwards by Horrocks's 30th Corps along what became known as 'Hell's Highway'. Kampfgruppen SS Richter, Segler and Roestel deployed on the 17th between the Escaut canal and Valkenswald. Then blocking attacks were made by Kerutt, Hoffman and Koepel on the 18th. Between Eindhoven and Nijmegen, Poppe, Ewald and Feldt, and near or in Nijmegen, Generals Reinhold, Euling and Henke made aggressive attacks. In the last vital four days, 22–26 September, many more attempts were made to cut Hell's Highway,

Lt Colonel August Baron von der Heydte, defender of Carentan.

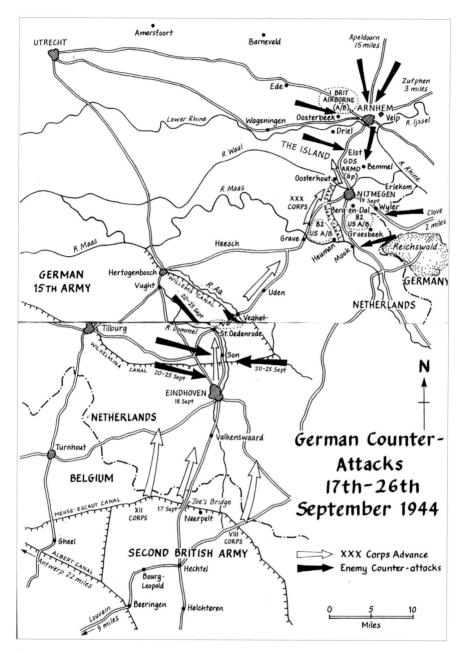

German counter-attacks, 17–26 September 1944.

causing General Horrocks much anxiety. Kampfgruppen Huber and Walther cut the road near Eerde. Then Von de Heydte and Jungwirth on the 24th, followed by Richter and the powerful armoured group Panzer Grenadier 107, caused havoc around Veghel. Jungwirth blocked the corridor at Koevering for most of 24–26th, but after that it was never broken decisively again.

Major Tom Craig OC 'B' Squadron 1st RTR passing Humber scout car in heavy rain, October 1944. (*Tank Museum 2556/C3*)

After Operation Berlin and the sad end of 1st Airborne, the two exhausted armies had a cold autumn and a very cold winter ahead of them. General Kurt Student's parachute troops had suffered heavily but remained in various kampfgruppen to deny the Allies further inroads into Holland.

Montgomery's army, on the west side of the famous Operation Market Garden, suffered bitter losses to 15th Scottish, 53rd Welsh and 50th Tyne-Tees in battles for canal towns such as Gheel, Mol, Lommel, Aart and Best. The history books concentrate on Operation Garden, which was perhaps more dramatic, but General Student's forces gave the long-suffering British infantry divisions a terrible mauling. Field Marshal Göring's fit young Luftwaffe units contributed unfettered Nazi enthusiasm. They probably didn't die for '*Der Grosse*', but they certainly died for their Führer.

CHAPTER 28

Who Won?

Bearing in mind that the Allied Command deployed Field Marshal Montgomery's 21st Army Group and the whole of the Allied Airborne Army to establish a firm bridgehead over the Lower Rhine, who won in that astonishing month of September 1944?

In any war the victors write the history books in the full flush of success, often turning defeat into a draw, perhaps even into a victory. And this is what happened.

Winston Churchill

In Volume VI of his awe-inspiring Second World War history, entitled *Triumph and Tragedy*, Churchill gave a perfectly accurate account of the various military actions:

Winston Churchill in a victory parade held in his honour in Brussels. (*L. Van Cauwenberg*)

Heavy risks were taken in the Battle of Arnhem, but they were justified by the great prize so nearly in our grasp. Had we been more fortunate in the weather, which turned against us at critical moments and restricted our mastery in the air, it is probable that we should have succeeded. No risk daunted the brave men, including the Dutch resistance, who fought for Arnhem.

This was accurate as far as it went, but on 9 October 1944 he sent a message to his good friend Field Marshal J.C. Smuts: 'As regards Arnhem, I think you have got the position a little out of focus. The battle was a decided victory, but the leading division, asking quite rightly, for more was given a chop ....' No mention of what Montgomery's 12 fine divisions were actually fighting tooth and nail for: a *substantial* bridgehead over the Rhine.

Adolf Hitler

The Russian summer offensive of 1944 was prominent in Hitler's list of priorities in September of that year. The Russians had overwhelmed the German forces in Roumania and Bulgaria and had driven up the valley of the Danube towards Hungary and Yugoslavia. Hitler's next priority was probably his immense secret build-up of three experienced armies, with which he planned, in mid-December, to burst through the Ardennes in Operation Wacht am Rhein. There were still ten million able German soldiers more or less willing to fight and die for the Fatherland. The plan for this clandestine but major offensive was to recapture Antwerp and thrust a scimitar into the Allied forces, cutting off half of the British and Canadian Armies and much of the American Army as well.

Hitler was furious at the loss of Antwerp. He realised, even if Montgomery and Eisenhower did not, the vital logistical importance of that immense port and ordered half of his terror V-weapons to target the city. He also ordered General von Zangen's 15th Army to reinforce and help protect the fortresses on both sides of the Scheldt. In the event Antwerp was not open for shipping until the end of November. Hitler must have been delighted that Von Zangen's successful 'Dunkirk had produced more than 60,000 troops to help protect *Festung Holland*'. He also wanted to buy time to reinvigorate the defences of the long and vital Siegfried Line, which had fallen into disrepair. This Field Marshal Model, his 'Fireman', and Generals Bittrich and Student succeeded in doing, and it was not until 15 March 1945 that the Allies broke through the line. It took until April 1945 for the Canadians and the British 49th Polar Bears Division to finally capture Arnhem.

Definitely, Adolf Hitler and his Third Reich had done rather well in September 1944.

Field Marshal Bernard Montgomery

Montgomery initially produced a bland statement after the battle praising the Airborne Division, citing the bad weather as an excuse and looking for a scapegoat. He not only put the blame for failure on the Polish Independent Brigade but also wrote to the CIGS, Field Marshal Alan Brooke, on 17 October and the Deputy CIGS, Lt General Sir Ronald Weeks on 20 November demanding (and succeeding) in having the brave but unlucky Major General Sosabowski fired. A most unsavoury episode. Later on the Field Marshal issued a full statement. The bad weather again! He also accused Eisenhower: 'If he [Eisenhower] had kept Patton halted on the Meuse and had given full logistic support to Hodges and Dempsey [Monty's second-in-command] after the capture of Brussels, the operations in Holland *could* have been an overwhelming success, for 1st US Army could have mounted a formidable diversion at Aachen and 2nd British Army could have attacked sooner on a wider front and in much greater strength.' But Monty did admit a mistake: 'The airborne forces at Arnhem were dropped too far away from the vital objective – the bridge. It was some hours before they reached it. I take the blame for this mistake. I should have ordered 2nd Army and 1st Airborne Corps to arrange that at least one complete parachute brigade was dropped close to the bridge, so that it could have been captured in a matter of minutes and its defences soundly organised with time to spare. I did not do so.' Monty then wrote: '… the 2nd SS Panzer Corps was refitting in the Arnhem area …. We knew it was there. But we were wrong in supposing it could not fight effectively. Its battle state was far beyond our expectation.' Poor Major Urquhart, the Intelligence Officer, was right all along.

Architects of victory? Field Marshal Bernard Montgomery, Generals Horrocks and Whistler. (*Imperial War Museum BU3986*)

Later on Monty wrote: 'I must admit a bad mistake on my part. I underestimated the difficulties of opening up the approaches to Antwerp so that we could get the free use of that port. I reckoned the Canadian Army could do it while we were going for the Ruhr. I was wrong.'

So Monty blamed (a) the weather; (b) Eisenhower; (c) in effect Major Urquhart and the Ultra information about Model's forces; and (d) the Canadians for not opening the Scheldt quickly enough. Oh yes, and the Poles! Monty might have mentioned why he did not meet Horrocks *prior* to Market Garden, but waited until 23 September when it was all over.

Lt General Brian Horrocks

'Jorrocks' wrote an engaging and sincere autobiography, *A Full Life*. He admitted: 'My excuse is that my eyes were fixed on the Rhine and everything else seemed of subsidiary importance. It never entered my head that the Scheldt would be mined and that we should not be able to use Antwerp port ... Nor did I realise that the Germans would be able to evacuate a large number of the troops trapped in the coastal areas across the mouth of the Scheldt estuary from Breskens to Flushing. Napoleon would no doubt have realised these things but Horrocks did not. His mind was fixed on the Rhine.'

Horrocks, like most of the British Army top brass, had an enjoyable three or four days of liberation in Brussels, during which he met the royal family.

'Jorrocks' admitted that 4 September was a key date in the battle for the Rhine, before Model, Bittrich, Student and Chill could block Operation Garden. He praised the airborne divisions, the Guards and Thomas's 43rd Wessex Wyverns but did not admit, of course, that he should have pushed the last two much, much harder.

Horrocks was still the best and the most liked of Monty's corps commanders and he commanded 30th Corps for the rest of the North-west Europe campaign.

Lt General 'Boy' Browning

After the long list of mistakes that this highly respected, decorated general made so that he personally could get into the battle, the outcome was that he was invested as a Companion of the Order of the Bath at Buckingham Palace. Then, in December 1944, he was dispatched to Burma as Chief of Staff to Lord Louis Mountbatten, Supreme Commander South-east Asia.

Major General Roy Urquhart

He later voiced criticism of Horrocks and his divisional commanders when he summed up the failure of 30th Corps to reach Arnhem:

> Even when one has taken into account every possible set-back, large and small, which occurred during our nine days north of the Lower Rhine, the fact remains that we were alone for much longer than any airborne division

Major General Roy Urquhart of 1st Airborne Division outside his headquarters, the Hartenstein Hotel in Oosterbeek. (*Imperial War Museum H-40947*)

is designed to stay. I think it is possible that for once Horrocks' enthusiasm was not transmitted adequately to those who served under him, and it may be that some of his more junior officers and NCOs did not fully comprehend the problem and the importance of great speed. By and large, the impression is that they were 'victory happy'. They had advanced northwards very fast and had been well received by the liberated peoples, and they were now out of touch with the atmosphere of bullets and the battle. As is always the case, it took them a little time to attune themselves once more to the stern reality of tough fighting against the Germans. At first, the opposition seems to have caused them a certain amount of shock and surprise.

In Urquhart's official report on the lessons of Arnhem, he wrote:

We must be prepared to take more risks during the initial stages of an airborne operation. It would have been a reasonable risk to have landed the Division much closer to the objective chosen, even in the face of some enemy flak … Initial surprise was gained, but the effect was lost because it was four hours before the troops would arrive at the bridge. A whole brigade dropped at the bridge would have made all the difference … Both the Army and the RAF were over-pessimistic about the flak. The forecast about the impossibility of landing gliders on the polder country was also wrong. Suitable DZs and LZs could have been found south of the bridge and near it.

Churchill tank carrying British infantry with captured German POWs on board (note their coal-bucket steel helmets).

Perhaps Urquhart should have expressed these sensible views strongly at the planning meeting. He never got further promotion.

General Eisenhower

Curiously enough, Ike claimed that he ordered and encouraged Market Garden although it was devised in its entirety by Montgomery. This was probably because the two US airborne divisions, the 82nd and 101st, fought valiantly and successfully and suffered heavy casualties.

Field Marshal Alan Brooke CIGS

He was critical at the end: 'I feel that Monty's strategy for once, is at fault. Instead of carrying out the advance on Arnhem he ought to have made certain of Antwerp in the first place ... Ike nobly took all the blame on himself as he had approved Monty's suggestion ....' As CIGS Alan Brooks should have advised Montgomery of his policy viewpoint *before* the Market Garden operation started.

The population of Holland

After the euphoria on 'Mad Tuesday', 5 September, the joy of liberation quickly turned into despair as their German masters exacted retribution. The long cold winter of misery set in. On 10 April 1945 Churchill wrote to President Roosevelt: 'The plight of the civil population in occupied Holland is desperate. Between two and three million people are facing starvation. We believe that large numbers are dying daily ... I fear we may soon be in the presence of a tragedy ....'

Whoever may have 'won', the gallant Dutch population certainly 'lost'.

CHAPTER 29

The Island, 'No Man's Land' and the Polar Bears

Towards the end of September, in the sad aftermath of Market Garden, there were three quite separate battle arenas.

In the Dutch Peel country 11th Armoured and 3rd British Divisions made slow but sure progress eastwards towards the river Maas. The villages of Zomeren, Asten, Deurne, Amerika, Oploo and Overloon were all captured in the late autumn and early winter.

Further north in the polder country of the Betuwe (the Island), between Nijmegen, Elst, Elden, Oosterhout and Valburg, there was a watery 'No Man's Land' with both Germans and British making small raids, often at night. 30th Corps held the Island with 50th Tyne Tees Division on the right flank, 101st US Airborne on the left partly guarding Nijmegen, and on the far right, 43rd Wessex facing the Reichswald. Both sides settled into a grudging static warfare, rather like Caesar's winter quarters with the barbarians on their doorstep. The Guards Armoured Division was in reserve. The Island was surrounded on three sides by the confluence of the Waal and the Maas, and on the west side by a canal linking these two rivers. The historian of the 8th Battalion Durham Light Infantry, stationed in the village of Aam, due north of Nijmegen, described the country as 'flat [and] marshy', reporting that 'the majority of the few large villages had been reduced to ruins by the fighting, which meant the troops had to rough it in the open'. The whole area was intersected by dykes, many filled with dead cattle. Most dykes were overflowing with the constant autumn rain. The numerous orchards were leafless and offered no protection for artillery observers, although the two churches at Schindle and Weiboche provided observation points. 'Men caught out in the open had to decide quickly whether an approaching shell would land close enough either to jump into several feet of water in the nearest ditch, or take a chance and press themselves flat in a foot of squelchy mud.'

The third battle area was the large rectangle north-east of Antwerp some 40 miles wide and 30 miles in depth. Operations Alan, Colin and Pheasant took place in October to capture and liberate Breda, Tilburg, Oosterhout and s'Hertogenbosch. As a preliminary Major General 'Bubbles' Barker and his 49th Polar Bear Division, with a Canadian armoured division and a Belgian and Polish unit, were tasked with the capture of the large town of Turnhout and with probing attacks north to Poppel on the way to Tilburg. The general

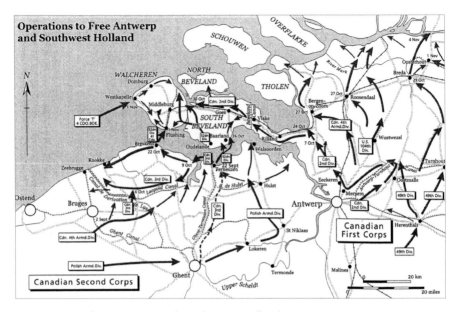

Operations to free Antwerp and south-west Holland.

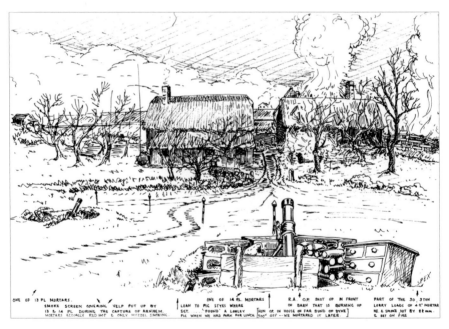

A 3-inch mortar position on the Island. (*Michael Bayley*)

kept a diary: '27 Sep. We have a bridgehead across the Antwerp–Turnhout canal. Not bad. On Thursday 21st we had completed two bridges over Albert canal by early am 24th and had a bridge over the Turnhout canal by 6am 25th. We took 10 officers and 508 men prisoner and killed and wounded quite

'A' Coy 4 Lincolns pass wrecked German anti-tank gun in Willemstad, Autumn 1944. (*Imperial War Museum B-11802*)

a packet. I must say I consider we are now complete professionals. Everything works like well oiled machinery.'

The Polar Bears started at Herenthout and Herenthals, and the 146th and 147th Brigades crossed the Albert canal on the 22nd and 23rd. All the bridges had been blown and barges sunk, so the 4th Lincolns crossed at East Ostmalle at midnight in assault boats in darkness and silence. Soon the Division captured Rychevorsel, Vlimieren and, on the 24th, the large town of Turnhout. The Recce Regiment and 7th Duke of Wellingtons were first in. For two days cheering, hand-clapping crowds shouted applause and thanks. Counter-attacks came and the 1/4th KOYLI were hard pressed. The Hallamshires were directed to take the Depot de Mendicité, a huge, formidable barrack block, part prison, part workhouse and part lunatic asylum. The depot, which lay on the road to Merxplas, was well defended by two enemy battalions. In the end it required the whole of 147th Brigade to capture the Mendicité: the Leicesters from the west and the 7th Duke of Wellington's and Gloucesters from the south. The Hallams put in a joint attack from the north and south. Corporal J. Harper won a posthumous VC for leading his platoon of Hallams in savage hand-to-hand fighting. At dawn on the 29th, in a silent attack because there were many inmates and patients mingling with the German defenders, the Polar Bears broke in.

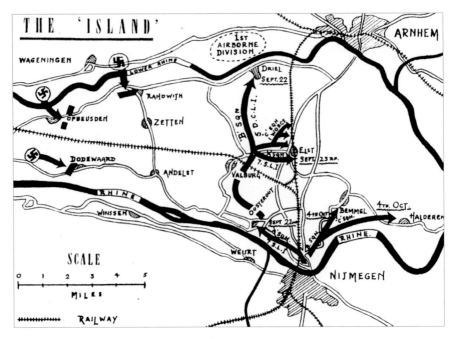

The Island between Nijmegen and Arnhem.

German column retreating from Meerssen, 7 September 1944. (*Stan Procter*)

The Polar Bear monument on the Kade, Roosendaal, Holland. (*Bill Hudson*)

49th Divisional memorial, Utrecht, Holland. (*Bill Hudson*)

The Polar Bears continued their advance north to Poppel and the Polish Armoured Division took over at most of the Dutch frontier. In the early winter they became known as the Nijmegen Home Guard.

*   *   *   *

The Polar Bears had a significant role to free many key towns in Holland from the Nazi rule by Dr Seyss-Inquart and Anton Mussert. The battles for Roosendaal and Utrecht are commemorated by large, friendly white stone statues of a Polar Bear. They helped liberate Willemstad and Breda and finally helped capture Arnhem in April 1945 and their Recce Regiment was first equal in the capture of Amsterdam on 7 May 1945.

*   *   *   *

The real heroes in the liberation of Holland were the Canadians in the 'Cinderella War'. In his book *The 85 Days*, R.W. Thompson wrote:

> ...the rain, driven by winds blowing half a gale, had seemed to join the dark evil sky to the dark evil land, so that the small space that had been won resembled the inside of a tureen squelching with mud and water like some foul stew. Even the dykes had lost their lines, crushed and churned into the grey muck heap of the featureless wilderness. There were no fires ... Men lived and died and slept always wet and caked with ooze. The first respect for

the enemy had given way to a bitter hatred, growing to an absolute loathing for the Germans had mined and booby-trapped the bodies of the dead [the author witnessed this in the village of Amerika in the Peel country]. The bloated bodies in the mud of the polders, and lolloping face down like filthy grey bags in the dark waters of the dykes, had proved as dangerous dead as alive. Bodies exploded at a touch to destroy men in their rare moments of compassion ... so they rotted and stank where they had fallen, of less account than the swollen carcasses of oxen with their legs sprouting upwards, symbols of the misery of that land reclaimed from the sea.

Nevertheless, despite the devastating misery that the Canadians endured in the Verdronken land, September 1944 was the great month of liberation. All of northern France, all of Belgium and much of the south of Holland were liberated – and finally escaped from the clutches of the Third Reich.

Detail from picture on p. 126. (*Imperial War Museum B-10170*)

Bibliography

Ambrose, Stephen, *Citizen Soldiers* (Simon and Schuster, 1997)

Bennett, David, *Magnificent Disaster* (Casemate, 2008)

Buckingham, William, *Arnhem 1944* (Tempus, 2002)

Churchill, Winston, *Triumph and Tragedy* (Cassell, 1954)

Clarke, Lloyd, *Arnhem, Operation Market Garden* (Sutton, 2002)

Delaforce, Patrick, *Monty's Northern Legions* (Sutton, 2004)

Delaforce, Patrick, *Smashing the Atlantic Wall* (Pen & Sword, 2005)

Delaforce, Patrick, *Fighting Wessex Wyverns* (Sutton, 1994)

Ellis, John, *One Day in a very Long War* (Pimlico, 1999)

Ellis, L. F., *Welsh Guards at War* (London Stamp Exchange, 1989)

Hart, Liddell, *Other side of the Hill* (Cassell, 1948)

Farrar-Hockley, Anthony, *Airborne Carpet* (Macdonald, 1969)

Frost, John, *A Drop too Many* (Sphere, 1983)

Harclerode, Peter, *Arnhem, a Tragedy of Errors* (Caxton, 2000)

Hastings, Max, *Overlord* (Michael Joseph, 1984)

Horrocks, Brian, *A Full Life* (Collins, 1960)

Howarth, T. E. B., *Monty at Close Quarters* (Leo Cooper, 1985)

Kershaw, Robert, *It never Snows in September* (Ian Allan, 1994)

Lewin, Ronald, *Ultra goes to War* (Penguin, 1978)

Middlebrook, Martin, *Arnhem 1944, Airborne Battle* (Viking, 1994)

Moorehead, Alan, *Eclipse* (Hamish Hamilton, 1945)

Moorehead, Alan, *Montgomery* (Hamish Hamilton, 1946)

Rosse and Hill, *Guards Armoured Division* (Geoffrey Bles, 1958)

Ryan, Cornelius, *Bridge too Far* (Hodder, 1974)

Shulman, Milton, *Defeat in the West* (Secker & Warburg, 1947)

Sosabowski, Stanislaw, *Freely I Served* (Kimber, 1960)

Urquhart, R. E., *Arnhem* (Cassell, 1958)

Wills, Deryk, *Put on your Boots and Parachutes!* (Deryk Wills, 1992)

Wilmot, Chester, *Struggle for Europe* (Collins, 1952)

Glossary

German and Dutch Terms

Abteilungen	Combat units
Abwehr	Military intelligence department of the OKW
Binnenlandse Strijdkrachten	Dutch Forces of the Interior
Bocage country	Terrain of mixed woodland, pasture, small fields and high banks
Brigadeführer	Senior SS rank
Fallschirmjäger	German paratroopers
Feldwebel	German rank roughly equivalent to British warrant officer
Festa	German garrison
Festung	German fortress or stronghold
Hauptsturmführer	SS rank equivalent to a captain
Hitler Jugend	Young and highly indoctrinated Nazis, fanatically loyal to Hitler
Kampfgruppe	Impromptu German battle group
Kettenhunde	German Military Police, also known as Chain Dogs
Kranken	Wounded convalescent formation
Kriegsmarines	Members of the German Navy
Landsturm Niederland	Dutch Nazi volunteers
Luftwaffe	German Airforce
Minnenwerfer	German mortars known by the Allies as 'Moaning minnies'
Moffen	Dutch equivalent of 'Jerry'

Nebelwerfer	Mortar gun designed to fire chemical shells
Obersturmbannführer	SS rank translated as 'Senior Assault Unit Leader'
Flak units	German anti-aircraft units
Panzerfaust	Cheap German one-shot anti-tank weapon
Panzergrenadier	German motorised or mechanised infantry
Panzerjaeger	Armoured units designed to fight tanks, usually SP guns
Schmeisser	German submachine-gun, also known as the MP-40
Schwerpunkt	Concentrated method of advance upon a focal point with co-ordinated armour and infantry and appropriate flank protection
Sicherheitspolizei	Nazi security police
Spandau	German machine-gun
Sperrlinie/ Sperrverband	German defensive blocking line
Stadtkommandant	German military governor of a town or city
Stonk	German word for a sudden artillery bombardment, also used by the British
Sturmbannführer	SS rank equivalent to Major. Translated as 'Assault Unit Leader'
Teller	Cylindrical, powerful anti-tank mine
Verdronken land	Flooded region in Holland
Volksgrenadier divisions	Emergency divisions created in 1944 to combat the German manpower crisis
Wehrmacht	The unified armed forces of Germany
Wolfschanze	Hitler's Eastern Front military HQ. Translated as 'Wolf's Lair'

Military Abbreviations

AA	Anti-Aircraft artillery
AAA	Allied Airborne Army
ADC	Aide-de-camp
AFV	Armoured Fighting Vehicle

AQMG	Assistant Quartermaster General
AVRE	Armoured Vehicle Royal Engineers; special Churchill tank
BEF	British Expeditionary Force (1940)
BLA	British Liberation Army
CAS	Close Air Support, usually by RAF planes
CIGS	Chief of the Imperial General Staff
CO	Commanding Officer
CQMS	Company Quartermaster Sergeant
CRE	Commander Royal Engineers
Crocodile	Churchill tank with flame-thrower
CSM	Company Sergeant-Major
DCLI	Duke of Cornwall's Light Infantry
DCM	Distinguished Conduct Medal
DF	Defensive Fire target
DLI	Durham Light Infantry
DSO	Distinguished Service Order
DUKW	Wheeled amphibious landing craft
DZ	Drop Zone for parachutists
FFI	Free French Forces of the Interior
FOO	Artillery Forward Observation Officer
GAF	German Air Force
GOC	General Officer Commanding
HLI	Highland Light Infantry
KOSB	King's Own Scottish Borderers
KOYLI	King's Own Yorkshire Light Infantry
KRRC	King's Royal Rifle Corps
KSLI	King's Shropshire Light Infantry
LAA	Light Anti-Aircraft artillery
LAD	Light Aid Detachment (regimental medical unit)
LZ	Landing Zone for glider troops
MC	Military Cross

MM	Military Medal
NCO	Non-Commissioned Officer
OC	Officer Commanding
OKW	Oberkommando der Wehrmacht
OST	Eastern Territories (Russians, Hungarians etc)
PBI	Poor Bloody Infantry
PIAT	Projector Infantry Anti-Tank
PIR	Parachute Infantry Regiments
PLUTO	Pipeline under the Ocean from the Isle of Wight
POL	Petrol, Oil and Lubricants
RA	Royal Artillery
RAC	Royal Armoured Corps
RB	Rifle Brigade
RDG	Royal Dragoon Guards
RE	Royal Engineers
REME	Royal Electrical and Mechanical Engineers
RHA	Royal Horse Artillery
RMO	Regimental Medical Officer
RSF	Royal Scots Fusiliers
RTR	Royal Tank Regiment
RWF	Royal Welch Fusiliers
SHAEF	Supreme Headquarters Allied Expeditionary Force
SOE	Special Operations Executive
SRY	Sherwood Rangers Yeomanry
TCV	Troop Carrying Vehicle

Index

Adair, Major General Allan, competent but uninspiring, 82; sanctions delay, 129; wrote Guards Armoured history, 130–1; in Operation Garden, 134, 136; at Malden conference, 137–8; got it wrong, 143; reaction to sight of The Island, 143; division's losses, 146

Antwerp, liberation impeded, 14, 15; author's welcome at, 15, 16; von Zangen on fall of, 17, 23; Hitler's reaction to fall of, 23; Hitler's directive, 24; von Zangen's 'deny the port' order, 25–6; Hitler designates as 'fortress', 28; Belgian resistance at, 28; Admiral Ramsey 'highly vulnerable' at, 29; 11th Armoured attacks, 31; capture of dock area, 32; capture of Commandant, 33–4; German POWs in zoo, 35–8; 4KSLI in trouble in Merxem, 39; Monty tells Crerar to open port, 49, 57; vital harbour opened, 59, 60; Monty orders opening of port, 61, 63, 72, 75, 76; fleshpots, 78-9, 133, 137, 169, 182, 183; liquid booty acquired, 186; 53rd Welsh garrison, 197, 212, 222–3; Hitler startled at fall of, 257; open for shipping, 258–9, 264; Gen. Horrocks' mind fixed on Rhine, 266

Arnhem, Dutch SS in battle, 16, 19; regional emblem, 20, 61, 65; Gen. Hakewell offer of help, 66, 72-4; Major Urquhart briefs aerial photographs of, 78–9; signallers frustrated, 83, 91; eminent journalists and reporters at, 92; main objectives, 93; FM Model's quick reaction to attack on, 96; RAF Dakotas shot down, 98; 'Black Tuesday', 99; 11 Para destroyed, 100; 1 Para overwhelmed, 101; 'witches cauldron', 103; Hagen's animal existence, 105; Lonsdale Force, 106; truce for wounded, 107; Frost's citadel, 114; Frost's war over, 115; lack of radio communication, 121; FM Model on capture of vital bridges, 122; Polish drop near Elst, 129, 134, 136, 138; Guards' 'we've got to try', 139, 143–4; Operation Essame 'situation critical', 150–1; Colonel Taylor's advice, 153; Gen. Urquhart's dissatisfaction, 154–8; Operation Berlin evacuation planned, 159; Wyverns carry out 'Berlin', 160–1; Gen. Horrocks' views on Market Garden, 162; casualties, 163; Polish Brigade plan, 172–4, 178–9; state of survivors, 197, 214; 15th Scottish plan, 236; Gen. Bittrich organises alarm groups, 241, 252; Gen. Student's Para division, 259; capture of, 264; Monty's excuses, 265; Gen. Urquhart's criticism, 266–7

Barker, Major General 'Bubbles', commands 49th (West Riding of Yorkshire) Division, 40; unhappy about Canadians, 45; meets German envoys from Le Havre, 47; on Operation Astonia, 48; plans to capture Turnhout, 269

Bernhard, Prince, becomes C-in-C Netherlands forces, 61; advises FM Montgomery, 63; worried about British tactics, 65–6; portraits of, 200

Bittrich, General Wilhelm, 264, 266; commanded kampfgruppen, 19, 20; joined by FM Model, 94; 96; Armoured Defence miracle, 101;

panzers battered houses, 103;
agrees to truce, 107; 136; realises
importance of holding Nijmegen,
138; protests to FM Model, 140;
quick reaction to show on ground,
257

Bletchley Park and Ultra, 81, 266, 276;
decrypts 100,000 Enigma machines,
9; reveals location of FM Model's
HQ, 20; 75; reveals Panzer Corps'
movements, 79

Browning, Lt General 'Boy', 102, 138,
157, 160, 180; deputy to Lt Gen.
Brereton, 71; detests Brereton, 72;
uses guile and deceit, 73; Monty's
adviser, 73; hijacks gliders, 74;
threatens Major Urquhart, 81; folie
de grandeur, 85; encourages Guards
recruits, 86, 88, 90; 'Instruction
No. 1', 92; no effective authority,
94; generals' conference at Valburg,
106; kept evacuation decision secret,
107; lack of courtesy, 108; at HQ at
Nijmegen, 110; drops on Groesbeek
Heights, 121; orders Gavin to capture
Nijmegen bridge, 126; sanctions
delay, 129; watches American river
assault, 141; partnership with
Horrocks, 162; 'Father of the British
Airborne Forces', 177; asks Sosab for
advice, 178; awarded Order of Bath,
266

Brussels, 29, 39, 49, 61, 72, 78, 131,
168, 182, 197, 199, 229, 234, 236,
253, 265, 266; 'Great Swan' to
capture, 11; Morehead describes
liberation, 14, 16; von Zangen's
plan, 22–3; BBC Radio Orange
broadcast, 63; 21st Army Group
HQ, 81; Guards Armoured arrival,
133; Wessex Wyverns garrison, 150;
ceremonial liberation parade, 169

Canadian Army, 13, 23, 45, 60, 76, 241,
256, 266, 269; Operation Jubilee to
attack Dieppe, 9, 10, 12; Herculean
task to clear Scheldt estuary, 25;
casualties, 39; Operation Totalise,
39; doomed attack on Dieppe, 50;

Defence Minister re 'Canloan', 51;
Lt Gen. Crerar commands, 53;
'Cinderella Army', 54; Spry's 3rd
Division, 54; Operation Wellhit,
56; abortive attack on Dunkirk,
57; capture of Calais, 58–9; Monty
blames, 75; Operation Spring,
131; Field Company help Arnhem
withdrawal, 161; composite
battalion in Berlin parade, 219; R.W.
Thompson praises 'real heroes', 274;
misery in verdronkenland, 275

Casualties, 32, 35, 42, 46, 48, 96, 111,
116, 117, 144, 145, 1666, 168, 169,
184, 225, 227, 228, 229, 253; Gen.
Horrocks' notes, 9; Colonel Dupuy's
notes, 10; Normandy average, 11; in
Antwerp, 39; from mortars, 41; at
Le Havre, 48; Canadians at Dieppe,
50; Canloan, 51; Canadians in
Normandy, 53; Russians in Berlin
offensive, 75; in Arnhem, 101; in
Oosterbeek, 107; 'Screaming Eagles',
120; 'All American', 129; 8th Corps,
131; Wyverns, 149–50; 'Butchers'
Bill', 163; 50th Div. in N. Africa,
164; replacements for 50th Div., 172,
175; 11th Armoured in Operation
Goodwood, 181; in Gen. Roberts'
victory, 186; 'virgin' division, 190,
192; 3rd Div., 197, 198, 199, 202;
Desert Rats, 210, 214; needless,
218; 53rd Welsh, 221–2, 231; 15th
Scottish, 234; Gheel battle, 235, 236,
240–1; Best battle, 245; US Airborne,
268

CHANNEL PORTS

Calais: 28; German 15th Army at, 22;
Monty orders capture, 57; defences
commanded by Lt Colonel Shroeder,
58; captured, 59
Boulogne: 23, 24, 53, 54, 55, 58;
'Wellhit' battle, 56; Monty orders
capture, 57;
Dunkirk: 23; von Zangen strengthens,
24; commanded by Gen. von
Treskon, 56; ferocious defence of, 57;
surrender of, May 1945, 58; Tyne-
Tees in 1940, 164; Monty's rearguard
in 1940, 193

Dieppe: 13, 42; Operation Jubilee, 12; Port Clearance Team, 49; Operation Rutter/Jubilee, 50; Canadians capture, 53–4

Le Havre: 13, 23; codename Astonia, 40; port defences, 42; Colonel Wildermouth commands garrison, 43; port facilities, 44; attack plans, 45; bombardment by RAF, RN and Army, 46; Liddell Hart's accolade, 47; Major Gen. Barker's report, 48; Hitler designates as 'Festung', 54

Rouen: leading port in France, 44; easy capture, 54

Churchill, Winston, angry at end of 50th Div., 13; at Quebec conference, 25; quoted by Gen. von Zangen, 26; on importance of Antwerp, 29; decision about fate of 51st Highland Div., 41; on Canadian Army, 50; on fate of Holland, 61; on SOE., 63; promises to Stalin, 109, 164; Desert Rats favourite division, 209; Potsdam conference, 219; victory parade in Berlin, 219; famous speech, 220; service dress, 220; *Triumph and Tragedy* quote, 263; victory parade in Brussels, 264

Crerar, Lt General Harry, commands 1st Canadian Army in Normandy, 53; summoned by Monty, 54; waiting for reinforcements, 55; Monty orders to capture key ports, 57; ordered to invest Dunkirk, 58

Desert Rats, 49, 175, 182; capture of Ghent, 11, 12; first armoured division into Normandy, 130; 'Jerboa' nickname, 209; foreign language, 209; Operations Goodwood, Spring and Bluecoat, 210; Operation Market Garden, 212–4; Operations Don, Alan and Blackcock, 215; Operation Plunder, 217; relief of Fallingbostel POW camp, 217; surrender of Hamburg, 218; in Berlin, 219; Churchill's speech, 220

Eindhoven, 206, 266; 'Screaming Eagles' target, 78, 116; Alan Morehead visit,

118–9; Horrocks' expectations, 134; Horrocks' disappointment, 137; Irish Guards reach, 137; Lowland Brigade pass by Philips radio works, 242, 244

Eisenhower, General Dwight, arrives in Normandy, 11; unaware of importance of Antwerp, 28; makes broadcast to Dutch people, 61; offers Airborne Army to Monty, 71; great skills, 76; re Market Garden, 81, 84, 268; quotes from his D-Day to VE Day report, 85; accused by Monty, 265

Gavin, Major General James, 126, 129; 'Slim Jim,' 121; Horrocks praises, 127

Göbbels, Dr Josef, 55, 72, 190, 192; lowers call up age, 19

Göring, Field Marshal Hermann, 71, 72, 96, 173, 224, 239, 257; produces six para regts, 17; Hitler worried about his own safety, 21; produces a training regt, 138; 'Der Grosse', 262

Hitler, Adolf, 9, 58, 72, 96, 176, 264, 278; Hitler Jugend, 10; shock at news of capture of Antwerp, 11, 16, 17; fortresses, 19; Wolfchanze HQ, 20; impressed by Model's escape, 21; fooled by Operation Fortitude, 22; orders Sheldt to be mined, 23; important new directive, 24; plans destruction of Antwerp dockyards, 26, 28; aware of Allies' logistical problems, 29; plans Operation Wacht am Rhein and orders Operation Wildemuth, 43, 44; designates seven Festung (fortresses), 53; dismisses Gen. Heim, 56; deploys paras in 1940 capture of Belgium, 71; Plan Orient, 164; 'worst day of my life', 166; 'Hitler's gone to Spain!' 169; rejects call for more para drops, 257

Horrocks, Major General Brian, 28, 39, 66, 74, 88, 94, 102, 107, 119, 137, 138, 149, 151, 276; comments on army in Normandy, 9–10; 'duntmaster', 11; meets Prince Bernhardt,

63; often sick but best Corps commander, 82; generals' conference at Valburg, 106; quotes from *A Full Life*, 120, 122, 124–5; mistake, 121; on Nijmegen battles, 126–7; order to Guards Armoured, 131; briefs 30th Corps officers on Operation Market, 134; Grenadier Guards attack in Nijmegen, 139; lost confidence, 141; 'a miracle', 143; describes terrain on 'The Island', 153; refutes criticism, 156; orders Gen. Thomas re Operation Berlin, 159; end of battle of Arnhem, 162–3; praises 50th Div., 167; Brussels victory parade, 169; seemed bewildered, 179; umbrage with Sosab, 180; capture of Mount Pinçon, 251; sincere autobiography, 266; Urquhart's polite criticism, 267

Island, The, location of, 16; Horrocks' description, 129, 144, 153; Model plans to capture, 163; description, 230, 269, 274; sketch, 270

Kampfgruppen, 140, 161, 179, 180, 207, 215, 226, 230, 257; emergency battle groups, 13, 19; Spindler, Moeller, Krafft, Knaust, Brinkmann, von Allworden, 96; von Tettav, 98, 99, 101; Bruhna, Krafft, 103; Henke, Euling, 113, 118, 122; Stargaard, Fuerstenberg, Greshick, Goebel, 124; Becker, Hermann, 125; Walther, von der Heydt, Kerutt, Segler, 136; Henke, Grundsberg, Reinhold, 138; Knaust, Brinkmann, 144; Zedlitz, 224; Erdmanns, Walther, 259; Ewald Richter, Hoffman, Roestel, Kerutt, Koepel, 260; Huber, 261

Model, Field Marshal Walther, 259, 260, 264, 266; continues as Commander Army Group B, 17; tells Hitler he needs to buy time, 19; nicknamed 'Hitler's Fireman', 20; Hitler impressed by escape, 21; von Stolberg reports to, 32; Ultra reveals HQ of, 81; prompt reaction to airborne attack, 94; achieves defensive miracle, 101; orchestrates final days of Arnhem battle, 103; retains control of Nijmegen bridge, 122; sends reinforcements to Nijmegen, 125; positions troops around Neerpelt bridgehead, 136; refuses to blow up Nijmegen bridge, 140; plans to recapture Nijmegen, 163; fortunate to have first-class commanders, 257

Montgomery, Field Marshal Bernard, 141, 249; unleashes 'the dogs of war', 11; involves entire 21st Army Group in Operation Market Garden, 13; unaware of importance of Antwerp, 28; replaces GOC of 51st Highland Div., 41; criticises Canadian commanders, 53; hopes to fire Gen. Crerar, 54–5; dismisses Prince Bernhardt's advice, 63; jumps at offer of American Airborne Army, 71; plans Operation Comet, 72; Browning trusted as 'airborne warfare' adviser, 73; brilliance, arrogance and confidence, 75; clashes with Eisenhower on military strategy, 76; plans Operation Market, 78; trusts Lt Gen. Dempsey, 79; ignores advice from Bedell and Urquhart, 81; chooses Guards Armoured to lead Market, 82; privy to aborted airborne drops, 83; 'thirsting' for action, 85; 1st Airborne, 'Forlorn Hope', 89; planning mistake, 121; chooses Desert Rats to be first armour ashore on D-Day, 130; on Gen. Thomas, 147; trusts 50th Div., 164; decides 50th Div. must be training division, 175; scapegoats Poles, 180; warned by Ultra in Operation Epsom, 181; commands 3rd British 'iron division' in BEF, 193; unrealistic plan to capture Caen, 195; plans Operation Plunder, 217; Berlin victory parade, 219; ensures 'virgin' divisions are physically fit, 232; regards Scottish divisions best for river or canal assaults, 234; praises 15th Scottish, 239; admits mistakes in Market Garden, 265; criticised by FM Alan Brooke, 268

Moorehead, Alan, 276; intrepid journalist, 14; on liberation of

Brussels, 15–6; on German POW, 19; on Breendonck concentration camp, 30; visits Antwerp, 200; describes Eindhoven, 118

Nijmegen, 78, 116; liberation impedes Allied troops, 15; Browning's HQ to move to, 74; faulty planning re capture of bridge, 79, 86; 'All American' Div. plan to capture, 121; German reinforcements arrive at, 122; battles for town, rail and road bridges, 124–9; Gen. Adair 'surprised' at, 138; Gen. Horrocks on Guards' attacks, 139–42; Sgt Hearst on bridge battle, 173; Capt. Stirling on railway bridge, 255; 8th Armoured Brigade on working with Americans, 256; 'Polar Bears' known as 'Nijmegen Home Guard', 274

OPERATIONS

Aintree: battle to capture Overloon and Oploo by 11th Armoured Div., 3rd British, 68
Alan: Desert Rats clear Middlerode, Doornhoeck, Berlicum, 215, 231, 269
Angle: 52nd Lowland Div. in Scheldt clearance, 59
Astonia: 54; all-arms capture of Le Havre, 13; Major Ward describes plan, 44; Brigade Major Crook on morale and civilian casualties, 46; garrison well prepared for surrender, 47; Major Gen. Barker on the battle, 48
Atlantic: Canadians' attempt to capture Caen, 18-20; July 1940, 53
Avalanche: 209
Berlin: 108, 159-61; 1st Airborne evacuation from Oosterbeek and Arnhem, 106
Blackcock: 256; 12th Corps operation to clear Roer area, 147, 215
Blackwater: 150
Bluecoat: 197, 210, 234, 251; Monty's only genuine victory in Normandy, 131, 149, 166, 169, 181
Charnwood: 3rd Div. attack on Caen, 11, 75, 196
Clipper: 163
Colin: 269

Comet: 78, 178; aborted minor version of Market Garden, 71, 72
Don: 215
Epsom: 181, 221, 248, 250; Wyverns and 15th Scottish in first Normandy battle, 11, 75, 83, 130, 148; major attack by 15th Scottish, 232–3
Express: 149
Forrard On: 251
Fortitude: 22
Fustian: 109
Goodwood: 11, 75, 83; Guards Armoured attack on Cagny, 130-1; 11th Armoured Div. led badly and suffer, 181; 3rd Div. flank protection, 196; Desert Rats as 3rd Armoured Div., 210
Greenline: 53rd Welsh third battle in Normandy, 221; 15th Scottish third battle in Normandy, 234
Haggis: 245
Heather: 202
Husky: in the Sicilian campaign, 41; 50th Tyne-Tees suffer badly, 164
Infatuate 1 & 2: 59; Canadian battles to clear Scheldt, 71
Jubilee: 12
Jupiter: 221, 234; Wessex Wyverns suffered badly in classic Monty battle, 11, 50, 75, 83, 148
North Pole: deception of SOE by German Abwehr, 63; Germans' cheeky message to SOE, 65

Polish Brigade, efforts to cross Rhine, 65, 70, 72, 78, 106, 112, 115, 138, 144, 158, 176–80

Resistance Movements, 28

Roberts, Major General 'Pip', 7, 29, 32, 36, 38, 39, 137, 181, 186, 190, 192, 226, 248

Sosabowski, Major General 'Sosab', 71, 74, 106, 107, 176–80

Stalin, Josef, 50, 75, 164, 176, 209,

Student, General Kurt, 17, 19, 71, 72, 78, 117, 136, 151, 184, 224, 239, 240–3, 257–62, 264, 266,

Taylor, General Maxwell (US Army), commands 101st US Airborne, 73, 74, 81, 116–20

Thomas, Major General Ivo, 143, 144; commands Wessex Wyverns in Market Garden, 106, 107; description, 147; in Normandy battles, 148–50; leading infantry formation trying to reach Arnhem, 151–62; Butcher's Bill, 163

Ultra – *see* Bletchley Park

Urquhart, Major General Roy, 71, 72, 74, 78, 100, 101, 153; Browning fails to advise about enemy armour, 81; description, 89; takes refuge, 94; 100, 101; establishes HQ in Hartenstein Hotel, 103, 105; sends emissaries to Nijmegen, 106; evacuation plan, 107; sad end to 'Forlorn Hope', 108; memoirs, 158; faint praise for Poles, 159; praise for Sosab, 176; alters Polish drop, 178; mistake re ferry, 179; criticism of 30th Corps, 266

US FORMATIONS
82nd Airborne: 85, 86, 121-9, 206; objectives in Operation Garden, 78; Gen. Adair assumes Nijmegen bridge captured, 138; praise from Gen. Horrocks, 162; heavy casualties, 268
101st Airborne Division: 85; plan for Operation Garden, 78; objectives including capture of Nijmegen bridge, 86; Bereton persuaded to change dropping plans, 116; Gen. Taylor leads from the front, 117; praised by Gen. Horrocks, 120

von Rundsted, Field Marshal Gerd, most dependable of Hitler's generals, 17; orders German 15th Army to hold all the designated fortresses, 23

von Zangen, General Gustave-Adolf, 53, 54, 72, 145, 211, 248, 258, 264; takes command of 15th Army, 22; conducts brilliant withdrawal, 23–4; strengthens garrisons of three major ports and Walcheren Island, 25; Hitler delighted with, 26

Also available from Amberley Publishing

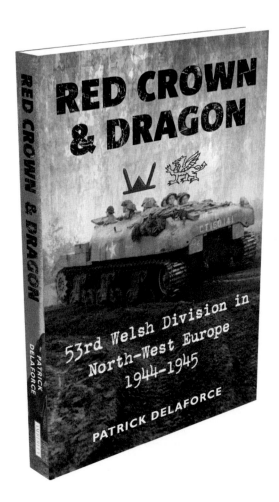

Red Crown & Dragon
53rd Welsh Division in North-West Europe 1944-1945

Patrick Delaforce

ISBN 978-1-84868-817-9
£14.99/$22.95

Available from all good bookshops or order direct
from our website www.amberleybooks.com

Coming soon from Amberley Publishing

Operation Eclipse
The Invasion of the Third
Reich 1945

Patrick Delaforce

ISBN 978-1-84868-948-0
Publication date: Dec 2010